A Trimaran Sails
the Seven Seas

Jerry Heutink

SHERIDAN HOUSE

First published 2000
in the United States of America by
Sheridan House Inc.
145 Palisade Street
Dobbs Ferry, NY 10522

Copyright © 1999 by Jerry Heutink

*A CIP catalog record for this book is available from the
Library of Congress, Washington, DC.*

Printed in Canada

ISBN 1-57409-106-9

TABLE OF CONTENTS

Acknowledgements

To Hetty, my wife and life's partner for fifty years. To Harry, my youngest son and first mate on board our beloved *Trillium II*.

Through Hetty's patience, sacrifice, and financial management, we were able to sail the Seven Seas for so many years. Even though she was not fond of the sea, she sailed with us often. She was on board when we made our first Atlantic crossing from east to west, and loved island hopping in the Caribbean. When we plied the Indian Ocean, Hetty accompanied us for three months. During the last year of her life, she corrected the Dutch version of this book.

Harry is a born mariner. He had an uncanny instinct in detecting the unforeseen dangers lying in wait for us.

Without Hetty's support and Harry's involvement, I could not have accomplished what I did. To both, I am deeply indebted and grateful.

Also, I would like to thank my present wife, Jennie, for proofreading the English manuscript and making the first corrections; Mary-Jo, her daughter, for the final editing; and Rena Potter, for typing it.

Harry and Hetty on board the Trillium II.

And last but not least, I would like to express my gratitude to the late Norman Cross of San Diego, California. He designed a ship so highly seaworthy and strong that no sea could break her.

Prologue

As an eight-year-old boy in Holland, I read only books pertaining to the sea and ships. When somebody asked me what I would like to be when I grew up, my answer was, without hesitation, "Captain on a big ship...!" I had a dream that some day I would have a ship and sail the Seven Seas.

In 1939 I received my ticket as a Radio Officer in the Merchant Navy. But Adolf Hitler rattled his sabre, and I had to bury my dream. When the war was over, shipping companies needed wireless operators, but by then I was married, and my wife was expecting. I could not leave her under those circumstances. Down went the old dream again, and the sea was forgotten.

The liberation of Holland by Canadian soldiers left strong ties between Holland and Canada. After the war, a hundred thousand Dutchmen emigrated to Canada. Immigration advised us to go to Barrie, Ontario, the Gateway to the North, and so we did. We settled, made friends, and quickly felt at home.

In 1961 I enrolled in the George Brown College (Toronto) course in celestial navigation, and in subsequent winters took courses in Radio-RADAR-navigation, coastal navigation, and meteorology.

In 1968 I took my first CPS course in piloting. I became a member of the Barrie Power Squadron, was invited to the "Bridge," and was sworn in as Squadron Commander in May 1974. Throughout those years, until 1977, I taught courses in piloting and navigation, not only in Barrie, but in the Penetang and Midland Squadrons, too. I loved it.

While I was teaching, I built a small trimaran daysailer and bought a 1952 Century-Coronado. The trimaran became a toy for my sons, and the Coronado was used extensively on Georgian Bay. Theoretically and practically, I was ready to go to sea, so I dug up my old dream.

In the early sixties, I encountered a trimaran for the first time. I thought it was a rather strange vessel, though it looked truly impressive—three boats built side by side with one enormous deck stretching across. This deck was considerably larger than that of a single-hulled boat.

A friend of mine built the Piver *Lodestar*. Piver designed and constructed the first trimaran and was said to be the grandfather of the trimarans. He earned his reputation by successfully sailing across the Atlantic Ocean from America to England. Of course, this attracted a great deal of attention. All who witnessed or heard about it shook their heads and wondered how Piver could have accomplished this feat in such a vessel built from plywood. Was he crazy?

Piver wasn't crazy. For thousands of years the ancient Polynesians had crossed and explored the world's largest ocean—the Pacific—in trimarans and catamarans. At that time, they were crudely constructed of hollowed-out tree trunks with makeshift outriggers made from heavy branches on one side—the catamaran. For more stability a second branch was attached to the other side; and presto, it became a trimaran. Primitive man conceived it; modern man named it.

My friend had an extra set of blueprints for Piver's 16-foot *Frolic*, a daysailer; I purchased the drawings and in a few weeks hammered and glued it together. It was enjoyable building it, and pleasantly rewarding sailing it on Lake Simcoe near our little town in Ontario. I even participated in an afternoon race of the local yacht club (and lost in grand style).

That same year, I bought many books on boat building, especially about multi-hulls. I read everything I could get my hands on concerning catamarans and trimarans. Many yacht designers had concentrated on these kinds of boats after Piver, and various plans now came on the market. It was difficult to make a choice, but eventually the big day arrived. I ordered a complete set of blueprints for the Cross-46, which, back then, was the largest trimaran. I have never regretted it.

On January 2, 1970, I cut the first board. Included in the blueprints was a list of materials needed. I had ordered the lumber all at once from a company in British Columbia, the forestry capital of Canada. Imagine my surprise when that big pile of lumber arrived. Every sheet of plywood, every special board carried a sticker that read: "Bruinzeel–Zaandam–Holland," a Dutch lumber company!

The work progressed well. I had my old friend helping me, and in August of that year I was finished with the two outer hulls, or floats. Through unforeseen circumstances, I was forced to postpone my project for two years. During that time, two other trimarans of the Cross-46 model were being built in Ontario, also by private parties. Norman Cross travelled to Toronto and gave a lecture on how to build boats from his designs. He gave me encouragement and invaluable advice.

In 1972 I resumed work on a full-time basis—ten hours a day, six days a week. Every so often my old friend, the shipbuilder, came over to help me or give me his welcome advice. Usually, though, it was a one-man job. Every evening before leaving the workshop, all the scraps, woodshavings, and sawdust were cleaned up. Tools that were worn out or dull received the necessary repairs, sharpening, or replacement, and were eagerly set out for the next day's use. The building in which I worked was an ideal workshop. It was equipped with professional machines such as bandsaws, table saws, and electric planers, etc. At home I kept a diary, recording the number of hours spent, the part of the ship I had worked on, and the materials used.

On the occasion of my parents' visit to Canada in July 1974, my mother had the honour of christening my ship-under-construction. This event took place in the workshop in the presence of many guests.

The completion, however, took another two years. Finally, in July 1976, she was finished. The interior was completely panelled in light walnut. Four tanks were placed in the bilges. We could carry 1,000 litres of water and 1,000 litres of diesel fuel. Radio and navigational equipment was installed and the masts were stepped with the sails folded around the booms. She was

Framework and longitudinals of a "float" or the driver of a trimaran. Note the curved frames; they make the hulls extra strong. Trillium II *has been punished by very heavy seas—there was never a cave-in.*

to be launched totally completed. After 8,500 man-hours of this labour of love, she sat ready in her cradle on the banks of Penetang Bay. One gentle nudge in her rear would be enough to glide her into her element.

The local press were present, radio reporters were mumbling into their microphones, and television cameras from

three stations were ready to roll. It was not every day one could witness the launching of a 30-ton trimaran.

Finally the *Trillium* slowly slid from her cradle toward the water. She crept one foot, two feet, three...and stopped. She was what is referred to as "frozen" in her cradle. With perseverance,

Trillium II *and* Jerry Heutink. *Here she is waiting to be painted.*

plenty of old grease from a fish and chip stand, and a hefty shove from a bulldozer, *Trillium* at last slipped into the waters of Penetang Bay. The sun had begun setting in the west, so it was too late for the usual ceremonies. Next day, Hetty smashed the champagne bottle over her bow, thus fulfilling the old tradition.

Trillium II— frozen in her cradle.

In March 1978, I went to the office of the registrar of ships in Toronto. I had *Trillium* properly registered for sailing in Ontario waters under No. 25E-7545. For me that was not enough. My dreams had taken flight to far-away lands and islands with pure white beaches, palm trees, and beautiful tanned girls. That meant I had to register *Trillium* for international waters.

When I told the registrar I had named my ship the *Trillium*, he rose from behind his desk and said, "*That* is the *Trillium!*" That *Trillium* was a steamship built in 1910, who had seen service as a commuter ferry before being outfitted as a pleasure vessel.

Disappointed, I asked the registrar, "Can I not name my ship *Trillium?*"

He answered, "Yes, you can, but make it *Trillium II.*"

Hetty smashes a champagne bottle over Trillium's *bow. Friends witness the traditional ceremony.*

What lay in store for our ship?

In future years, she would sail many times toward horizons where blood-red or golden suns sank into the skyline, and colourful, windblown clouds turned the western skies into a festival of unequalled beauty. Our good ship *Trillium II* cruised from the midsummer night's sun in northern waters to the breathtaking, heavenly beauty of sundowns during tropical monsoons. She sailed the Seven Seas from east to west, north to south, and back again. We made charter trips on the North Sea, in the Mediterranean, the West Indies, the Carabic, and the Far East. Four times we crossed the Atlantic Ocean, once via the northern Great Circle route in early spring where we were assailed by a mammoth wave in the Bermuda Triangle.

Six times she crossed the Bay of Biscay, once in October. There we encountered a seven-day storm of Beaufort 8–9, with gusts of 10–11.

I don't think Norman Cross ever suspected that one of his ships would ever undergo the torture that *Trillium II* survived. Not even a hairline crack ever appeared in the joints between the three hulls. In twelve years of constant sailing the seas of the world, *Trillium II* never sustained any severe damage. She always reached her destination—always.

Harry, my son and first mate, and I loved our ship very much. We could trust her and we understood how reliable she was. She would pull us through the harshest weather conditions and the wildest storms. She had her whims, like any other ship, but she never failed us. Even in a gale-force Beaufort 11, we did not doubt her ability to pull us through. She and we were one. We had built her with care and love, and sailed her with pride. Every screw and board were familiar to us, and her whims were overlooked. We gave her a soul and a will, which she had made known by her refusal to glide from her cradle.

Once, in a storm during the Fastnet Race in which many yachts broke up and sunk and sailors perished, we didn't have so much as a scratch. We had listened to the weather reports and prepared on time. That had made all the difference.

This book is a personal account of twelve years at sea. It is a book about a ship and the sea, a skipper and his first mate, about exotic lands and unusual people, tropical islands and carefree natives, about chartering and paying crew, sunrises and sunsets. The voyages were a dream come true.

The finished product. A proud ship, ready to be launched. 8,500 hours went into her construction. Harry stands on the foredeck.

Plans and Construction of Trillium II

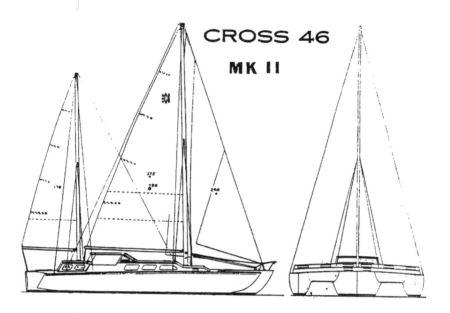

CROSS 46 MK II

Specifications

Length Overall	46'6"	Displacement	19,500 lbs
Waterline Length	43'0"	Payload	6,500 lbs
Beam Overall	25'3"	Auxil. Power	45–55 HP
Draft	4'3"	No. of Berths	8–10
Sail Area (working)	780 sq. ft.	Headroom	6'3"

Design Features

THE CROSS 46 is designed to accommodate a party of eight to 10 persons and is an ideal boat for cruising, living aboard, or charter work. Privacy, which is essential aboard any boat, is assured in the five double staterooms, two of which have their own private head. The main cabin is 12.5 feet long and has ample room for the dinette and galley areas. The forward cabin is separated from the main cabin by the head and shower. The two rear staterooms are separated from the main cabin by a cockpit the full width of the boat. Access to the rear staterooms is made directly from the cockpit. A head and hanging locker separate the two rear cabins. A recreation cockpit is located in the stern of the main hull and is ideal for fishing, swimming, or skin diving. The large deck area is well suited for sail handling, moving about, or sunning. There is plenty of storage space located throughout the boat.

The combination of the ketch rig with a moderate working sail area, low aspect ratio, fin keel, and spade rudder pro-

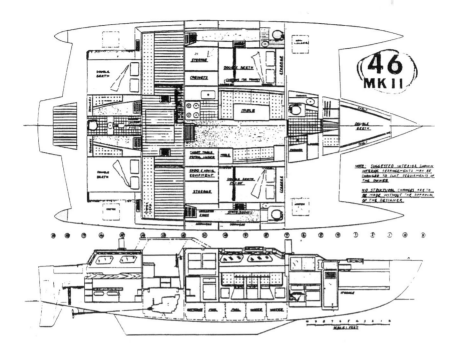

vides a boat that is easy to handle. It has good directional stability and comes about easily. The sail area can be increased with the addition of a genoa and mizzen staysail. Even with the fin keel the draft is not excessive.

Construction

THE HULLS are of the round-bottom type using double/diagonal plywood planking.
- Frames are laid out on and cut from sheet plywood.
- Bulkheads are plywood and Douglas fir (or other boat-building lumber).
- Beams are marine plywood and Douglas fir.
- Stringers and longitudinals are Douglas fir (or other boat-building lumber).
- Deck, cabin, and fin keel are plywood.
- Fastenings are bronze anchorfast nails, staples, and marine glue.
- All exterior surfaces are covered with fibreglass, dynell, or vectra.
- Spars are spruce (aluminum optional).
- Standing rigging and fittings are stainless steel or bronze.

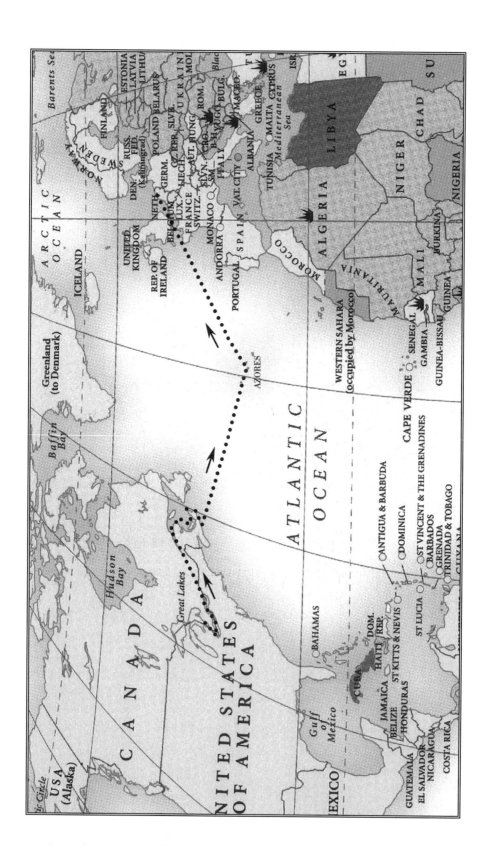

From Canada to Holland

Sailing in the Mist

Since our departure from Penetanguishene, Ontario, the wind had dropped and Ethel, our diesel, rumbled underfoot. It was strange that no one had thought of giving the engine a name before, but suddenly, there it was—Ethel. She was called that until we replaced her years later with a Volvo-Penta, a stronger diesel. The Volvo-Penta never received a pet name.

This was the beginning of a long cruise with *Trillium II*, but we never dreamed that it would be a voyage of twelve years across seas and oceans.

We were headed for our native land, Holland, a small country on the other side of the Atlantic Ocean. As the saying goes, "God made the world, but the Dutch made Holland." It is a land of dunes and polders, broad rivers and straight canals, willows beside water-courses, and rows of tall poplars on the horizon, bent by prevailing winds. Many age-old farms hide behind giant oak trees and greenery. Towering cumulus clouds are white against pastel blue skies. Sunlight streams over green meadows dotted with black and white cattle.

It is the land of Rembrandt and Hobbema, Van Gogh and Peter Paul Rubens, painters *par excellence* of the Dutch landscape and its inhabitants. To this land we would go first.

Holland was still a long way off. While the sun sank on the western horizon, we passed between Giants Tomb and Beckwith Island in Georgian Bay. Twilight on this latitude did not last long. At most, we had another hour of gradually fading dusk. The crossing to the Bruce Peninsula would take all night. We had sailed this part of the bay before.

Georgian Bay and Lake Huron

*An historic photo—*Trillium II *leaves Penetang Bay, the very beginning of her voyages over the Seven Seas.* Trillium II *never returned here.*

Our greenhorn crew—Harry, my youngest son, as first mate, and Dave and Frank as deckhands and cook, were excited in anticipation of what lay ahead.

The evening was warm and balmy, and the waters of the bay as smooth as glass. The air was still, and even at that hour, had a pearl-grey clarity. Slowly the horizon faded away and the sea and sky merged. Not a ripple disturbed the water, except where the screw thrashed it into a long wake of foam. At half a mile distance, we passed two small islands called the Western Islands. They were nothing more than rocky humps with some scraggly cedars growing out of the cracks. However, around those clusters lay underwater reefs of hard, rigid basalt. A ship would be a total loss if a collision should occur. One look at the chart was enough to understand the dangers. We gave the Western Islands a wide berth.

Cooky had supper ready, and for this special occasion we stopped Ethel. This would be our first official meal aboard *Trillium II* on our intended international cruise. We ate on deck, but spoke little. Such moments must be savoured; they are few and far between.

It was time to bring Ethel back to life, and the boys cleaned the galley without protest. Harry took the wheel and pointed our ship on its west-nor'west course. Everyone gathered on deck to enjoy the enchanting evening. The doors of the wheelhouse were left wide open so Harry could be part of the group. Dave strummed his guitar while Frank blew a trumpet melody in minor. The tune did not disappear in the air, but seemed to hover around us on that calm, peaceful evening.

The first bright stars twinkled high above us in the ebony sky. Stars are the guiding lights for the navigator, assisting him in finding his path across the oceans. We set our course to the red flashing light of the beacon on Hope Island. Closing in, we noticed the dark shadow of the rocks and passed at a safe distance. Abeam of the light, we changed course to Cape Bruce and slowly Hope Island faded away over our stern. From then on we would sail by compass. No more flashing red, white, or amber lights of beacons to show us the way.

The boys came below to watch the new skipper play with his navigational toys. "Fellows," I told them, "this straight, thin pencil line on the chart is the course we need to follow to reach Cape Bruce. I hope you will all steer a good course without zig-zagging or straying from this pencil line." As an afterthought I added, "Keep your eyes not only on the compass, but also look aft every so often. If the wake is a straight line, you are a good helmsman."

The moon was in its first quarter and we should have seen it in the southeast. But all we could see was a dark circle of water around us, and in the distance a thick grey wall seemed to be closing in. Fog!

Visibility reduced rapidly, but above us the stars sparkled in abundance. Moments later, the moon peeked over the encroaching mist. The moonlight transformed the ring of black water into a silvery mirror. We could see no further than a hundred metres ahead, but luckily we were not yet in a shipping lane.

This night sail captivated us as never before. No one wanted to sleep. As the moon rose higher and higher, it cast a wide beam of pure silver toward the ship. We sailed on through the night. The moon, high in the sky, made the wall of mist around us more transparent and visibility improved somewhat. Around the midnight hour, we had a very unusual experience. The ship sailed straight into an enormous swarm of large, nocturnal moths. By the thousands they landed on the decks, creeping all over us, getting in our noses and ears. A plague descended upon us and we tried to escape inside. Frank, at the wheel, had been too late to close the doors and the pests had already invaded the ship's interior. The attack lasted for an hour. We travelled at a speed of six knots, and the swarm must have been six miles long. Months later, we still found their dry, grey corpses in nooks and crannies.

Early the next morning we felt a slight wind and the fog lifted at times. Now we had double lookouts because we were in the tanker lane from Parry Sound to Tobermory. A tanker cruising at a speed of twenty knots could appear from below the horizon and be right on top of one's ship in ten minutes. It did not leave much warning time.

Patches of fog hung around us and we started to search for the beacon of Bruce Peninsula. We should have seen it by now, or had we missed it? Thoughts of meeting a tanker were constantly on our minds. Suddenly, out of nowhere it appeared like a lit-up Christmas tree almost on top of our stern. Turning the wheel hard to starboard, we gave him the right of way. Our little nutshell was no match for that enormous hulk of steel. Relief washed over us. Our rival had passed us, and we were exactly on course. We had deep water under our keel, and that makes a seaman very happy.

The sun rose and split the sky wide open with arrows of pure gold. By full daylight we could see the grey cliffs of the north coast of the Peninsula. These cliffs were 200 metres high, so we could keep track of them even in those foggy conditions.

Our faith was shattered. Mist banks closed in again and visibility was reduced to zero. We set Ethel on dead slow and hoped for the best. Under normal conditions we should have reached Tobermory by noon, but that goal would have to be forgotten.

Unexpectedly, we sailed into a large pool of sunlight and a view of the coastline. For a few hours we stormed full speed ahead, but about a mile from Tobermory we were enveloped by fog once more. This time we were in a narrow stretch of water with large clumps of rocks on both sides. We didn't dare move ahead, but to remain dead still in the water was even more risky. A serious decision had to be made. There were buoys on either side of the shipping lane, but we couldn't see them. We drifted a bit and luckily *Trillium* nudged a bright red buoy. We felt safe now because we knew we were on the edge of the shipping lane. I slung a painter around the buoy and checked the drifting. We heard the foghorn of Tobermory loud and clear.

Ethel had been on standby, and lazily idled in her cosy, white engine room. For a moment, the grey fog dissolved, and Ethel jumped to life; *Trillium II* was on her way again. Like a ghost ship, a heavy cruiser burst out of the fog on our other side. He hailed us and we explained the critical conditions, and questioned him about the weather he had just travelled through. He had come from Tobermory, and told us that the harbour was closed in with fog. With gas handles forward and engines roaring, he took off. We waved goodbye and hoped the best for him.

After intermittent periods of stopping and starting, we finally reached the entrance of the harbour. Far over the starboard we beheld Lake Huron, blue and scintillating in the sun. The entrance was blocked by a ferry, but by careful manoeuvring I piloted *Trillium II* into the inner harbour. Many yachts were moored at the quay. Our entry caused much activity, so there were enough hands ashore to catch our mooring lines. It was 2:00 P.M., and we were thankful and relieved that we had arrived safely.

Not long after, another ship entered the inner harbour. It was our friend from that huge plastic cruiser. His American flag hung listlessly from the poop. The skipper seemed to have lost his bravado, and timidly found himself a spot in the back of the yacht harbour.

For three days we were held prisoners along with all the other yachts. Every day a few more boats would pull inside. Tobermory did not have much entertainment, but that did not bother us. We had plenty of work to do.

We did not know at that time what we were in for. For three weeks we would have a fight on our hands with the greatest enemy of the mariners—fog.

The crew was content socializing with the crews and passengers of the other yachts. The marina became like a commune, with parties going on here and there. Our crew considered this quite an adventure.

We bunkered the second day, and the boys did some shopping in preparation for our next trek. On the third day, our lookout on the mole reported that all was clear as far as the horizon. Our mooring lines were thrown on deck, and Ethel growled at first contact. We were the first to put to sea. Adieu, Tobermory.

ON BOARD the other yachts, activity began, and a few followed us to their regained freedom. Through the narrow, buoyed Devil's Rock Channel, we reached Lake Huron in about an hour, and we considered ourselves lucky that we had passed through it in such clear, beautiful weather. We wondered how the tankers of 10,000 tons managed to make it through this channel without any damage.

That pleasant weather didn't last any longer than the last buoy. First, the skyline disappeared, and soon we were again closed in by heavy fog. This time the concern was not as great. We had plenty of sea room, and the channel with those devilishly dangerous rocks was far behind.

We followed the thin pencil line on the chart with the aid of the radio direction-finder. Tuned in to Sarnia Radio, we linked compass and direction-finder. *Trillium II* travelled a straight, unerring course, as the crow flies, to Sarnia.

For a day and a night, there was no visibility, and sounds were muffled by a damp blanket of air. At the end of the second day, a golden shine broke through the grey fog. Not long after, we saw the bridge over the St. Clair River. We had made it! Georgian Bay and Lake Huron lay behind us, and before us were Lake Erie and Lake Ontario. The St. Lawrence River waited to carry us to that great body of water, the Atlantic Ocean.

Fog chased us as far as Lake Erie, where we were punished for daring to sail in zero visibility. We were grounded on a shelf of slate. From Point Pelee, we were heading to Long Point, and we must have crawled too close under the coast. We had been

Adieu, Tobermory

running at half speed with all men on the lookout, but with no warning we ran aground. The boys set the sloop overboard, and rowed around the ship to see what could be done. Grinning happily, they reported, "No damage, Skipper. We'll have her afloat in no time. It's a piece of cake. Just watch us."

They took one of the new anchors, rowed out far, and dropped it overboard. Then they wiggled the anchor until the flukes took hold behind some slate. Frank had stayed on board *Trillium II*, and when given the sign by Harry, he wrapped the biter end of the line around a winch, and by turning the handle the ship inched out of its trap. Slowly she slid back into deeper water, and in no time she was floating again. I sighed with relief—it could have been much worse.

Now what? Where were we? Tatters of fog still hung around us. The anchor was now free from the slate, and Harry brought it around to the bow where he dropped it so *Trillium II* wouldn't run adrift. Meanwhile, the afternoon progressed. No one liked the idea of hanging around in this no-man's land for the rest of the day. As always, luck is with fools. Out of the shadows loomed a runabout with two anglers. With surprised expressions they approached, and asked what we were doing in that wilderness of water and rocks. Grinning sheepishly, we admitted that we didn't know where we were or how we got there.

The men scratched their heads and told us we had ventured deep into a swampy area with rocky islets, a quagmire of peat bogs, and armies of mosquitoes. Open water was at least one hour away.

Our smiles faded, and we faced each other with looks of astonishment and terror. How in Neptune's name had we come this far without hitting rocks or grounding in the morass? We had been very, very lucky to slide up on that slowly-rising shoal of smooth slate.

The men were friendly and offered to pilot us back to the open waters of Lake Erie. Just as they had said, it *did* take over an hour to get back.

We thanked our pilots profusely, and congratulated each other on escaping unscathed the labyrinth of waterways, islets, rocks, and underwater obstacles. How we had strayed so far off course, deep into the swamp, remains a mystery forever concealed in the mists of Lake Erie.

First Atlantic Crossing

The Welland Canal has eight locks. One entrance is located at Port Colborne, and another at Port Weller. The locks in between bring the total lift to 326 feet, connecting Lake Erie and Lake Ontario. Even the biggest lake vessels have access to the Great Lakes. Opened in 1932, the canal by-passes Niagara Falls. Large American cities such as Buffalo, Detroit, Cleveland, and Chicago are within reach of all other Maritime shipping from the Atlantic Ocean via the St. Lawrence River.

West to East

It was late evening before we got the go-ahead at the Port Colborne lock. The bridge rose and the green light indicated permission to enter. The sun had set and the shore lights flickered on, magically turning the evening into a very peaceful, pleasing, and romantic event.

Over the marine radio, the lock-master directed us to the far end of the lock, bows against the lock doors. A laker entered promptly at our heels. She was in ballast, lying high on the water. It was a mighty sight to watch her approaching. We sensed some uneasiness as she came nearer. If her skipper overshot the mark, we would be smashed to splinters. She kept coming and our uneasiness grew near panic. We waved frantically to the figures behind the windows of the laker's bridge towering high above us. They waved back.

Port Colborne– entrance to the Welland Canal. The lock-master let us wait until more ships had arrived to be sluiced. through.

One metre from *Trillium*'s stern, the laker stopped dead in the water. Three thousand tons of steel stopped just in the nick of time. We all breathed a sigh of relief. Had it been bravado or good seamanship, a show of rare performance or harassment? Probably a bit of each. Nevertheless, we experienced a terrifying moment.

In the wee hours of the morning, we had reached the lock at Port Weller. Lake Ontario lay ahead of us, in that half light just before sunrise. In the nearest yacht harbour I sent the boys to their bunks for a few hours of sleep. It had been a nerve-racking 24 hours. First the adventure of running aground, and then the near collision with the laker.

Our destination, Toronto, was on the other side of Lake Ontario. It was still thirty miles and a few hours of hard work for

Ethel. There was no wind whatsoever. The boys could go on shore leave, and Hetty would be joining us for a couple of days.

In the afternoon, the skyline of the city rose above the hazy horizon. We had noticed the CN Tower long before. With its 1,850-foot freestanding tower, it is the highest building in the world. But we saw more than that. An ugly, poisonous, green-orange cloud hovered over the city. We shuddered to think that people living below that cloud breathed this polluted air day and night.

Skyline of Toronto with the silhouette of the CN Tower under the evening sky.

On the Toronto Islands we found a suitable place to stay for a while. *Trillium II* was moored in a park under the shady boughs of some large trees. Hetty arrived on board with our daughter, Tina, and her friend, Lynn Dekkers. We enjoyed recounting our adventures to the guests. It awakened the wanderlust in the girls, and we agreed that they could come on board for the cruise down the St. Lawrence. They would board the ship in Kingston. Long before, Hetty had made it clear that she would not come along for the Atlantic crossing, but would fly over to Holland to wait for us. We respected her wish. Not everyone likes the sea.

The girls boarded in Kingston, where we were moored on a quay with a view of the barred windows of the famous jail. Sailing down the St. Lawrence was a splendid experience. The weather held, and we had a breeze to fill our white sails. We passed thousands of green islands and many houses with colourful roofs. I highly recommend it to all the sailing fraternity. With the welcome help of the river's current, we ran ten knots under sail. Our crew enjoyed themselves immensely.

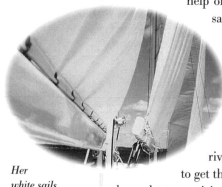

Her white sails put Trillium II down the St. Lawrence with a groundspeed of ten knots.

The St. Lawrence River has four enormous locks, and we had paid months in advance for the privilege of employing them. At first, we were slightly apprehensive about the undertaking, but all went well. Ethel, our old diesel, gave up somewhere in the middle of our cruise down the river, but we found a small harbour and a place to get the engine repaired. We were invited by a nearby yacht to participate in the yearly festival, Christmas in June. One of the houseboats was decorated with a rooftop tree, and the party was even attended by Santa Claus himself.

Our next stop was the yacht harbour of Expo 67, in Montreal. We danced that evening to polkas of the "oompah" music of an imitation German band in an imitation German beerhall. Between waltzes and polkas, we drank good German beer out of imitation German beer steins: long live wine, women, and song.

That summer, we sailed on the beautiful Bras d'Or Lakes on Cape Breton Island and tried our hand at chartering. We made enough to pay for the harbour fees and food before realizing that September had arrived, and it was too late for crossing the Atlantic. On Prince Edward Island we discovered a spot to stay for the winter. Our crew left ship, including Lynn Dekkers, who had sailed with us all the way down.

Baddeck, Nova Scotia— our summer harbour.

We hoisted *Trillium II* ashore at McDonald's Lumberyard, and hooked up to hydro before winter set in. Harry and I found jobs, and we braced ourselves for a harsh winter. We covered the ship's deck and wheelhouse with plastic sheets, and forced hot air through the bilges to keep the water tanks from freezing. On very cold days, when the outside temperature dipped below –25°C, we had a propane heater going in our living quarters. That kept everything nice and cosy.

Wintering in the Maritimes

By the time we had decided to winter in Charlottetown, we already had made many friends. Their doors were always open to us. We met Andy and Dorothy who promptly recruited me to build a rec-room in their basement, and their TV and radio repair shop needed expansion and renovations. These jobs would last me all winter.

The day we arrived in Charlottetown's yacht club, we met Joost and Ruth Roggeveen and became good friends. Joost was a direct descendent of the 17th-century Dutch explorer, Admiral Jacob Roggeveen, who on Easter Day in 1722, landed on Rapa Nui, or Easter Island, in the South Pacific. Ruth was a Prince Edward Islander and had grown up on her parents' farm.

Our ship enters Charlottetown, PEI to winter, high ashore at McDonald's Lumberyard. We pass the Canadian Coast Guard cutter, Trapper.

When Hetty came aboard in the fall, she brought Sally Ann, our old dog, with her. She was quickly promoted to "ship's dog." Sally Ann, with her spindly legs, soft furry coat, and black eyes, was, at the unbelievable age of 17, still a virgin. Would-be mates

Harry shovels the first snow from the deck; Tupper *in the background.*

were always met with growls and flashing, pointed teeth. No wonder her cowardly lovers were scared away.

I always took Sally to Andy and Dorothy's house when they invited me to dinner, and she became great friends with the Roggeveens as well. It was Andy and Dorothy who took Sally to the vet when she became seriously ill with cancer; we sadly buried her in Joost and Ruth's garden when she died on April 29.

A week later Hetty and Harry returned from a visit to Ontario, and in June we took our mooring lines in and said farewell to Charlottetown. *Trillium II* would never return, and Sally stayed behind, in the rich, red earth of the island. Before we left I planted a Russian olive tree on her grave.

From Halifax to Holland

TRILLIUM II was once again in her element. Harry checked the sails, and Ethel received a necessary tune-up and cleaning. I installed myself behind the navigation table and set our course to Halifax. We waved goodbye to all our friends on PEI and sailed into the blue yonder. Canso, on the northeast point of Nova Scotia, had a lock. From there, unfortunately, we were forced to sail through fog to Halifax.

Halifax had noticed us on their radar and guided us into the entrance of the harbour. We bunkered oil, took water in, and bought large quantities of supplies. Our new crew was ready and raring to go. The day before departure, Hetty left on a first-class flight to Holland. She deserved special treatment after that long winter in Charlottetown. We drew our lines in and set sail for Holland.

While crossing the Labrador current, once again we encountered dense fog. It persisted until we were abeam Sable Island. This time we laughed. We now had radar, and were able to see through the mist thanks to this indispensable piece of electronics.

Frank and Lyn Dekkers, our first crew mates, look aloft when hoisting sail.

Before we left Penetanguishene we had made arrangements with a Barrie radio station to keep in daily contact and report our progress via our shortwave radio. They would produce a regular program and a running commentary of *Trillium's* voyage. A similar radio schedule was agreed upon with the Charlottetown Amateur Radio Club. We maintained these engagements for a while, but communication broke down as we grew tired of it. This prompted the radio station in Barrie to notify the Canadian Coast Guard, and we were reported as "lost on the Atlantic."

The sun was shining brightly. Waves jostled our ship in a pleasant rhythm toward the Azores. The wind endlessly filled our white sails. All was well aboard. When the harbour-master in Horta, on the Azores, relayed to us the Coast Guard's message, we looked at each other and smiled.

Lost on the Atlantic... Found in the Azores

As we approached the Azores, visibility had reduced to approximately one mile. We could not see the islands, but we certainly could smell them.

A few days before, we had had radio contact with a merchant ship. The first mate had encouraged us to visit Flores, the westernmost island of the Archipelago. According to him, it was a beautiful island; and Santa Cruz, on the east side of the island, had a small harbour.

We were thrilled! Our first landing on an island paradise... perhaps with charming, olive-skinned women on clean, white beaches. But no island appeared out of the misty gloom. Our daydreams shattered to pieces. What on earth had happened to our position at sea? Where were we? North, south, or abeam Flores? The ship was shrouded in a veil of fog, yet a sweet fragrance permeated the haze. It wafted dreamily over the decks, seducing our senses. Was it the smell of flowers? Flowers? Flores? Of course! We were downwind of the island, and the honeyed sweetness of her flowers would lead us in. As we sailed upwind, the scent became stronger and stronger. After ten miles of fragrant piloting, the island of Flores slowly appeared out of the sea. The sun shone on her volcanic cone and lilac flowers crept up the mountain slopes.

Carefully we closed in on the coastline. After two miles, the harbour of Santa Cruz came into view. In the meantime, the ocean had changed her character. Wavelets became waves, and waves turned into a long, rolling swell. Between two crests, we disappeared into a canyon of water. Luckily, the enormous waves were gradually sloping and didn't break. We dropped sails and rode the peak of the billows. When lifted high to the top, we could see the harbour. When the ship plummeted down we were surrounded by water. Somewhere in the distant north a fierce storm must have raged, and the swells were an awesome remnant of it.

I radioed the harbour and a reply followed immediately in a

language (Portuguese) we could not understand. A moment later, we heard the voice of a woman informing us that a barque with pilot was on the way.

Not too far off, we noticed the brave vessel teetering on the crest of the gigantic waves only to disappear moments later in a trough between two mountains of water. That helmsman was a master in seamanship. Shortly the barque drew along-side us, and the two ships rose and fell simultane-ously. The pilot, a young man of about thirty, jumped over and without much ado took the wheel and brought *Trillium II* on a course beam-to the waves. The barque retired from sight, and we followed. Near the harbour our pilot took a wide turn and guided our ship care-fully through the entrance.

The little harbour of Santa Cruz on Flores— open and with little protection from the ocean. We navigated toward the island with the aid of the per-fume of millions of hydrangeas.

The harbour was nothing more than a tiny stretch of water between the quay and a row of rocks connected by enor-mous concrete blocks to keep the sea out. The crew of the barque took our lines and fastened them to points on the quay, and on the opposite side to rings in the rocks and concrete. We danced free and safe in the middle of the harbour where two ships were like-wise moored. One was a Dutch schooner, the other, a German yacht.

Once everything was ship-shape, there was time to get acquainted with our pilot, Umberto. He explained that his father, Augusto, was the captain of the barque. Augusto was not only a fisherman, but also the chief of the island. On behalf of his father, Umberto extended to us an invitation to join them ashore for a drink.

I gratefully offered Umberto a bottle of Canadian whiskey, but he politely refused any payment for bringing *Trillium II* into the harbour. We were overwhelmed by the generosity of our hosts; it was unheard of. We encountered many gestures of hospitality, and were invited to the chief's home and allowed the use of his luxu-rious bathroom! The floors and walls were covered in flamed Carrara marble. The king-sized bathtub was made of marble tiles with gold fittings. There we were, the whole crew, sipping the chief's port wine. One by one, we faded from sight to enjoy a soak and a scrub in that wonderful, super-deluxe bathtub.

We stayed for a pleasurable week and received many invita-tions from the islanders. Not one evening was spent aboard. We met the crews of the Dutch schooner and the German yacht. We even participated in a wedding and were guests of honour at a funeral. Every morning a sloop came alongside our three ships to deliver a gift of potatoes, vegetables, or a generous piece of cheese.

In our flag chest we did not carry a Portuguese flag, so I asked Umberto where in Santa Cruz one could be purchased. It is customary to fly the flag of the country one visits. There was no such store in Santa Cruz, which caused us some uneasiness. We did not want to be rude. That afternoon, a woman rowed up beside us and presented us and also our Dutch and German friends with hand made Portuguese flags. She refused payment.

To the left, a German yacht; in the middle, a Dutch schooner; and at right, Trillium II. *Our arrival was an event of great importance. We were received as kings by the friendly islanders.*

On a lovely Sunday morning, Augusto delighted us with a tour of the island. In the back of his truck he had placed crates for seats. The crews of the three visiting ships were present. We were given the grand tour, all the way up to the crater of the dead volcano. Along the way we beheld the unimaginable splendour and richness of purple hydrangeas. It was their sweet scent we had noticed from twelve miles out at sea. Some were blue, and others had a rosy hue. Augusto steered the truck down a narrow country road where a small bush of white hydrangeas bloomed. He cut a few and presented each lady in our company with a bouquet, saying, "These are the only white hydrangeas on our island."

Sweet island hospitality

The vistas were remarkable. All around us glittered the deep, blue ocean. Far down the mountain lay Santa Cruz, where our ships seemed like toys in a miniature harbour. As we had learned already, Augusto did not want any financial compensation for the day we spent with him. A "Muchos gracias, Augusto" was all he was willing to accept.

Our stay on this charming island had been especially memorable. We didn't want to wear out our welcome, so after an emotional farewell we took in our lines and set course to Horta, on the island of Fayal.

Horta had an enormous open harbour, but also a concrete pier behind which we could hide from the rollers of the Atlantic. There were many yachts of several different nationalities, and we

The harbour of Horta in the Azores—a very fine view of the city. To the left, a well-protected mole. Trillium II *moored there next to a world-solo sailer from the Netherlands.*

felt at home among them. Included was a yacht from Harlingen, Holland, and also the *Bylgia* with Eilco Kasimir, a Dutchman, who was a world solo sailor. He had arrived two days before we did, and was busy catching up on his sleep. We moored next to the *Bylgia*. Soon we became regular guests at Café Sport, world renowned by the sailing fraternity. We donated a Canadian flag with the name of *Trillium II* painted along the hoist of it.

In the distance, far beyond the horizon's lip, Holland awaited. Eilco had become restless. He was on the last leg of his solo cruise around the world and yearned for his homeland. We departed at the same time, and sailed together for half a day. A strong nor'wester blew, creating rough seas. The *Bylgia* heeled far over and Eilco quickly radioed us: "I envy you. Your ship sails upright, but look at me. My starboard railing is under water!"

Then he disappeared into a black raincloud and we never saw him again.

We continued on in extremely bad weather for the month of July. In the Bay of Biscay we encountered a gale so forceful it set us off toward the French coast. Before we ran into trouble, we overheard Quessant Radio talking to fishermen at sea. A bearing on that station showed us we had crossed the Bay and could set course to Plymouth. There we would stop for a much deserved rest from the sea. *Trillium II* and the crew had earned it—especially the captain.

From Quessant to Plymouth was not a great distance, but under the English coast we were once again faced with fog. Luckily the Eddystone lighthouse became dimly visible and we were able to sail straight into the harbour. We searched in vain for the *Bylgia*, but later heard that she had made a landfall in St. Peter's Port on Guernsey.

When we turned into the yacht harbour, we were greeted by a crowd onshore. Cameras flashed and questions were fired at us about a Trans-Atlantic race. We were sorry to disappoint the spectators and race officials, but *Trillium II* had not been in any race at all. However, she had crossed the Atlantic all the same. Here yet another harbour master also told us we were lost at sea!

HETTY FLEW over from Holland intending to sail with us for the rest of the summer. Harry and I were very pleased with her decision. Part of the crew had paid for the cruise as far as Plymouth and had left the ship. We explored the town, but after finding nothing of interest, we departed. In one run, we reached Vlissingen, in Holland. The statue of Netherland's greatest admiral, Adriaan de Ruyter, welcomed us. With a great sense of pride, we realized we had actually sailed in a trimaran all the way from Canada to Holland; from the birthplace of *Trillium II*, Penetanguishene, to Enschede, birthplace of the captain. Hetty, Harry, and I sat down to confer and lay out the plans for the next three months. We had much to choose from. We listed the Dutch canals and rivers at the top of our itinerary. Also included were the North Sea, Denmark, and Germany. From there, we would travel back to Holland via the rivers Rhine, Ijssel, and Twenthe Canal, ending at our destination, Enschede.

After rounding up some paying passengers, we sailed the first short leg from Vlissingen to Middelburg on the island of Walcheren. This island had witnessed much fighting between Canadian soldiers and German troops in November 1944. Now it was quiet, peaceful, and full of sunshine. *Trillium II* entered the little canals of the town of Middelburg and moored not far from the heart of the busy centre. The town hall, partly destroyed during the war, had been completely restored to its original grandeur of 16th-century architecture and beauty. However, the streets in the shopping centre were completely strewn with litter. Where was the clean, tidy Holland that I remembered so well? We were shocked and ashamed, especially about the condition of the town of Middelburg. I felt compelled to apologize to our American guests on board.

Cruising the Dutch waterways was a splendid adventure. We visited Veere, a quaint, old fishing village in Zeeland, and fell promptly in love with it. We were beguiled by the doll-like houses with windows of little, square panes and the clean, white lace curtains behind them. To wander through that low, glossy green door seemed to us like a step into a long-ago past.

We also made a stop at Willemstad, in the province of Brabant. The old fishing harbour had been transformed into a yacht harbour. When we arrived, it was completely full of Dutch and German yachts. The courteous harbour-master, dressed in a contemporary suit, chased several of the boats from their moorings to make room for the odd trimaran with its Canadian flag waving proudly. We thanked him profusely. "Bravo, harbour-master. We won't forget you," we called from our deck.

Sailing down more rivers and waterways, we bypassed Rotterdam and headed for Gouda, the town famous for its cheese and its specialty, Gouda waffles, which we bought at a delightful, old-fashioned shop on the quayside. With a steaming cup of coffee, the waffles tasted delicious. When the door of the shop was opened a chime could be heard. We could not resist opening and closing the door a few times to listen to that nostalgic sound. It brought back many childhood memories.

Trillium II *in Dutch waters—Willemstad in Brabant. A friendly harbour-master found us a spot in the full harbour. That beautiful windmill is still in use.*

Gouda had no harbour to speak of. The quay was built along a narrow canal, and with *Trillium*'s beam of eight metres we took up a large portion of it. Later, a tugboat with a number of barges in tow found the channel too constricting. The captain of the tug, standing in the door of his wheelhouse, hurled such an exquisite string of Dutch expletives and abuses our way that we were so totally flabbergasted and speechless, we forgot to retaliate.

From Gouda, we followed the river Gouwe Aar with emerald-green pastures on either side. On the horizon were many pointed church steeples like fingers reaching toward heaven. There was little or no shipping, and the only soul we met on the water was an angler in a rowboat. It was so rural, peaceful, and serene. We set Ethel on slow and glided through waters that reflected the blue skies and white cumulus clouds. When we reached the lake district, we thanked Ethel for her good service, and under full canvas we sailed from one lake into the other. By evening, we looked for the yacht harbour in the Nieuwe Meer (New Lake) just south of Amsterdam. We had many old friends living in or near Amsterdam, and when they learned of our arrival they made a point of visiting us. We were invited to their homes, and most importantly, to their bathtubs!

A week flew by quickly. To enter the canals of Amsterdam, we had to negotiate a lock to bring us up from the lower water level of the Nieuwe Meer to the higher level of the canals. We had already spoken to the lock-master, a very friendly and helpful man. He arranged everything for us. On the day of departure, he told us to be at the lock at midnight to pass through his sluice. On a chart, he had mapped out in blue ink the route we needed to follow through the Amsterdam canals to reach a railroad bridge named the Hembrug. It would be open for only twenty minutes, between the last train from Amsterdam and the first train coming back in. "Twenty minutes," said the lock-master, "no more!"

It was inconceivable that we could traverse the winding canals through the middle of that huge city. We were concerned about all the bridges, hundreds of them. Would they open for us? Would we be at the Hembrug on time? At the lock at midnight, our friend assured us that he had phoned ahead and all the bridgekeepers were ready for us. The lock doors yawned sleepily upon our approach, allowing us to enter. It was exactly midnight.

Trillium II would then proceed into an adventure that was unparalleled in the annals of boating. First we sailed along in the quiet waters of tree-lined canals. Here and there a lonely lamp-post would break the intense darkness under the trees. Harry turned on the spotlight and swung it back and forth. Hetty, also, was on the lookout. She had sharp eyes and good night vision. Gradually, it became lighter and busier ashore. Before we realized it, we were in the centre of the city. Neon lights flashed and blinked on both sides of the canals. It was so confusing; at times we were unable to distinguish them from the bridge lights. When we were given the green light, trams waited to cross, and late party-goers stared with wide, unbelieving eyes. Was this huge, two-masted sailing vessel actually in their canal? In colourful Amsterdam slang, we received many juicy remarks from the denizens of that city.

We were expected at the Hembrug at 4:00 A.M. and we reached it with time to spare. In a large basin, many barges and Rhine vessels waited with their diesels rumbling. We found a vacant ring in a huge wooden post and fastened a line to it.

At 0400 hours precisely, a train thundered over the bridge. As if by magic, the massive steel construction swivelled on its centre buttress dam. The barges were the first to go through. As latecomers, we had to wait until last. The bridge closed behind us, and not long after a train came from the other side to pass. It was timed to the second.

We were then in the Ij, a large body of water with many harbour complexes for different purposes. Even the largest sea-going vessels could reach the Ij via the Noordzee Canal through the enormous locks at Ijmuiden.

Midnight in Amsterdam

In the early light of dawn, we saw the filigree silhouettes of numerous warehouses and cranes against the sky. We knew that to the west the Ij ended and the North Sea canal began. But that was where the heavy shipping took place. We were searching for the entrance of the Noordhollands Kanaal, east of our present location. In the beginning of the 1800s, the Dutch had dug a canal from the Ij north to Den Helder. Soon it could no longer carry all the vessels to and from Amsterdam. When the North Sea canal replaced it, the Noordhollands Kanaal became a recreation area for anglers and sport boaters. That was the waterway we were looking for.

In spite of our sleepless night, we decided to carry on. The canal flowed directly through the middle of the town of Alkmaar, another cheese centre with many tourist attractions. We stayed for a couple of days, attracting much attention in our strange vessel.

From Alkmaar to Den Helder, the landscape grew monotonous: green fields dotted with black and white cattle. Den Helder is a naval town where the Dutch war fleet is concentrated in a harbour open to the North Sea. We were invited to be guests of the marines for three days. On the fourth day we thanked them for their hospitality and headed our ship toward the North Sea. I set our course north of the islands that border Holland and Germany.

By morning, we had reached the mouth of the river Elbe. We then proceeded to Brünsbuttel and the locks that would lift us into the Kieler Canal, known now as the North Sea–Baltic Sea Canal. Once through, we found a small yacht harbour with just enough space for *Trillium II* to stay a day and a night. A ship chandler in a dory rowed up alongside and showed us a handy list from which we could order fresh victuals.

The next morning we motored through the canal that slices the counties of Schleswig and Holstein in half. We were flanked by picturesque scenery, including many Holstein cows grazing leisurely in the lush, green fields. Using locks had become such a routine that we no longer felt apprehensive. In no time we passed through the locks at Kiel, and the Baltic Sea lay in front of *Trillium*'s bows.

Sitting at my navigation table, I pondered which way to take to Copenhagen; the direct route, or the longer, scenic route. The decision to travel the long way was made quickly by the crew. They wanted to visit Flensburg, an old Hansa town, half Danish and half German, and then cruise among the islands. I agreed, keeping an eye on the chart of the Baltic.

Flensburg was somewhat disappointing, and we departed with no regrets, and set course to our next destination, Svendborg, on the island of Fyn. While our guests explored the city, Hetty and I boarded a train for Odense, the hometown of the famous writer of fairy tales, Hans Christiaan Andersen (1805–1875). Outside the museum housed in the story-teller's family home was a terrace under an old sycamore tree. Hetty and I had coffee and a Danish pastry there, thinking about how, long, long ago Hans Christiaan must have sat there to write his tales.

We walked around the old mediaeval town, sat on a park bench, and I took some snapshots of life-sized statues—beautiful women in the nude—that lined the pathways.

Later we boarded the old chug-a-chug again and the steam engine huffed and puffed us back to Svendborg in a dreamy, sleepy kind of ride.

On the ship we found Harry and our crew bent over the navigation table discussing several routes to Copenhagen.

SEPTEMBER BEGAN with nice, balmy summer weather. The sun still shone warm and golden in the evenings. It was time to try a bottle of Skoll in Copenhagen and pay our respects to the charming mermaid posed on a rock in the outer harbour. At a wooden dock in the city's main park, we found a fine spot to bring *Trillium II* alongside. And the mermaid was only a few steps away. She was smaller than we had envisioned, yet so beautiful with her fishtail draped delicately over the rock.

Copenhagen beckons

Soon after, however, we moved to the inner harbour, right in downtown Copenhagen. With its sidewalk cafés and shops, this city had more to offer our young sailors than Flensburg or Svendborg. The beer was refreshing, and the boys admired the blonde Danish girls.

It was a damp, rainy day that Hetty and I visited the Tivoli, a world-renowned amusement park, while the crew sought their entertainment in places where those Danish beauties might be found. The park seemed to be as dull as the day, and we did not enjoy it as much as we had hoped. Children under the watchful eye of their parents had fun, but we left and made our way back to the ship. Arm in arm we strolled under an umbrella on which the raindrops played a melody.

Mermaid sitting on a rock overlooking the harbour of Copenhagen. Isn't she lovely?

The next day was dry and sunny with a freshening wind coming from the northwest. The boys and I agreed it was time to leave Copenhagen. In the Sund, a strait between Denmark and Sweden, we ran under full sail at 15 knots, past Malmö in Sweden, and headed for the neck of land off the Island of Mon. The wind had freshened some more and upon rounding the neck we were confronted by a gale from west-nor'west. With sails trimmed flat and the diesel at full power, we were unable to round the corner. Finally, we decided to back off and lie a-hull behind the steep and very high cliffs of Mon. Overhead the storm raged, but *Trillium II* lay anchored safely close to shore in smooth, calm waters.

InnerHarbour, Copenhagen. Trillium II parked in front of the old warehouse from Hansatimes, now a hotel.

At daybreak, we tried once more and made it to a little fishing harbour on the island. Here we waited five days for the storm to abate. The harbour-master called on us each morning to bring a weather report and to collect the harbour dues. The first day we paid, he knotted a coloured ribbon onto our steering wheel. The second day, I presented him with a bottle of Canadian scotch and that paid for our stay as long as we liked.

Our paying guests and crew nagged me to buy some fish. I talked to some fishermen who were puttering about on their idle ships. For forty dollars, I received a helping of eel for at least ten people. The following morning I set out again, but this time I took a bottle with me. It did wonders. I returned with a crate full of whitefish. Spirits are very expensive in Scandinavian countries, and a bottle of whiskey can open doors that would otherwise stay closed.

The crew not only ate fish that night for dinner, but also for the next four days. They ate fish until it came out of their ears, and at last Harry disposed of the remains over the side of the ship. The seagulls had a feast. On the morning of the fifth day, the harbour-master brought good news. The waves did not smash over the mole anymore, and the centre of a low of 960 millibar had moved from Norway to Russia. The storm had passed.

DURING THE violent weather we had been studying the sea charts. If we sailed to Lubeck, also an old Hansa town, we could enter the inland waterways of Germany. However, it would be necessary to take our masts down. Bridges in Germany, contrary to those in Holland, did not open. They were solid fixtures in the landscape.

Everyone was enthusiastic about the plan, and as it turned out, it was a wise choice. We were able to observe much of the German countryside. We made use of a few locks, including one with a screw system that lifted us twenty metres, making us almost dizzy. Finally, we ended up in the river Rhine at the city of Wezel.

The Rhine carried us swiftly into Holland. As we neared the cut-off of the river Ijssel, we had to put the diesel in reverse to slow *Trillium II* down. Otherwise, the strong current would have dragged us past, and we would have ended up in Arnhem.

The Ijssel wound through the beautiful countryside on that day of perfect weather. The skies were blue with puffy, white clouds, and a fresh, cool breeze ruffled the water. Everyone, except the man at the wheel, stayed outside or sat in the open cockpits to enjoy the splendid scenery. This was Holland at its best.

By late afternoon, we arrived at the lock at Eefde, but the light was red and the doors were closed. We cast our mooring lines around bollards and waited, and waited, but nothing happened. The lock-master's booth remained vacant. We became impatient, so I jumped ashore and followed a narrow path toward the lock. The door of the building was ajar and I could see the coloured lights on the control board. After a short time I discovered a house. Lo and behold, there was the lock-master puttering in his garden. Humbly, I approached him. A lock-master is a powerful man. He could make you wait forever. A captain might be the authority on board his own ship, but a lock-master is the boss over all those buttons inside his domain.

I explained the situation, and asked him politely if he could sluice us through. "Certainly not!" he replied indignantly. "It is Saturday afternoon. The locks will be closed until Monday morning."

I stood dumbfounded. We certainly had not counted on this. My mind raced as I decided what to do. Should I grumble and complain, or be polite? I resorted to the latter. "Mister Lock-master, we have travelled on my ship across the Atlantic Ocean all the way from Canada. We would like to go to the town where I was born, Enschede. Our relatives and friends are waiting in anticipation to welcome us. Must we wait here until Monday?"

Home again to Holland

That our relatives were waiting was complete nonsense, of course, but it seemed to soften him up. Then I had a second idea. "Mister Lock-master, how does a bottle of Canadian whiskey sound to you?"

He pushed his shovel into the earth, looked me in the eye, and said, "You are a manipulator, that's what you are. Now, go back to your ship and start your diesel. Wait in front of the lock doors and I'll open them up."

In the basin, I handed him the precious bottle, which he accepted with a big grin. "Hurry up," he told us. "There are three more locks. I have phoned the lock-masters and they are expecting you. Go full speed."

We celebrated our journey from Penetanguishene Canada to Enschede, Holland with a delicious cake from Grandma Heutink.

We thanked him and accelerated the throttle to full speed as he had commanded. Skippers from barges moored alongside the canal had come on deck to find out what all the commotion was about. We knew the lock-master would have a lot of explaining to do on Monday morning.

At the next three locks, the green lights were on and the doors open. We passed through without much ado. We had the liquid offerings ready, and I said in a neighbourly tone, "Cheers, Mister Lock-master. Enjoy this spicy Canadian drink tonight when you are relaxing at home." It had cost us four bottles of whiskey, but it had been worth it.

When we arrived at the yacht club in Enschede, it was already dark. We were greeted in a soft-spoken dialect. It had been so many years since we had heard it, it sounded like music to our ears. We heard something else, too; the soft drumming of rain on our decks.

Finally, we had reached our goal. We had sailed from Penetanguishene, in Canada, all the way to Enschede, in Holland. It had been an extremely long but eventful voyage. We were elated, yet satisfied it had come to an end.

Grandma Heutink was waiting for us, the coffee ready, and a huge cake with big letters that read "Welkom in Holland."

Chartering to Helgoland (1)

**Getting
acquainted
with a Rock**

There was much work to be done on the day before departure. *Trillium II* would venture out on her initial charter cruise to Helgoland and Denmark. The final chores seemed to take forever. Harry had slugged and toiled for several days to have all the provisions on board for the sail on the North Sea. The bar was well-stocked. It was important to make a good impression on our paying guests, who also functioned as crew. They would be treated like royalty.

The time had come to set sail. All the guests were aboard. An appointment had been set up to have the drawbridge opened on Friday evening. Once through, we would enter a wide canal that connected Leeuwarden, the capital of the Dutch province, Friesland, with Harlingen, our home harbour. Large locks separated the canal from the Wad Sea.

The crew had taken possession of their cabins, unpacked, and waited eagerly on deck to watch the take-off. The agent and his wife stood on the wooden landing stage ready to wave their farewells. Harry was given orders to let go fore and aft. As he threw the mooring lines on deck, one end of the aft line glided back into the water. No one noticed it. When I shifted the diesel engine into reverse, the end of the rope was sucked into the propeller and tangled around the shaft. The diesel was smothered, and we were dead in the water. I signalled to the bridge-master as Harry examined the situation. The agent wore a worried smile and the novice crew seemed alarmed. This was certainly not a very good start.

Only one thing could solve our problem. Harry donned his wetsuit and scuba gear because the water was cold and dirty. He dove underwater and cut the rope from the shaft piece by piece. After a half-hour delay, we motored through the bridge and entered the canal. The crew was all smiles. They were under way.

By the time we arrived at the locks, the red light shone and the enormous sluice doors were closed tightly. We would have to wait until six o'clock the next morning for them to open. Several lines were slipped around a mooring pile, and the crew and I settled in for the night. Soon a barge came in, and the disgruntled skipper muttered something about lazy lock-keepers. He was an impatient man, but he had to wait just like everyone else.

The crew consisted of three men and two women. Lucìenne

was a friend of Harry's, and Roelie, a young lady from Almelo, a town in eastern Holland. Roelie's dream of taking a sea voyage had come true. Bob, the owner of a café-bar in Haarlem, had been at sea before.

Harry prepared a steaming pot of soup, and with some crusty bread, it made a tasty and enjoyable meal. A hefty dinner was out of the question, because the next day we would be on the Wad Sea and the North Sea—seasickness always hovered around the corner.

Long before 6:00 A.M. we were up and about. We could see the sluice doors wide open, but the light was still red. The lockmaster was a man of the clock. He would open the doors at precisely 6:00 A.M. and not one minute sooner. The barge skipper had his diesel engine rumbling, and as soon as the light jumped to green, he was under way. With a smile and a wave of his hand, he passed us. We were slower getting started. The crew had trouble with the mooring lines, but by and by we were free of the pilings and followed the barge into the basin of the lock. The doors closed and clicked shut behind us.

The light of dawn glowed softly above the green pastures of the flat Friesian countryside. When the sun broke through the morning mist, we could feel its warm rays on our faces. Soon we could see the Wad Sea glimmering in the bright sunshine. High tide flooded in and we struggled against it. In the slenk, a deep channel marked by buoys, the current ran strong but we stayed on course. Beware the skipper who loses control of his ship there. The current would drag him over the Pollendam, a low concrete breakwater, and make mincemeat of his ship. We kept a sharp eye out for the buoys, and six hours later we entered the North Sea through a slenk called Noordergat, located between the Dutch islands of Vlieland and Terschelling.

Cruising on the Wad Sea was a beautiful experience, but without charts it could be deadly. One should follow the slenks, clearly marked, have a tide table close at hand, and stay off those waters in heavy fog or stormy weather. I had pencilled a line on the chart from the Noordergat to TE-5, a large buoy north of Terschelling. There we would change to an easterly course and follow the ships going to German North Sea harbours. Because it was our first time sailing this route, Harry and I agreed to follow the green buoys to the German Wad Island, Norderney, and, abeam its lighthouse, we would cross the channel and set a northeasterly course to Helgoland in the German Bight.

The pleasant morning sun had disappeared behind a layer of

stratus clouds, but a west wind of Beaufort 4 assured us of a good sailing day. We kept the buoys in sight but stayed just outside the channel. That was the domain of tankers, container ships, and merchants. The crew was enjoying the voyage, as the ship steered itself. We passed the Dutch islands one by one, marking the time in the ship's journal each time we were abeam of their lighthouses.

AS *TRILLIUM II* danced along the gentle waves, Roelie's dream was shattered. She became the first victim of seasickness. She huddled in the open cockpit, shivering despite her warm coat, looking like a small, lost bird. Now and then, she would hang over the bulwarks. The sea was not for everyone.

A rough crossing on the North Sea

Dusk fell as we passed the last of the Dutch Wad islands. Thereafter, we kept an eye out for a series of east Friesian islands that belonged to Germany. June is the time of the midnight sun, and it did not get completely dark. When we were abeam the light of Norderney, we changed our course to the Rock, Helgoland. In the northern sky was a broad band of greyish-yellow light to indicate the position of the sun under the horizon. The wind had freshened, and under full canvas we made nine knots. It was heaven for an old salt, but hell for Roelie.

As we followed the green buoys, big ships passed us in a continuous stream, almost stem to stern. We heard their diesels and saw the board lights, like tiny stars moving up and down with the cadence of the ship. The hulks were huge black shadows rolling to and fro. On the starboard side, far toward the mainland, were also moving lights. They came from the coasters that tried to make a living carrying freight to the smaller harbours.

Before we crossed the buoyed channel, we had checked our radar to find a gap in the endless string of bobbing lights. To cross would take at least twenty minutes at full speed. We did not want to confront heavy tankers or container ships.

Once across, the distance to Helgoland was a mere 28 seamiles. Because the wind had freshened again, we took the mainsail in and proceeded on foresail and mizzen with about six knots. We didn't want to arrive in Helgoland too early in the morning. The seas had built up somewhat, and when a heavy wave cannonaded broadside into *Trillium II* and spray swept the decks, our passengers stared at Harry and me, a question in their eyes.

Roelie remained in the corner of the cockpit, too far gone to even care. She wanted to die. In the wee hours of the morning, the light of Helgoland peeked over the horizon. The lighthouse stood high upon a rock and on a clear day can be seen from afar. At 7:00 A.M. we saw the vague silhouette appearing out of a nebulous lip of horizon, and at 9:00 A.M. we swung into the harbour. Over the marine radio the harbour-master directed us to a spot on the quay, where we fastened our lines to bollards at least ten metres above our heads. We had to climb a steep, iron ladder with slippery rungs covered in seaweed and algae.

Exploring the Rock

The harbour-master reminded us that the fee would be ten German marks daily. The full complement was on deck, including Roelie. She was as lively as a fish in clear, cool water. She could not believe that she had been so sick out there on the North Sea.

Early tourists strolled along the harbour works and pointed at *Trillium II* and her flag high up in the main mast. The red maple leaf fluttered proudly in the sea breeze. It was not long before questions were fired at us. They wanted to know if we had come all the way from Canada and if we had crossed the Atlantic Ocean on that ship. We answered them politely. They stared at us with awe and disbelief. Shaking their heads, they made room for other tourists and the game of question and answer was soon repeated.

Helgoland was a duty-free harbour, with a population of 2,200. Their livelihood came mainly from tourism. One hundred and fifty years before, the island was a health spa for wealthy Germans. Prior to that time, the Helgolanders tried their hand at piracy now and then.

The lower village included the harbour works, the promenade, the Kurort Hotel, as well as souvenir shops, cafés, restaurants, and a modest sea-aquarium. On the sea boulevard was a bandstand. On top of the rock was the upper village where the natives lived in bungalow-type houses which had been rebuilt after the war. Many people in the upper village rented rooms to vacationers to make an extra mark or two.

No automobiles were allowed on Helgoland, and even bicycles were banned. Freight was transported by small, silent, battery-operated wagons. The air was pure and smelled faintly of fish and the sea. A hiking path wound all the way around the Rock. Walking at a leisurely pace, it could be completed in under two hours. The sea vistas were extraordinary, even for a seaman. Because of its iron content, the rock itself was reddish. With her base in the surf, the 'Lange Anna,' rose like a lofty pillar. Birds flocked to Helgoland to breed. Their nests clung to rock ledges and recesses. When nesting time was over, the bird families disappeared, not to be seen again until the next spring.

Sheep, belonging to no one and all, grazed freely. In the fields, one could still recognize bomb craters from World War II, though overgrown with grass and weeds.

In summer, huge, white passenger ships anchored far off in the roadstead. Sometimes there were five or six coming from Bremen, Hamburg, or Denmark. At 10:00 A.M. they would unload their passengers and bring them ashore with tenders or longboats, and pick them up again at four in the afternoon. Those day visitors usually stayed in the lower village. Their first stop would be to the restaurants to gorge themselves on coffee and Black Forest cake or other rich pastry. The very hungry ones would begin with sauerkraut and sausages.

Helgoland in the German Bight–the freestanding rock is called "Lange Anna." In the lefthand corner is the upper village of Helgoland, and in the roadstead the daily cruise ships that drop off hundreds of daytrippers for cheap and tax-free shopping in the lower village.

Afterwards, they raided the shops and boutiques to buy tax-free Dutch gin, Dutch cheese, or the latest Paris fashions. Cigars, also from Holland, were the favourite bargain of the men. Later, exhausted from all the shopping, they would relax at a *conditorei* (tea house). An attractive waitress dressed in the local costume of elaborately embroidered blouse and simple black shirt served platters loaded with cakes and pastries.

During the invasion of the day trippers, the natives hid in their bungalows in the upper village, and the vacationers remained in their hotel rooms. But after 4:00 P.M. both natives and island guests made their appearance. People strolled or relaxed on one of the many terraces, drinking the German beer served in tall glasses, with its foamy, white collar.

Next to the Rock was a vast sandbar. Dunes decorated the edges where little waves played with beach shells. The sandbar was separated from the main island by a deep channel, through which even the large passenger ships could pass. A small ferry cruised between the two islands regularly. The island was the domain of a nudist colony, but guests from Helgoland were always welcome to join the party provided they had paid the admittance fee of five marks. To pay that amount for the privilege of walking bare-bottomed amidst other naked men and women seemed rather steep. The crew of *Trillium II* declined the friendly invitation.

Because it was our first cruise to Helgoland, I invited my crew to come ashore, where I treated them to coffee and pastries at one of the numerous sidewalk cafés. It was an expensive proposition and I resolved not to repeat it if we ever returned to the island.

While the crew roamed the lower village for tax-free goodies, I headed for the local weather station to talk to the meteorologists. They assured me the next four or five days would be good sailing weather, sunny, wind Beaufort 3–4, and calm seas.

When I returned to our ship, Harry, on deck watch, was chatting with a man, a true Helgolander. He told us some of the history of the island. In the 30s and early 40s, Adolph Hitler attempted to make a submarine base from the rock and moved the natives, against their will, back to the mainland. Unfortunately, for the Nazis, Helgoland lay within reach of the allied bombers so Hitler's plans were abandoned. After the war, the island became practice terrain for bombers from NATO countries. Later, the original Helgolanders returned, rebuilt their village, and settled down as of old.

We learned a great deal from Uwe. He exchanged local information for sociability on board our ship. He became our friend, and it paid off handsomely during subsequent stays on the island. Every time he caught sight of *Trillium II* in the harbour, he extended an invitation to his home. Through him, we didn't fall prey to the tourist industry and were able to buy provisions for a reasonable price.

I informed our guests that we would sail early the next morning. Our destination was the Wad Islands of Denmark. Roelie appeared concerned. She hoped she would not get seasick again. We tidied the ship for the night and turned in. Our first impression of Helgoland had been favourable. We would definitely return.

Chartering to Helgoland (II)

Our cruise to Great Yarmouth, on the east coast of England, had been quite pleasant. The guests were all from the province of Friesland, and the camaraderie was excellent. They bought a mascot for *Trillium II*, a little furry toy monkey, called Jopie. Where that name originated, nobody knew. We hung the stuffed animal over the navigation table, where it stayed for ten years. Now Jopie decorates the bed in our apartment.

Back in Harlingen, at the yacht harbour, Harry and I prepared the ship for another cruise to Helgoland. Provisions were brought aboard, water tanks filled, and diesel fuel bunkered. This seven-day trip would last from June 23 until June 29. The agent had recruited four paying guests; not many, but better than none. There was a married couple to whom we gave the entire starboard cabin, and also a Friesian, who could not convince his wife to join him and their teenager daughter. Just before we were ready to sail, the daughter broke her leg and had to cancel the trip and her dream of sailing to Helgoland.

Saturday afternoon, prior to our departure, I phoned my wife in Canada. Her birthday was the next day, and while we were at sea there would be no way to reach her. Harry and I wished her a happy birthday and promised we would toast her when we arrived in Helgoland.

Back on board, customs officers were waiting to clear us out. Harry poured them a drink of Dutch gin with a *plaatje* on top. That meant the glass was so full, that one could not lift it to drink but had to slurp the top off first. Our friends honoured this tradition like true connoisseurs. They were quite amiable and knew us from previous trips. They also knew we were completely trustworthy.

By evening we were moored in the yacht harbour of West Terschelling, where we enjoyed a pleasurable evening ashore. Early the next morning, after a good night's rest, we sailed with the ebbing tide through the slenk, Noordergat.

The weather on the North Sea did not appear hopeful. Low-hanging clouds scudded along the sky and a strong west wind pushed the white horses eastward in endless rows. With the wind abaft, *Trillium II* did not steer well, and Harry had a difficult time keeping the ship on course. When the wind freshened some more, we took the mizzen and mains'l down and let the foresail do the work. *Trillium II* steadied on her course, but before dark a full-blown Beaufort 8 made life on board miserable. Our guests disappeared below to curl up in their bunks, regretting having spent so much money on a sea cruise. The waves continued to smack into the ship; the sound alone made the guest crew shiver with fear. They thought we would never make it to Helgoland. Storms on the North Sea in summer seldom blow harder than Beaufort 8, but it was more than enough for our frightened passengers.

Another rough voyage on the North Sea

We did not want to arrive at Helgoland in the middle of the night, so we took all our sails down. Because we were in the German Bight, we could safely ride out the storm. The seas were extremely rough. Sheets of water flew across the decks, but *Trillium II* still made headway. In order to slow down, we hoisted a heavy-weather foresail and locked the wheel in a hard-over position. Then the ship skated backwards and forwards. The forward motion was negligible. The masts swung savagely, causing the lights on top to streak wildly across the dark sky. However, our strong, stubborn ship had no problem with this kind of weather.

On Sunday, the day loomed out of a grey sky in the east. Harry and I had contemplated hoisting more sail and setting course to the Rock. In safety harness, he ventured onto the deck. By now, our passengers were too ill to help, so single-handedly Harry set our normal working jib and mizzen. With an altered course and the wind veering more to nor'west, *Trillium II* gathered speed. I hollered to him over the Tannoy, "Good work, my boy, good work!" He waved to me and made his way across the decks, moving the snap-hook of the harness from guy-wire to guy-wire. The ship stampeded like a wild mustang trying to throw Harry overboard, but to no avail.

We realized by now we could not be far away from the island. At approximately six o'clock that morning, we saw the dim silhouette of the Rock against the grey sky. As we closed in on the island, we observed the waves breaking on the shoreline in towering geysers of boiling water. We circled the island at a safe distance, until the concrete piers came into view. But it was not the piers we saw, but sheets of water breaking with thunderous violence over the concrete, attacking the harbour entrance again and again.

Harry roused our guests, urging them to forget their seasickness and to help him on deck. Slowly they came and Harry assisted them with their harnesses and life vests. What they saw a quarter mile ahead turned their faces deathly pale. They had hoped for a pleasant cruise on a calm, sparkling sea with the sun beating down to tan their skin. They had not imagined crossing the North Sea with waves pounding *Trillium II* ceaselessly. As they stared at the witch's cauldron, horror filled their eyes. I assured them that our paradise lay beyond the hell. They did not appreciate my joke.

At the piers, people watched our approach, peering through binoculars and shaking their heads in disbelief. They expected the ship of mad sailors to smash against the piers at any moment. We were insane, there was no denying that. But we trusted our ship and our seamanship.

Harry took down the mizzen, and with the help of the crew, he hoisted the storm jib while I started the diesel. Deep in the water the rudder had a good bite and listened to every change of the wheel. The storm jib pulled, the diesel pushed, and ground seas carried us upward and smashed us down again. Within this

fury of wild water, *Trillium II* stayed on course and kept proper speed. Spray swept over the decks, splattering against the windows of the wheelhouse and hindering my view of the outside world.

Suddenly the welcoming arms of the piers enfolded us. *Trillium II* sailed nonchalantly into the calm water of the harbour basin. We had made it. For a moment, we could not believe that our ordeal had ended. There were no more roaring winds or cracking, raging waves, only the cheers of the onlookers.

By jib alone, we ran before the wind to the end of the harbour. Harry and his helpers took the sail down. Even on bare poles the ship still flew ahead, so I used the diesel to check her speed. The harbour-master directed us to our usual spot on the quay near the ladder with the slippery rungs. Our guests could breathe freely again. Someone brewed a pot of tea, and buttered some Dutch rusks. Harry and I left the guests to themselves and turned in. It had been a strenuous night and morning. We were exhausted.

BECAUSE OF THE STORM, we had forgotten Hetty's birthday. It had been drowned in heavy seas and smothered in Beaufort 8, but we would celebrate it anyways.

Trillium II in the harbour of Helgoland— behind her a local fisherman who supplies the Kurort Hotel with fresh fish daily. The big trawler is from Denmark.

Celebrating Hetty's birthday in her absence

My thoughts travelled back. A year before we had been in Halifax, on Canada's east coast, having dinner together at a quay-side restaurant. From the window we could see the replica of the famous Nova Scotia schooner, the *Bluenose II*. We had toasted Hetty with a glass of vintage Matheus Rosé.

Now we found ourselves in the harbour of Helgoland, and Hetty was back in Canada. We had no Matheus Rosé on board, but we would grace the table with a bottle of '77 Riesling. Since this was a special occasion, I did the cooking that day. I cooked a custard pudding with red currant sauce, setting the bowls on the navigation table to cool. They were flanked by polished wine glasses and the bottle of Riesling. There were also bottles of rum, Dutch gin, and beer. When the sun was over the yard-arm, the guests could help themselves to a drink. They were sensible and pleasant company. On the grill the butter was browning, waiting for the pork chops. Passersby could smell the delicious aromas wafting from *Trillium*'s galley. As I put new potatoes into the pressure cooker, Harry prepared a special salad. The vegetable served was red cabbage with applesauce. As an appetizer, I had made a tomato consommé, which I kept hot under the blankets in my cabin.

First mate Harry and two of our guests. In the background the cruise ships anchored offshore in the roadstead of Helgoland.

We took our seats around the festive dinner table. After I had dished out the soup, I asked for a moment of silence, and then wished everyone *bon appétit*. It all looked so pretty and inviting, it was hard to believe that less than 24 hours earlier, we had been battling a storm on the North Sea. Harry uncorked the wine and filled the glasses. We raised our glasses to an oil painting on the bulkhead, where Hetty was pictured as an 18-year-old girl. She wore a wine-coloured dress with a dainty Flemish lace collar. Her delicate, young face was framed with dark blonde hair, a becoming curl on her forehead. I longed to be able to turn back the clock and relive the days of our youth.

Following the exuberant toast to Hetty, forks and knives clicked and clattered noisily as the guests ate heartily. The dishes were cleaned up by the guests without any objections. Helgoland boulevards beckoned us to take a stroll and, who knows, maybe a drink and a dance in the Kurort Hotel later that evening. The air was cool, so we donned jackets and heavy sweaters. Our guests sauntered along the boutiques and shops comparing prices. Forgetting about the hidden island tax, they commented on the low costs. They purchased mainly cigarettes and bottles of Dutch gin.

On the boulevard, young Helgoland girls handed out sheets of green paper with the German lyrics of old, sentimental songs about sailors and the sea. In the bandstand was a male barbershop choir dressed in wide navy pants, striped shirts, and red scarves tied around their necks. A sailor's cap perched jauntily on each head. In front of the barbershoppers, a group of children fidgeted as they waited for the show to begin.

The sky was grey and a chilly sea breeze blew. Now and again we felt raindrops. The storm had eased, and the sea around the island rippled. In the distance, a streak of late sunlight peeked through a tiny opening in the clouds, painting a golden pool on the surface of the water. On the horizon, a tanker rode behind her anchor, waiting for a pilot to guide her up the Elbe and into the harbour of Hamburg.

Harry starts preparing dinner. The galley is across from the navigation table. The view through the louvred doors is into the wheelhouse. Harry was not only a very good first mate but also a cook who could dream up the most exotic meals.

The children's choir was first to perform. They sang the well-known songs about sailors and their lovers, and the crowd that had gathered around the bandstand sang along. The old, heartfelt songs of the sea brought back many memories. Both young and old stood arm in arm spellbound, listening to the voices as they sung of the sea. Several elderly ladies opened their colourful umbrellas, not wanting the rain to spoil their expensive hairdos. Children frolicked about, having lost interest in the singing.

A group of young people from the Friesian country of Holland enjoy dinner on board Trillium II.

Not far from Harry and me sat a young couple, madly in love with each other. She whispered something sweet into his ear, and he pulled her close and placed a soft, little kiss on her forehead.

Young love was both enchanting and romantic.

The children's choir finished its program, and then the men, dressed as sailors, took their turn. They were accompanied by piano and accordion. The popular music made the people on the benches sway from side to side. Harry and I happily joined in. It was an entertaining and amusing evening.

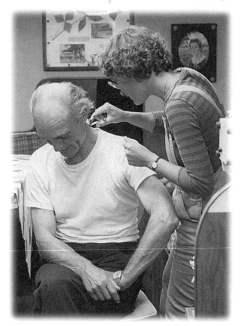

A crew member trims the skipper's hair.

The breeze from the North Sea remained chilly. In the distance, we could see a tiny triangle of sail. As it approached, we could see a real sailboat entering between the piers. This time, there were no wild seas and no applauding onlookers.

The Helgoland singers and musicians were tireless, and with resounding gusto they began their second collection of songs. Harry and our crew walked away. They had heard enough about sailors and their maidens, seagulls, and waves.

With the last breath of the accordion and the applause of the crowd, the audience dispersed. German men wearing sailor caps on their silver hair, and their stout wives, returned to their inns or hotels to play cards and drink schnapps or beer. The young folk went in search of some entertainment in the lower village. There they would have good, clean fun. Helgoland was a decent island. What happened after the drapes were drawn was anyone's guess and nobody's business.

With my crew, I headed for the dignified Kurort Hotel, where there was ballroom dancing to a live band every night. We ordered beer, which was served in large steins by a jolly Fraulein. "Cheers!" We lifted our voices and our glasses and thrust our upper lips into the foam. We danced to the tunes of familiar waltzes, foxtrots, and polkas on a smooth, teak floor.

How long had it been since we had danced to the tunes of 'Dance Macabre' on a pitching, heaving deck? Had that been yesterday or was it yesteryear?

Close to where we were seated, an attractive and charming lady sat alone. Her sea-grey eyes had been staring at us (at me?) for some time. I made my way over to her table to ask her for a dance. We waltzed in the customary three-quarter tempo and then I invited her to join our table. Soon there was a cheerful and amiable atmosphere. Her name was Frieda; she was the widow of a German naval officer, and she lived in Hamburg. She had stood on the breakwater that morning when we had struggled against the wind and water to find shelter in the harbour. Frieda admitted to us she had been terrified, wondering if we could make it inside safely. She paid us so many compliments, we were embarrassed.

We raised our heavy beer steins to her. "Prosit, Frieda!" Then we toasted all the sailors in the world. She asked if we planned to return to Helgoland. We answered in the affirmative. That summer, our agent in Harlingen had arranged two more trips to Helgoland. Frieda's eyes shone. She promised to be there when we came back.

The genoa pulls the ship over a sunny North Sea. Two danforth anchors are clipped on deck, ready to go.

The next day when we left the harbour, Frieda waited at the pier to bid us farewell. Little did we know then that she would accompany us on many cruises on board our good ship *Trillium II*.

Winter Intermezzo

We had enjoyed a beautiful summer, chartering with our ship to Great Yarmouth in England, Helgoland in the German Bight, and visiting the Wad Islands of Denmark. Not always had we been booked full, but every cruise had been pleasant. We had learned about ports, people, and traditions of many European lands. We had made friends with Uwe from Helgoland, Frieda from Hamburg, the customs officers from Harlingen, and many more. One voyage to Great Yarmouth had not been completed because of inclement weather—we didn't dare enter the channels between the gravel banks, even if they were buoyed. The hard, unyielding banks made a direct approach to the harbour impossible. Reduced visibility, rain and fog; it was unnavigable. Our paying crew had taken it in good stride. As compensation we sailed back across the North Sea and paid visits to some Dutch islands in the Wad Sea: Terschelling, Vlieland, and Ameland.

Now summer was almost over, it was necessary for Harry and me to decide what to do with the ship. Could we leave her in the water? Winters in Holland were not severe, but we didn't want to risk getting frozen in. Our agent came up with the perfect solu-

Christmas in Holland

tion. He had located a place in the marina where she could be hoisted ashore. Thankfully, we accepted his offer.

Through some friends, Harry found a job as an electrician in a town not far from Harlingen. Hetty, back at her job as book-keeper at my former business in Barrie, Ontario would join us for the winter. We had made arrangements to stay with my mother. She was alone and would love to have us around for company.

Soon, we settled into life ashore. Christmas and New Year loomed up on the horizon of time. On the Saturday before Christmas, it was still dark at eight o'clock in the morning. In the lane beside Mother Heutink's house, the globe on the green lamp-post glowed softly through the rain. The weather was unusually mild, and only 8°C. The doves in the tall poplar trees behind the house cooed as if it were spring.

Church in the middle of our native town of Enschede in the Netherlands. Once upon a time "Ye Olde Market" was held at the foot of the tower.

The sun had reached its lowest point on the zodiac, and its path along the heavens was short. It rose in the southeast and set in the southwest. Twilight at this latitude was long. At about 3:00 P.M. daylight waned, and at 5:00 P.M. it became totally dark. Though winter had begun, it seemed as though we would have no snow or ice. Christmas would be green that year.

Mother Heutink had set the breakfast table festively for the season. There was tea with Dutch rusks, raisin bread, and warm, fresh, crusty, white bread straight from the bakery. Three different kinds of cheese were served, and the cold cuts made my mouth water. The elaborate breakfast was a part of the hospitality of Holland. The selection and quality were hard to match.

Hetty and I thought about our homeland, Canada, so very far away. We reminisced about blizzards, and of the sun glittering like diamonds on freshly fallen snow. We talked about Springwater Park near Barrie, Ontario, where we took afternoon walks under snow-covered trees. Swans drifted gracefully in a pond, trying to keep the water from freezing. In the evening, we beheld the glorious splendour of golden beams as the sun descended behind the trees.

We also spoke about *Trillium II*. She waited for spring in the far north of Holland, to be refitted for another season of chartering.

Harry, my first mate, came to spend Yuletide with us in

Enschede. We would have more overnight guests: our older son, Fred, his wife, Janet, and their two adopted Korean daughters arrived later that evening. The little house bustled with the friendly greetings, kisses, and slaps on the back.

Outside, the heavens wept. Heavy raindrops splattered against the window panes, but inside we were cosy and warm. Fred and his brother were deep in conversation, Hetty chatted with Janet, and the little girls busied themselves with their dolls and colouring books. Grandma Heutink puttered around in her galley.

In the morning large pieces of cake topped generously with real whipped cream were served with coffee. Harry and Fred helped themselves to a second slice, and we all wondered

The "Heutink Clan" has been traced back to the 13th century. This rural paradise outside the city of Enschede is called "Heutink's Corner." Our ancestors were farmers. Skipper Jerry broke the tradition to become a seaman.

if they would have room for Mother Heutink's dinner—turkey with all the trimmings. We needn't have worried. They made short work of it.

That evening there was carol singing at the church in the old market square. Many choirs from the area participated in the event. People flocked to the ancient church, and it was so crowded that chairs had to be added along the sides and in the aisles. Behind the pulpit stood five adorned Christmas trees, and the sanctuary was lavishly decorated with flowers and plants. The florists had brought the leftovers from the Saturday market, and added some fresh from the greenhouses.

There was a special presentation that night performed by the midwinter hornblowers. It is an old tradition dating back to Germanic pagan times. The horns, made from strips of wood, measure anywhere from one to two metres. Farmers and their sons use them at the end of December (midwinter), placing the end of the horns over a well. The deep, melancholic, vibrating sound echoed over the surrounding countryside. An answer would soon resound from neighbouring farms. While walking over the barren fields in the still, grey twilight, one could hear the mystic, secret sounds in the

Restored old farmplace in a winter setting: "Heutink's Corner."

desolation of a wintry land. The sombre tones are meant to repel the dark forces of winter when the sun sets lower and days became shorter and shorter.

We heard the sonorous timbres echoing from the depth of the church dome. The hornblowers dispersed throughout the building, each one blowing in turn. Spellbound, we listened, captivated by sounds issuing forth from the centuries of times gone by.

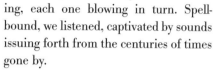

Midwinterhorn.

After the midwinter horns, the choirs took their turn, and before long everyone joined in. No microphones or electronic amplification were necessary. The churches of old had been built by artisans with knowledge of natural acoustics. When one person sang, it sounded as though a whole choir was singing. For an hour all were united in music and melody of the Yuletide season. We left the church with peace in our minds and our hearts.

A New Year dawns

THE DAYS between Christmas and New Year remained dark and rainy. The sun hid behind a cloud deck, low and grey, hovering over the world.

Somewhere the sun shone hot and bright. Hetty and I went to a travel office to collect brochures. In no time we had an armful of books about the sunny south. The brochures were picture books for grown-ups, and they were free for the taking. Back home, on the sofa close to the hearth, we gazed longingly at white beaches, hotels with swimming pools, and the deep, blue sea in the background. Under palm trees, beautiful, tanned girls lay in the tropical sun. We were enticed to run back to the travel agent to book one of the dream trips.

Aye, but what about *Trillium II*, ashore in Friesland, waiting for us? She would carry us to the same beaches so beautifully pictured in the brochures. Would it be soon, when spring was just around the corner?

The next day would be New Year's Eve. It would be a good time to drink hot toddies, eat well, and talk about the past with its many memories and events. Was it only a few short months ago that we had sailed in stormy weather on the North Sea? Did we actually make it across the Atlantic Ocean with the Coast Guard from Halifax reporting us missing on the high seas? Looking back, it all seemed so unreal. Was it longer ago, in another life?

On the last day of the year, snow had arrived during the night, with strong winds still from the east. It had piled up in corners and Jack Frost reigned with glee. Tonight, the old demons would be chased away with 'boerhorns,' discharging old muskets, firecrackers, and bombs.

Young people and children were already out on the streets in the morning, trying out the first noisy firecrackers and sparklers. At dark, the men would bring out the more powerful stuff.

Frozen waterways from horizon to horizon, and the Dutch skate from village to village, from sun-up to sundown.

The streets were deserted in the afternoon. Icy blasts howled around corners, but inside it was cosy and warm. Christmas trees were lit and would stay decorated until Epiphany, January 6, according to tradition.

In the kitchen, Mother Heutink heated the *Glühwein*, a spicy, red wine, and a tradition which has been kept alive through the centuries. Then, the clock chimed 12 o'clock. "HAPPY NEW YEAR, EVERYONE!"

Trillium II sailed through these same waterways in summer.

Glasses tinkled as we toasted each other. The hot toddy tasted delicious. Outside, all hell broke loose.

Children waved their sparklers furiously round and round in the air, while teenagers lit the more expensive fireworks. Safely behind the picture window, we watched the grand spectacle. High in the sky, the heavens burst open in the shape of a fan, spreading sparks of white, red, orange, and blue. The revelry lasted for hours, and the happy occasion had cost the Dutch people a tidy 40–50 million guilders on fireworks.

Until four o'clock in the morning, we heard the explosions. Then the stillness returned. Malicious ghosts and pagan gods had received their send-off. Soon the sun would return and the days would grow longer once again.

And in the far north of Holland *Trillium II* waited patiently, waited for the spring days to come.

Voyage to Vikingland

Sailing with Georgie and Wullum, Bas and André

From Harlingen, our home harbour in Holland, over the Wad Sea to the North Sea was directly north. As usual there was a nor'west wind. With the course set north, we would have to struggle against it.

After studying the charts and consulting with first mate Harry, we decided to sail west over the Wad Sea, then via the Dutch Wad island, Texel, to the North Sea. In this way, the wind would come in slightly for'ard the starboard beam and ensure us a pleasant ride over small, foamy wavelets. Later we would sail into the quaint fishermen's harbour of Oudeschildt on Texel to spend the evening in the cosy canteen of the yacht harbour. Our crew was in full agreement, and by afternoon we were on our way.

The sun had already sunk below the western horizon when the windmill of Oudeschildt rose up out of the Wad Sea to guide us to the harbour. It would probably be dark before we reached the marina. Harry and I were familiar with the Wad Sea and its manifold beacons and markers that indicated where the shallows and slenks (channels) were located. At twilight, the beacons twinkled red, white, green, and amber. On such a beautiful night, with all the lights guiding us along our way, it was so dreamy, so romantic.

It was late when we arrived at the yacht harbour, but the harbour-master had reserved a place for us right beside the canteen. We were well known because of our many cruises to Great Yarmouth in England. It was customary for us to stop for a night before crossing the North Sea. The harbour-master bade us welcome and *Trillium*'s crew found a spot at an empty round table in the canteen, or sailor's pub. Hundreds of little flags drooped from the ceiling, colourful and fascinating.

The harbour-master was also the landlord of the establishment, and his wife held sway in the galley. On one of our previous cruises to England, I had met her mother, a delightful young lady not yet sixty. Together we had spent a pleasant evening in a quiet corner of the canteen and had felt a mutual attraction. Thoughtfully, her daughter had set a candle in an old wine bottle in the middle of the table. It made it so romantic.

I had dished up a few sailor's stories and had not only looked deep into my beer stein, but also into her beautiful brown eyes. Had I seen her soft, smooth cheeks turning a healthy, rosy colour? It must have been the wine, of course.

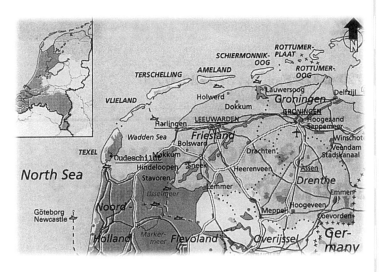

The Wadden Sea was Trillium*'s playground for two summers with Harlingen our home harbour and Oudeschildt on Texel the starting point for many a sea voyage. From West Terschelling we sailed charter cruises to Helgoland, Denmark, Norway, and Sweden.*

This time she was not present. I had hoped to see her again but alas, one cannot always be lucky. I asked the daughter to convey my greetings and love to her mother.

Our four male guests were soon accustomed to the world of "yachties," especially the two young men, Wullum and André. They thought the trip was all very exciting and they did their utmost to behave like real seamen. They even tried to bribe Harry to stay another day in the harbour. Harry looked at me and I winked. "Okay! Tomorrow afternoon we leave." Wullum cheered and dipped his nose into frothy beer placed before him. It was not a favour. How were they to know that tomorrow afternoon we would leave at high tide to catch the ebb tide in the Marsdiep, a channel between the mainland and the island of Texel. It was good seamanship, and no more.

Sunday morning in the canteen was also pleasant. All the tables were occupied when we entered, but it was no problem. People moved over and made room for the crew of the Canadian yacht. Many of the yachties attempted to shake off the hangover of the previous night by consuming endless cups of strong, black coffee. After the coffee, the harbour-master treated me to a Dutch gin and I also accepted one from my crew. That was my limit. There would be no drunken captain on board *Trillium II*.

At neap tide we left the harbour and set course to the Marsdiep. The ebb stream was starting to run and carried us at a good clip along the south coast of Texel until we changed course at the south point of the island. The wind filled the sails from port side and we had to keep an eye on the breakers over the Noorderhaaks, a large, shallow sandbank with the consistency of concrete. In the olden days of sailing, many a ship found a grave there. We passed without a mishap and then the open sea lay ahead of us. Just before dark, we crossed the shipping lanes and from there on we had the sea to ourselves all the way to Norway.

The Wad Sea—on the horizon the Dutch island of Texel. To find the harbour of Oudeschildt we always navigated towards the windmill. The entrance was close by.

The crew consisted of four men. The eldest was Georgie, who was 59 years old. He volunteered to cook for the entire two weeks of cruising. We were not sorry about this gesture, because what he did in our miniature galley was magic. The meals were excellent. Then there was André, his twenty-year-old son, who had red hair and moustache and was nearly seven feet tall. Wullum was of the same height. The headroom of *Trillium II* was only six feet, three inches in the cabins and saloon, and those two beanpoles had to walk with their heads down. Wullum walked with a bad stoop anyway, and when he had wheelwatch, his back became as round as a hoop. André was the opposite. When he had the wheel, he leaned all the way back until his arms stretched out in a straight line. Everybody has his own peculiarities, and that breaks the monotony at sea.

Then there was Bas. At 34 years of age, he had a boyish face, and was almost completely deaf. When spoken to, he always replied, "Wasseggu?" (Wadoyousay?). Because of his hearing problem, he was a lonely figure and did not participate much socially. He was also slow in everything he did. His nearsighted eyes stared from behind very thick glasses. We hoped this trip to Norway would give him some pleasure and amusement. He sure needed his spirits lifted.

The second night at sea the wind backed from nor'west to west, and with our northerly course we seemed to fly over the waves. In the early morning hours she veered back to nor'west and became brisk. The sky stayed blue, not a cloud to be seen, and the barometer was steady and high.

In the course of the day, we got a fair blow and the seas became higher. By afternoon the wind reached the force of a heavy storm and the waves took on a nasty, green colour with white horses all around us. The sun kept shining, but life aboard became wet and unpleasant. Mountains of water smacked into our hulls with frightful claps. We carried too much sail, so Harry and the two beanpoles scrambled onto the deck outfitted in safety harnesses and lifejackets. They changed jib number one to jib number two, reefed the mains'l halfway and took the mizzen down. With reduced sail, *Trillium II* soared on and we made good time. From the north came endless rows of transparent water mountains throwing the ship off course time and time again. Our crew became seasick and worthless. Wullum could not stand the violence of wind and seas any longer. He disappeared into his cabin and burrowed himself under the blankets. The sea separates the boys from the men and there was no room at sea for boys. Poor Wullum. And he had seemed so sure of himself back in Oudeschildt!

It had become impossible to keep our course toward Norway. We had fallen off to an easterly course, and after a few hours we saw the Danish coast appearing on the horizon. Straight ahead of us lay the harbour of Hantsholm. We called the harbour-master over the marine radio for permission to enter his harbour. He insinuated that the harbour was already full, and with the raging storm it would be better to stay outside at sea. Harry wouldn't take no for an answer. No one may refuse a ship entrance in a storm. He then told us he had us on his radar, and gave us a course to the approach buoy, a mile from the harbour entrance. Once again he advised us to stay outside and ride out the storm, because the situation in front of the harbour was so serious that no sane man would even try to fight his way through. Monstrous waves were beating against the piers.

We were on the approach course. There was no turning back now. A quarter mile ahead were the flogging waters of a witch's cauldron. It was Helgoland all over again.

We would try our well-proved method of storm jib to keep the bow on course, using diesel power to push the ship. At the same time, the screw delivered a water stream along the rudder for perfect steering control. Harry wrestled with the sails alone. His deck-hands were knocked out by seasickness and fright. When the storm jib was up and pulled taut, Harry anchored himself on the

Harry, with his keen eyesight, keeps all his attention to the buoys. What's coming up there ahead of us? Aha, it is a cardinal buoy and it shows we have to pass to the north of it. And the girl? A penny for her thoughts!

forestay and gave directions. Sheets of water washed over him relentlessly. What my first mate did on the foredeck was priceless, and I followed his signals obediently. A few hundred metres before the harbour entrance, an enormous ground-swell rose up behind *Trillium II* and carried us along on the crest with neck-breaking speed. With the diesel in reverse, the wave passed underneath the ship and we sank so deep into the oncoming trough that we were swallowed from sight as the fishermen and others watched our approach from shore.

A final wave thrust us between the outstretched arms of the piers, and then there was the stillness of the harbour, as in Helgoland. We were also given an ovation, this time not from the soft hands of vacationers, but from the tough, calloused hands of the fishermen.

Hantsholm, Denmark. Breakers near the protecting piers. We entered Hantsholm Harbour when a gale from the northwest made life miserable on the North Sea.

The harbour-master emerged from his booth and directed us to a mooring spot in the already overcrowded harbour. He stated in perfect English, "It was a mighty sight to see you storming in, but just before the piers I didn't see you anymore and I was afraid you hadn't made it." He did not charge us any harbour fees.

Hantsholm was a fishermen's port and everything was paid for by the Danish government. Fishermen from several different nations had sought refuge from the storm. We even saw a few Dutch boats, including one from Harlingen, and another from Terschelling. A German barkentine had moored across from us—a three-master from the glorious times of seafaring when there were wooden ships and iron men. There were also several yachts and, of course, *Trillium II* as the last ship in out of the storm.

Wullum appeared out of his molehill under the blankets and our other guests came on deck, too, still shaken and dazed. Harry rummaged in the galley and made us a pot of tea and some sandwiches. It had been a long time since our last meal.

In the evening we all went ashore to visit a seaman's bar at the quay. The fishermen from Terschelling were also present so we joined them. The dark, oak-panelled bar was an authentic seaman's pub. Heavy wooden tables were bolted to the floor and the chairs would survive if used in a fight. Wullum behaved incorrigibly. He carried the conversation, and at the same time eyed a couple of heavily made-up girls who were serving beer.

The music blared. Some girls from town came in and joined the Danish fishermen. We and the Terschellingers looked on. The beer was expensive (four guilders for a bottle of Carlsberger). Oh well. Cheers, and let's be jolly!

Our friends from the island of Terschelling were not enjoying themselves. They were hopping mad about the prices and annoyed enough to start throwing those heavy chairs around. It was time for us to take our leave.

Hantsholm was not very exciting. A few doors down the street was a café with the jukebox playing softly. An attractive, friendly girl tended the bar. Wullum and André did their best to impress her and, by the looks of it, it seemed to work. We presumed that after many years behind the bar, she knew how to handle her customers. Nevertheless, the beer was just as expensive here. Disappointed, we shared a taxi back to the harbour.

Wednesday morning at eight o'clock the sun was warm and the wind had calmed down to a breeze from the north'west. The Danish fishermen next to us became restless. The ship from Terschelling had already gone to sea, and we also planned to pick up our mooring lines. The German barkentine was just ahead of us and the Danish fishermen were in our wake. It was a sight to behold, all the ships leaving port in keel-line. The barkentine sailed on a southern course, and we watched her sails falling from the yard arm and filling with a sweet, light wind.

Back on course to Norway

Georgie, our cook for the trip, made split-pea soup for lunch, with rashers of bacon. He cut up a large, smoked sausage into six equal pieces, and with slices of bread we had a meal fit for a king. Bas, sitting beside me, slobbered and shovelled the soup into his mouth by bringing his face down to his bowl. Even with the ship dancing over playful waves, he did not spill a drop.

In the afternoon, Harry and I studied the nautical charts of the Oslo Fjord. Land could not be far away. Our guests asked the unavoidable question, "When will we arrive?" Twenty miles out they climbed on top of the wheelhouse. Each one of them wanted to be the first to shout, "Land ahoy!" But it was the radar that spotted land eight miles ahead. Soon after, the jagged coastline of the Oslo Fjord came into view. The Norwegian *Pilot* offered ample information on how to navigate these waters. By evening the sun had arched down toward the northern horizon. We were on latitude 58°N (approximately the same as Hudson Bay or the Yukon). Daylight changed to twilight, and at midnight the newspaper could still be read on deck.

When we moved deeper into the fjord, the mountainous coast showed its dark, ominous profile against the light sky. It was a marvellous sight. The sun shone upward against a cloudbank and the colour changed from gold to yellow to orange and later to mauve, with the sky a pale pastel blue. The air was still. The sails had been stowed. The only sound we heard came from Ethel, rumbling in her engine room.

Moments later we passed a lighthouse high upon a rock. Its beam flashed through the still, clear sky. It was strange to see this guiding light sweeping across the translucent heavens. We could tell from the lighthouse at port, the beacons on the rocks, and the houses at starboard that we had entered the ship's channel.

The sea became as smooth as a mirror, and the silence of the evening was miraculously beautiful. A three-quarter moon rose out of a southeast skyline. No stars were yet visible. In the north, a mellow, orange sun wavered above the mountain tops deciding whether to sink or stay put. Strings of lights twinkled down from the mountainsides to the waterline reflecting brightly and colourfully in the water. The evening was so breathtakingly awesome that Georgie stopped talking in mid-conversation, and the boys perched atop the wheelhouse where they could quietly take in the scenery and the peaceful atmosphere.

Grönningen Lighthouse, entrance of the Oslo Fjord. The light swings around at a reddish transparent sky. Time: about 11 o'clock at night.

Harry picked up the microphone and reported to Kristiansand Harbour Control that we had just passed Grönningen lighthouse. He kindly requested permission to enter port. There was an immediate answer: "Permission granted." However, that port was still five miles deeper into the fjord. Small motor vessels closed in around us and people started waving and shouting, "Welcome to Norway!" They had spotted the Canadian flag flying proudly from the top of the main mast. They sailed along beside us like a welcoming committee escorting us into port.

A brief stop in Kristiansand

In the meantime, the sun had made up her mind and disappeared behind the mountain tops. Twilight changed to a deeper dusk. We rounded the cape and Kristiansand appeared in full splendour of her city lights. The chart of the fjord had shown an average depth of 600 feet or more, but closing in to the quay, our depth sounder showed a mere five feet. That was scanty for our draft of six feet plus. *Trillium*'s keel scraped through soft mud, but luckily we did not run hard aground. Many onlookers watched our approach. Our crew cast the lines ashore and willing hands looped them around bollards. A customs officer awaited and stepped aboard when the ship was secured. The formalities were few and quickly finished. We offered the man a drink and even a second one was appreciated. He informed us that a hundred metres farther down the quay was deeper water. We moved the ship and, indeed, we were out of the mud bed.

A native folk dance group walked by clad in splendid embroidered costumes. Upon seeing our strange, foreign vessel, they stopped. The accordion player struck up a merry melody and the group commenced dancing. It was so graceful and elegant that we applauded loudly. With a deep bow in our direction, the band disappeared into the midsummer night. Our young people also wanted to go into town in pursuit of blonde, Norwegian girls. But it had been a long, long day, so the skipper retired to his bunk.

At the breakfast table the next morning, plans were made to explore the city and do some sightseeing. Who would do the ship's chores, the shopping and cleaning? In all cheerfulness, our guests divided the tasks at hand.

It was a gorgeous day. The Norwegian sun was warm and there was no wind. The main street of Kristiansand was long, with many shops and sidewalk stalls. It was a pleasure to walk there, but the prices made us shudder. How could people afford it, especially the food? One kilo of tomatoes cost at least $6.00 Canadian. A chunk of cucumber, three or four inches long, was $2.50. We shook our heads in disbelief. Everything was three to four times as expensive as in Holland or Canada, except for a banana split. That cost only a few dimes, and besides that, it was delicious. Prior to our next cruises to Scandinavia, we would load *Trillium II* with food supplies until there was no waterline visible.

The Nordic women were blonde beauties, tanned and bronzed by the midnight sun, and they would look a man square in the eyes. That was refreshingly different from the women of the Azores, who would pass by with their eyes fixed to the ground. Give me a healthy, straightforward, Norwegian girl any time and, not to forget, a smiling, Dutch country girl with rosy cheeks.

Oslo Fjord—Boaters were out in full force to shout, "Welcome to Norway." They had seen the Canadian flag high up in the mainmast of Trillium II.

Harry and Georgia had stayed on board that morning and when I returned with the boys, we saw the ship from far away. They had spanned the lines across the decks, and blankets and bed sheets fluttered in the breeze that came down the mountains. Somehow it had a festive look, like a collection of flags strung up in the masts.

In the evening, we decided to "do the town." The younger generation was friendly enough to take the old skipper and Georgie in tow. Bas sacrificed himself to stay on board to keep an eye on things. Georgie began to bleat in anticipation of a jolly evening spent in a bar or café. Wullum and André went ahead, trailblazing with long, awkward legs. They were going to show the skipper and Georgie the nightlife in Kristiansand. We followed the leaders.

Well, that nightlife didn't turn out too badly. We finally ended up in the centre of town and from there we could easily find our way back to the harbour and the ship. In case we over-indulged, we could always find a taxi. As it turned out, the price of beer was so exhorbitant, there was no danger of that!

Some guests, like fish, begin to smell after three days ...

A NORWEGIAN CRUISE takes two weeks, and we had plenty of time left for touring on the return trip. After Kristiansand, we made a landfall in Lillesand, also in the Oslo Fjord. From there we would visit Hantsholm, again and then sail to Helgoland. Maybe Frieda would be there.

Bas had behaved himself modestly the first week on board. Sometimes, after the ship's bell had sounded for meals, he had to be called two or three times, and then at the table he was overly timid. He hardly dared to put butter on his bread. We had to persuade him to get his share of the meal.

After that first week, it became a different story. He could take care of himself, and no longer needed our protection. He ate a whole loaf of bread in one sitting, spread lavishly with butter. His short-sighted eyes scanned the table for something to put on the next slice. Would it be Dutch cheese or Norwegian jam? His towering masterpieces looked like Dagwood sandwiches. At dinner, he scraped and cleaned all the pots and pans, the others egging him on.

We encountered an unfriendly North Sea after our departure from Lillesand, so we set sail directly for Hantsholm. Seasickness reared up once more and we did not want to expose our guests unnecessarily to that fierce, cold sea. *Trillium II*, small and fragile, danced her way over the green, hostile waves until the waiting arms of the Hantsholm piers welcomed her. Without much ado, the harbour-master, now used to our caprioles in entering his port, showed us a mooring spot next to a German vessel. The good entrance we had made was immediately spoiled by Bas's bungling with the lines. *Trillium II*, at that moment, was dead in the water and strong winds pushed her toward the middle of the harbour, away from the German craft.

I shouted to Bas to throw the lines to the German ship, where willing and helpful hands were ready at the railing to catch them. He didn't hear me and did not understand what he was supposed to do. Harry skillfully jumped up and seized the line from Bas's awkward hands. Immediately, the German crew grasped it and slowly we were pulled alongside. When all was properly secured and we had thanked our German neighbours, we made our way down below where Georgie was brewing tea. After an earful about his blundering on deck, Bas promised to be more attentive.

Having Bas on board was an adventure in itself. We discovered he had a secret habit of stealing food. On his way to the saloon he would snatch an apple from the fruit basket, look around, and when he thought no one had noticed, he would take two more and drop them into the pockets of his oversized pants. Then he would retreat to his cabin, happily munching the stolen fruit.

That was not the only antic performed by Bas. He had found Georgie's bottle of Dutch gin. When no one was in sight, he slyly poured himself a large glass and downed it in one gulp. Wullum, who shared a cabin with him, reported that Bas undressed completely twice a day and powdered himself from top to toe, spending extra time on his manhood. After he was dressed again, he would take his medication.

Last, but not least, and for us not so hilarious, we found out that Bas had guzzled 60 single-serving cans of V-8 juice. Every nook and cranny aboard a ship is utilized for storage and every bunk had built-in lockers. We had stored those 60 cans in one of Bas's lockers. When we checked later, back in Harlingen, there was not one can left. How in the name of Neptune had he managed that stunt?

Georgie and Wullum had become fast friends, but were always in each other's hair. Wullum would promptly nibble at the bait which Georgie dangled in front of him. That pleased Georgie tremendously, and he bleated to no end.

André was the lazy one. When he had installed himself on the settee, he would sit on his backside with his long legs sticking out so everyone would have to climb over them to get by. For one reason or another, André was allowed on board for half of the passage fare. This did not prevent him from being first in line at dinner time to load up his plate. When it was time to clear the table and do the dishes, he disappeared into his cabin. Wheelwatches were done very reluctantly when it was André's turn.

Trillium II lay quietly beside the German yacht and the crews visited back and forth. The wind had increased a bit and strummed the rigging in an endless melody. For the next 24 hours, a Beaufort 8 was forecast. In planning ahead, Harry and I agreed to set course directly to West Terschelling, but that was not to Wullum's liking.

We had promised our guests a landfall at Helgoland. Well, Helgoland it would be, but not before the weather had improved considerably. Wullum constantly nagged at us to get under way, but we pointed out to him the white water smashing over the concrete piers. We followed the lead of the Danish fishermen and stayed either on board or at the quay-side café. If they left, we would also go, but not before. Out of boredom, the sulking crew left the ship to drink beer at the bar where the tables were nailed to the floor.

Harry and I will not soon forget that summer on the North Sea. One depression after another came from the Atlantic. Between Scotland and Norway, the North Sea acted like a funnel increasing the wind velocity. We won't forget the pounding seas or the endless rows of storms. That sea has caused much suffering over the ages. Charts had been marked with crosses to indicate wrecks where ships and crews had met a watery grave in the bights and sonts and on the sandbanks of the Wad Islands. But there was also glory: the glory of entering a harbour safely out of a storm; the glory of reaching one's destination as it had been planned by the navigator; the glory of beholding a sunrise encircled by green sundogs, or at night the fluorescence of plankton where the propeller had churned the water to foam; the glory of the stars and planets sweeping across a velvety sky and the moon drawing a golden path of light toward the ship. These things make a sailor happy and content with his life at sea.

The weather had turned handsome, and with a good wind aft over starboard, we made good time from Hantsholm to Helgoland. Thanks to Bas, we had another poor showing when mooring *Trillium II*. We had completely given up on him. He would never learn. There was also something strangely wrong with Georgie. He bleated constantly without any reason. Had the sea got the better of him? Some people crack up from the immensity of water and sky.

In the afternoon our guests, all perked up, ventured ashore to sample Helgoland beer and ogle Helgoland girls. Harry and I remained aboard to give the galley a good cleaning. Georgie was a good cook, but our little galley showed a lot of neglect. When everything was spic and span, Harry and I went ashore to look for Uwe, our Helgolander friend. We were happy to find him at home ready for company and tales of the sea.

As the end of the cruise was in sight, and a stop at the island of Terschelling was planned, we left Helgoland the next morning. Again, it was not to the liking of Wullum. However, the captain never argues with his crew or guests. I explained to him the rules of the ship and the sea, and expected him to obey.

Foremost and uppermost in the mind of a good captain is the safety of the ship. If the ship is safe, the people on board are also safe. The skipper is a lonely man. He cannot share his responsibilities with anyone, and only he can make decisions that everyone else must abide by.

Some landlubbers do not understand that, and sometimes think that the captain is a mean ogre demonstrating his authority. What they do not know is that the skipper always sleeps with one eye and one ear open, to guarantee the ship's safety. Therefore, the skipper also sails alone from one horizon to the next, from one harbour to another, until in the end, he sails into his last harbour.

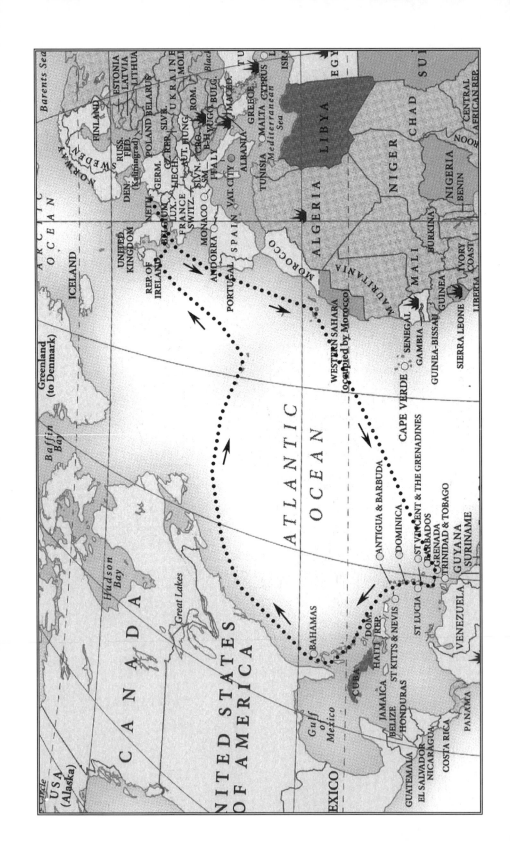

From Holland to the Caribbean and Back

Madeira

We sailed beneath the Azores High, an enormous area of high barometric pressure with the centre over the Azores. We were becalmed, making no headway at all.

Seven days of stormy weather

Until that time, our cruise to the beautiful island of Madeira had been filled with unfortunate setbacks. First we had been delayed in Plymouth for repairs to Ethel, our faithful old diesel. Then, in the Bay of Biscay, we encountered continuous gales from October 4 to October 11 so that our progress was only 120 miles in seven days.

Now the Atlantic Ocean was as smooth as glass, the air stark still. After rounding Cape Finistere on the northwest point of Spain, we picked up the Portuguese northeast passat for a short while with both current and wind in our favour.

For a few hours heavy rains persisted, and suddenly we were in the doldrums. The sails swept listlessly across the deck. We were thankful for one small blessing. The current carried us toward our destination free and clear at three miles per hour. In 24 hours we were 72 miles closer to Madeira.

After the seven stormy days in the Bay of Biscay, we had sought refuge in the harbour of La Coruna, located on the north coast of Spain. Despite the beauty of the city, the harbour was so filthy and crowded it made us shudder. *Trillium*'s white paint disappeared under a film of slick, black oil. For the privilege of mooring there we paid dearly with many pesetas.

The promenade was bedecked with various cafés, terraces, and bars where the *cerveza* (beer) and Spanish cognac were surprisingly inexpensive. Our annoyance about the oil slick in the harbour was quickly forgotten when we gazed upon the lovely signorinas strolling by. Even with a dark shadow on their upper lips, they were attractive, graceful, and charming. Their short skirts showed off their black lace stockings and they wore high, spiked black shoes.

La Coruna was cooled by the wind blowing from the Atlantic. The heat of midday disappeared, and by evening, sweaters or jackets were worn when sitting at the outdoor café. Gradually our interest in La Coruna faded, so we set sail again, hoping the restless waters of the ocean would clean the filthy oil from the sides of the ship.

In the doldrums, sweaters and jackets were soon exchanged for lighter clothing. The girls adorned our decks in their colourful two-piece bathing suits. It had become subtropically warm and the ocean was an incredible shade of blue. The atmosphere aboard ship was enthusiastic. Even the cook sang as he prepared meals in the tiny galley. As we sailed past Porto Santo, an island without harbour but with unbelievably white beaches, we knew that Madeira was not far off.

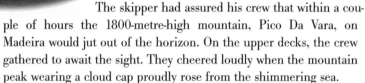

After a seven-day storm on the Bay of Biscay, we arrived safely in the fishermen's harbour of Cedeira. A rainbow greeted us with a promise of better weather.

The skipper had assured his crew that within a couple of hours the 1800-metre-high mountain, Pico Da Vara, on Madeira would jut out of the horizon. On the upper decks, the crew gathered to await the sight. They cheered loudly when the mountain peak wearing a cloud cap proudly rose from the shimmering sea.

Six days after departing from La Coruna, we arrived at Funchal, the seaport of the island. Thanks to the gulf stream, we had made good time. Suddenly, in the middle of the harbour, the diesel quit and we were set adrift. Harry tossed the anchor overboard to check the drift. He jumped into the warm waters, and dove down to inspect. Soon he emerged with the message that a plastic bag had become tangled in the propeller and had smothered the diesel. No wonder Ethel had given up. Harry cut it loose piece by piece. We stayed at that spot overnight. We were in no one's way.

The morning after, we moored next to a derelict hull of an old inter-island trader, biding our time until the harbour-master arrived to give us clearance. We needed to go ashore. The last crust of bread had been eaten two days before, and our supplies needed to be replenished.

According to the *Pilot*, the harbour works had been under renovation since 1970, but all we saw was an unsightly mess of broken pilings, eroded embankments, and rusty, bent railings in crumbling concrete.

Reflecting back, we were impressed with our good ship, *Trillium II*.

She had made her way through the Atlantic Ocean, the North Sea, the Baltic Sea, the English Channel, and the Bay of Biscay. She had been strafed by gale-force winds, and held her own in angry, turbulent waters. We, her permanent crew, had also learned a lesson or two. The most important one was that she wanted to be left to herself in tempestuous seas. She knew best.

When wind, weather, and waves were all against us and we could no longer handle the situation, we would lash the wheel hard over, drop all sails, and allow *Trillium II* to ride out the storm herself. She would find the correct position in respect to wind and waves. Then she could dance around naturally, unaffected by internal forces such as rudder, engine power, or sail. One watch was sufficient in the wheelhouse. The other crew members could play cards or read below.

Radio contact with other vessels was quite frequent. Once we had a pleasant conversation with a passing Norwegian freighter. Before signing off, her captain remarked, "You people are lucky to have the freedom to rove far and wide across seas and oceans. I would change places with you any time." It happened so often that professional seamen were envious of us boat-bums.

Wherever we sailed, we also had our friends of the sea. Dolphins kept us company for hours, frolicking in our bow waves. A baby dolphin flanked by its mother and an aunt was always a touching sight. We noticed that they always showed up before a storm. Was that their way of warning us of a change in the weather?

For a few days, a little bird joined us. It had a coat of grey feathers, with a yellow breast and a small pointed beak. Now and then she would strike down and settle herself on the railing or deck house, but not for long. She seemed to find enough food from the sea. For five days she stayed with us, then she flew away, never to return.

Nights at sea can be miraculously beautiful. The sky is clear and each star is distinct. The masts and rigging sway to and fro in cadence with the movements of the ship. When the ocean begins to radiate the colours of the rainbow, the spectacle is complete. It is absolutely mesmerizing.

There we were, in the harbour of Funchal on an enchanting

After the storm, the weather improved fast. View at a shallow inner harbour at low tide. We were anchored outside with the fishermen.

island in the subtropics. The splintered pilings did not invite us to moor there, so we clung with a few lines to the old derelict. We were eager to go ashore but didn't dare. We had no permission yet from the immigration authorities.

Where was the harbour-master?

A friendly aspect of the sea— our friends the dolphins kept us company, sometimes for hours. This picture was taken near the Azores.

FOR HOURS we had laid up against that old barge and kept our eyes on shore. Labourers were busy working, cement mixers turned round and round, and bulldozers pushed heaps of rubbish ahead of them. Was it true after all that the harbour would get a facelift?

Several other yachts were moored nearby. Their skippers stood on the quay talking to one another. Apparently they had received clearance. Soon a stocky fellow strutted toward the group of sailors. He looked very impressive, wearing navy pants and a white short-sleeved shirt adorned with gold decorations and chevrons. We knew that he must be the harbour-master. He gestured excitedly in the direction of our ship and also to the other yachts, but we did not understand what he meant. In the span of a few minutes, he had pointed our way several times. It seemed as though he wanted us to move, until he signalled us to stay put. Harry and I clambered across the deck of the old barge to join the company of the other yachtsmen. From close up, we could see three gold bars on his shoulder epaulets and assumed he was a commander or other high-ranking officer. It was hard to understand him since he spoke little English. Because of all the gold on his shirt, we kept quiet and listened submissively. Finally it got through to Harry and me that he would pick us up at 10:00 A.M. to take us to an office. For now we could return to our boat. We were warned by one of the skippers not to take the time of the appointment too seriously. It could mean today, but it could also mean tomorrow or the next week.

The harbour-master did not show up until 3 o'clock that afternoon. Harry and I were ordered to bring all the "passports." The other crew members had to stay aboard. The harbour-master did a lot of talking but we could not understand him. Every time we crossed a street or rounded a corner he would say, "Tisseway, tisseway." At the end of the trek, we came to the office for immigration on the Avenida do Mar—the sea boulevard.

Behind a desk sat a pleasant young man who handed us a stack of forms to be filled out. He was very helpful and was able to speak English. While we attended to business, our good friend, "Tisseway," stood timidly at the door, captain's hat in hand. When we left, we had documents signed, sealed, and delivered. We were granted permission to stay on the island for three months and had been charged only 30 cents per document.

The harbour-master led us to another building, where the entrance was heavily guarded by two soldiers armed with automatic machine guns. Nervously, we followed our guide to an office of the harbour authorities. A heavy-set man in uniform barked at our guide, "Get out!" He was ordered to wait out in the hall. The military man informed us that the harbour was under his control and there would be no fee charged for our stay on the island. We were welcome to visit for as long as we wished. Any weapons on board must be turned over to him, but we had only signal pistols so were allowed to keep them.

Outside the office door, Tisseway waited patiently. As soon as we stepped onto the street, he donned his gold-braided sailor's cap. We had discovered his secret. He was not a harbour-master at all, but an errand boy for immigration and harbour control authorities. Through his black hair were threads of silver. We guessed his age at about 50 years. The shirt he wore was immaculate, and upon closer inspection we realized it was adorned with the regalia that could be purchased at most souvenir shops along the quay.

Harry and I admitted that he had been helpful and deserved to be paid for his services in some way. When we invited him aboard for a beer, he accepted with noticeable pleasure. Once on deck, he shook hands with the crew and introduced himself as João Nunez. He explained that all his friends called him Johnny and asked if we would also call him that. "You people are now my amigos, aren't you?" he said.

We agreed to call him Johnny, and he insisted on referring to me as "Capitano." We quickly became accustomed to his broken English. We wanted to befriend Johnny. He knew everything and everyone along the harbourfront, and that would definitely be to our advantage.

As we relaxed on the settee, enjoying a cool beer, Johnny

João Nunez, the harbour-master of Funchal

volunteered a great deal of information. First, he proudly announced that he could not read or write, but he did have a captain's diploma. We expressed our doubts, thinking he must be bragging. Out of his shirt pocket he produced a grubby piece of paper with his photograph on it, proclaiming that João Nunez was permitted to handle small boats within the harbour territory. We acted surprised and complimented him. Johnny basked in the attention, pleased with the tremendous impression he had made on us.

I sent him ashore with a bottle of Canadian whiskey. He was so delighted that he was back early the next morning before any of us had climbed out of our bunks. Eagerly, he scrubbed the decks, ran errands, and did shopping, always returning with the change. He was not only the devil's advocate for harbour authorities and immigration, but he became the handyman on board *Trillium II*.

One afternoon Johnny urged me to come ashore with him. "I show you somethink nice. Come, come. Have a drink on me." Curiously I followed him, and soon we arrived at a dirty neighbourhood. In a slum-type street, he entered a bar and ordered a bottle of wine. "Somethink nice" was nothing but an establishment with three or four Portuguese beauties already on the other side of twenty-five. The manager was a nasty-looking woman with sharp, beady eyes. The vinho was so sour, it made my eyes water. Three of the girls joined us, and an attempt at conversation was made in halting English. I was asked to treat the girls to a glass of brandy. When it was served, I snatched the glass from one of them, sniffed it, and tried a sip. The brandy was nothing more than coloured water. I had had enough of this racket. I paid the sour woman for the sour wine and quickly left.

Johnny followed me outside, moaning that the bottle of wine had not been finished and I had not made use of the generous services of the girls. Now he would not earn his usual commission. I made it quite clear to him that I was not concerned about his earnings and I was not interested in services like that. Johnny did not accompany me back to the ship, but his parting words were, "Tomorrow, Capitano, I bring you present."

As usual, he was there early the next morning to swab our already-clean decks. While we sat in the saloon eating breakfast, he came in. From the pocket of his crisp, white shirt, he pulled a silver chain with a pendant in the shape of an anchor. I was expected to hang it around my neck at once and for days he made sure I was wearing it. He promised to bring one for Harry, too.

In the meantime, his daily visits were not so welcome any

longer. Often he would try to pressure us into doing something we were not interested in. Many times he hinted that he would like to come along on our cruises. After all, he did have a captain's diploma, didn't he?

We wondered about his personal life, and whether he was married, but questions about his home life were always evaded. I pictured his wife as one of the sloppy women dressed in black, including knit stockings and customary head scarf, standing in the portico gossiping with other women. In most of the Latin countries, the females are very attractive until they are married. Then babies are born and with each birth they seem to lose some of their charm. For the most part, they are not involved in public life or in the men's world.

The men spent time with their friends, drinking vinho. It seemed they could stand for hours at the café bar with no noticeable effect. Whether Johnny had a wife or not, he was always clean and neat. Each day he wore a fresh shirt and his navy pants were pressed. Maybe he had a nice wife who took good care of him and didn't look at all as we had envisioned her.

We had not mentioned our departure date to Johnny. Very early on a Monday morning, we slipped quietly out of the harbour. I wondered again if we would ever see the 'harbour-master' of Funchal again. Even the fact that he was only an errand boy and a recruiter for a bordello brought a smile to my lips. He had been quite a character. We felt a bit guilty not having said, "Saludos, Johnny."

Adios, João Nunez...

Santa Cruz de Tenerife

Santa Cruz de Tenerife was the filthiest and most impossible harbour for yachtsmen we had ever encountered in all our years of sailing the Seven Seas. As an introduction to this story, here is an excerpt from our ship's journal:

Yachts not welcome

Unhappiness from the moment we sailed into the harbour. Waters oil-polluted, floating scum, dirt, garbage, and animal corpses. Unfriendly watchmen and harassing harbour officials. Harbour control radio manned by people who do not (or won't) speak English and are rude and unhelpful. We are

slapped from one end of the mole to the other by officials.
A yacht is on sufferance in the fisherman's harbour of Santa
Cruz. <u>No</u> welcome received from the "Royal Yacht Club of
Tenerife." No drinking water available for yachtsmen for
2-1/2 days per week. Harbour officials not on duty from
Friday noon until Monday morning. Water taps on the quay
shut off during that period. Period.

In short, that is how it was on sunny Tenerife. Since we had
left Funchal on Madeira without saying goodbye to Johnny, the
"harbour-master," 250 sea miles had passed under our keel and
now we were precisely on course by dead reckoning only. The
flash of Tenerife light peeked above the horizon's edge at three
o'clock in the middle watch. At a course of 180 degrees true, the
light twinkled five degrees over the starboard bow.

Far to the north lay Madeira. Tenerife loomed up ahead of us.
Only a couple of hours of sailing and we would reach the harbour
and throw our mooring lines over bollards. We had perused the
Pilot for information about the harbour of Santa Cruz but found
nothing out of the ordinary. Also, we had brought some travel
brochures we had picked up in Holland, but those folders just concentrated on hotels, swimming pools, palm trees, and the usual
Spanish beauties draped on a beach. They were nice to look at, but
of no use to us at that moment.

At 6:00 A.M. we rounded Punta de Anaca, and an hour later
the city became visible through some wisps of sea mist. Santa Cruz
lay like a capricious tangle of buildings against the side of a mountain. Higher up, rocky outcroppings were black and uninviting,
the hills bare, with no trees or greenery whatsoever. Instantly, we
became homesick for Madeira with its flowers, lush green valleys,
brilliant sunshine, and rain in the mountains.

At 11:00 A.M. we sailed into the main harbour of Santa Cruz.
A gigantic sign bade us "Welcome from the Real Club Nautico." It
was the first, and also the last, welcome.

Yachts belonging to club members were moored at buoys;
there was no room for visiting yachts. There was no one at the
deserted clubhouse to greet us. We were not impressed with the
"welcome" given by the Real Club Nautico in Santa Cruz.

We motored deeper into the harbour and passed three white
cruise ships at a huge mole. Those giants dropped off 2,000 passengers at a time, letting them loose to shop and sight-see. They
were a most welcome source of American dollars. Hoping to find

a suitable place for docking, we floated between barges, traders, and trampships to no avail. Back to the yacht club, but the silence there was deafening. Nobody hailed us from their shore.

A cracking was heard from the marine radio and someone shouted, "Yacht American. Yacht American. This is harbour control!" We glanced around, trying to see which American yacht they were calling, but saw nothing. We had clearly, for everyone to see, a large Canadian flag on top of the main mast and a smaller one at the stern. We were not Americans. The call came again. Harry grabbed the microphone and spoke, "This is a Canadian yacht, *Trillium II*. Did you call us?" They *did* mean us and we were told to leave the harbour immediately. Then Harry asked where we could find a place to stay. From some gibberish, we understood that somewhere along the coast was a fishermen's harbour and to look for tankers and oil tanks on the shore. "But get out of here!" we were told.

As we sailed along the coast that morning, we had noticed some tankers but had not seen a fishermen's harbour. Nevertheless, we honoured the orders of harbour control, left that unfriendly place, and began to seek out somewhere more inviting. But to no avail. We saw no fishermen's harbour at all. Back to the first harbour we sailed, right by the control tower in quest of a nook where we could throw our lines around bollards. Immediately control tower began to shout, "American yacht, get out of this harbour!" Harry turned the volume of the radio to zero. In a far-away corner, we found some barges at a quay and proceeded to moor alongside them. In Europe, it was a normal procedure. Even the barge skippers helped to catch the lines and fasten them to cleats aboard their ships. It never presented a problem there. Here it was a different matter. All around us we saw angry faces, and arms flailing wildly, plainly meaning, "Get out!"

Harry called harbour control to ask permission to stay in the forsaken corner. But all we heard was, "Policia!" "What kind of harbour is this?" we asked ourselves. Why had they threatened to call the police? Was it just because we had tried to find a spot for docking or mooring? Who did we have to thank for this extreme rudeness and hostility?

Now Harry was more furious than ever. He blared into the microphone, telling them that we would take our "American" dollars where they would be welcome, and calling them a name I won't repeat. Our only reply was another rude warning, "*Policia!*"

We knew it was time to leave and try again to find the elusive fishermen's harbour. This time, we were more successful. We headed straight for the tankers and found a small pier protecting a little harbour from the sea. Fishing vessels were lined up on the quay, as well as a few yachts. Dead slow, we entered between some buoys and motored toward the yachts, which were moored five deep beside each other. Two kind young people beckoned to us. We could tie up alongside their yacht. As it turned out, they were two people after my own heart. They had come from Germany, and were on a world cruise.

When we had first entered the harbour, we had not noticed the foul smell from stoke oil and floating scum. All around us were chunks of driftwood, plastic bottles covered with thick layers of lumpy oil, old ropes, bags of garbage, and even bloated animal corpses. We shuddered.

It was not the yachts' crews who had dumped that filth into the water. Just as the other visiting boats, we placed our green and yellow bags ashore to be picked up by garbage collectors. The local fisherman were the culprits of the stinking mess.

The next morning, while still seated at the breakfast table, we heard someone jump on our deck. The harbour-master knocked at the door. We invited him in, and it was obvious that he was for real. He breathed authority. He was not Johnny from Funchal on Madeira. He wore authentic gold stripes, and sported a huge revolver. Here was Mister High-and-Mighty himself, from his steel-toed boots to his enormous uniform cap. We were duly impressed, but also angry because he had crossed our deck with shoe soles full of steel. He was business-like, but not the friendliest man we had ever met. From his pocket he pulled a bunch of papers which the captain had to fill out while he waited. He declined a strong drink, but accepted a cup of tea. Our passports would be checked later in the day by immigration officials, he informed us. With a "Gracias," he left with the completed forms and climbed on board the yacht of our German friends. We heard him clomping over their deck.

During the night, at high tide, our lines had sagged into the water, and stoke oil had done its work on our clean, white, nylon lines. They were so filthy, slippery, and unmanageable, we could have cried. Not only that, high tide had brought with it oil which covered the shiny, white sides of the ship and also the white legua-nas (bumpers). With tears of anger and powerlessness in his eyes, Harry entered the saloon to report the bad news. It was ten times worse than La Coruna.

We were not the only victims. The other white yachts were also plastered with the filth. All around us we heard moaning. The clotty oil slicks could be scraped off the sides, but the paint would always show a brownish yellow discolouring. Our lines had to be thrown out. Goodbye to many American dollars.

Now we had a choice to make. Should we pack up and leave, or stay on account of our paying guests? They wished to go ashore to explore Santa Cruz. Reluctantly, we decided to stay. A pent-up anger boiled inside me. In the next few days we realized that we yachties were barely tolerated. The fishermen and other local vessels had priority, and we were continuously pushed from one side of the harbour to the other by uniformed *officios*, all armed to the teeth. When one of those dictators told us to move, we had to move. He started to swing his revolver when we questioned him about where to go. Where we went was of no interest to him.

On the quay, hydrants were installed at regular distances. If there happened to be room, we could come alongside to top up our water tanks. At noon every Friday, they were turned off until Monday morning. There was no water for foreign yachts. During the week, we met a man with a cart full of hoses. He used a key to turn on the taps of the hydrants. A reasonable man, he helped us when he could.

After days of abuse, shouting, and provocation, we could take no more of Santa Cruz. We planned to leave on Saturday morning. On Friday afternoon, prior to our departure, Harry wanted to fill our tanks. The water man had just shut off the hoses. Harry negotiated with him for the loan of the cart, and the man also lent him the key to turn the hydrant tap on. While Harry was busy connecting the hose, he saw Mister Officio approaching, complete with rubber stick and revolver. Not sure what to do, Harry continued and inserted the key into the hydrant. The officer stood beside him twirling his stick. He barked at Harry in unmistakable Spanish and ordered him to return the hose cart and key to the shed. Absolutely no water after 12 noon on Fridays. That was the rule.

For us, it was the last straw. Santa Cruz de Tenerife could go fly a kite as far as we were concerned. We would leave, and even though our water tanks were only half full, we would manage. Gladly we would depart from this cursed place and look for greener fields and blue, clean, clear waters.

This dirty black line on the safety net is the result of a few days' stay in the oil slick of the harbour of Santa Cruz de Tenerif. Advice to the sailing fraternity: leave ten sea miles between you and that port.

A word of advice to our brothers in the sailing fraternity: Sail with a wide, wide circle around that place. If you have nothing to look for there, stay away. Do not even attempt a landfall. You will not be welcome. Move on to beautiful Los Cristianos. It is almost paradise, and the harbour-master there is friendly, speaks English, and even a little Dutch.

He does not wear a revolver or carry a rubber stick.

A Night in the Devil's Passage

A hopeful start in a lovely little town

Santa Cruz de Tenerife lay behind us. A calm breeze pushed us along the coast of the island. The monotony of bare rocks and low, extinguished volcanoes was our only scenery. It was a desolate and cheerless sight. At Punta Rasca we changed course and before long the wide bay of Los Cristianos could be seen. We took sails down and motored into the bay. What a sight it was! A dream of sunshine, palm trees, and white sandy beaches. Gleaming white yachts bobbed at their anchor chains. In the distance, dark mountains arose, arid and colourless. At the foot of the mountains were villages of white casas and cream-coloured hotels. These were the dream palaces for tourists from cold, northern countries.

A small pier enclosed part of the natural harbour of Los Cristianos. Docking at the pier was prohibited for foreign yachts. The space was reserved for the ferries from Las Palmas and Gomera. With a friendly harbour-master, we made arrangements to take in water and diesel fuel. That had to be done in daytime while the local fishermen were at sea.

French, English, German, and American yachts were anchored in the bay next to one another. We followed the trend and let out enough anchor chain until we were neatly lined up with an American yacht, bows pointing seaward.

Los Cristianos was a small fishing village, but to accommodate the ever-increasing tourist trade, it had become a modern little town with many hotels, apartment buildings, and a core of the usual cafés,

Trillium II in Los Cristianos. After the bad reception in Santa Cruz de Tenerife, we found this beautiful place on the south coast of the island of Tenerife. We were more than welcome; there was lots of room to anchor in the bay, and the water was crystal clear, inviting us for a swim. The friendly harbour-master was trilingual. He not only spoke Spanish, but also fluent English and Dutch.

boutiques, shops, and terraces. No cars were allowed. The promenade was sheltered under broad-leafed palm trees. The village
square was close to the beach with a view of the intense, blue
waters of the ocean. Here, yachtsmen from around the world gathered to drink the sweet, black coffee. Mostly German and English
could be heard, spoken by passersby.

Over the centre of the island hovered a large cumulus cloud,
its underside almost black. Day and night, it was always there. Yet
along the coastline the sun shone brilliantly.

Frequently, swimmers would come over to our ship for a
friendly chat. They were curious about where we had come from
and where we would be going next. That was how we became
acquainted with three young Canadian
people. They had taken a year off from
their studies at the University of British
Columbia and were touring Europe.
They had flown over from Madrid,
Spain. As usual, we smelled money and
invited them aboard.

We had already planned to go to
Gomera, an island west of Tenerife.
Taking only half a day's sailing, it would
be a nice weekend trip. Harry proposed
this to the young men and soon the
deal was made. That night they would
come aboard, settle themselves, and
early the next morning we would take
off. With a look of contentment on his
face, Harry placed a healthy stack of
American dollars into the ship's kitty.

*The village square from Los Cristianos. Here we
had our morning coffee on a terrace and chewed
the rag with friends from other yachts. Los
Cristianos was often the starting point for the
crossing to the West Indies.*

The open stretch of ocean between
Tenerife and Gomera was twenty sea
miles wide. Twice a day a ferry crossed
the channel known as Devil's Passage.

The name should have warned us.

EARLY IN the morning, our new
crew hoisted the anchor as Harry
looked on. Expertly, he showed them
how to handle the sails. Once out of
the sheltered bay there was a slight
breeze to fill the sails. We were still in

*The German Corner. Many people from Germany
have apartments in the Canary Islands and spend
the winter there to escape the dreary weather in
their homeland. Somehow, this beach was annexed
by them. One German couple adopted us and we
received many dinner invitations. Los Cristianos,
we miss you.*

**It could only
happen to us**

the lee of the island and its 3700-metre-high mountain, Pico da
Teide.

Once out from under the lee, the character of the ocean
changed. The calm waters became mounts of high waves without
crests. We were in the passage. The ocean, restricted by the two
islands working as a funnel, had only one way to go. Up, up, up.
One moment we soared to the top, the next we plunged into a
huge, deep trough of onrushing water; we assumed it was because
of a storm far to the north of us. This was a performance of the
Atlantic Ocean, of might and unbridled energy. Oddly, at the time,
it was not even an angry ocean. There was no wind, and the sky
was a pale blue. High above were translucent cirrus plumes warning us of winds to come. A French yacht had left the bay at the
same time as we did, following in our wake. Now it was mostly hidden between the rollers.

In no time the boys were sick. After emptying their stomachs
into the ocean, they disappeared to their cabins. With wide, frightened eyes they had seen the spiel of water and waves and realized
how small we were in this expanse of unlimited power.

As we tottered atop a gigantic roller, the harbour and town of
Gomera could be seen, but it seemed we had made no headway.
Every wave dragged us farther southward. In the afternoon, the
wind began to blow from the north. It was clear to us that we
would never make it to San Sebastian. White horses surrounded
us like an army of unstoppable mounted warriors. The ferry from
Los Cristianos passed us, obviously in difficulty. She held her
course to the harbour but was pounded to no end. Breaking waves
flew high over her superstructure. Her powerful diesels held the
ship on course. For us, only one thing could be done: fall off to the
south. Our French companion was nowhere to be seen. Hopefully
he had returned to Los Cristianos in time.

Sick as dogs, our guests lay in their bunks, completely
unaware of what was going on. We could smell the vomit through
the companionway doors. Harry put up a bit of sail and we backed
off to the southwest.

The devil had us in his grip. He threw our good ship hind and
far. We had occasioned storms in the North Sea, the Baltic Sea,
and the Bay of Biscay, but there was one obstacle between the
devil and total destruction and that was the seaworthiness of
Trillium II and her will to survive. Harry and I believed it as sure
as the Rock of Gibraltar was English dominion. With sail power
and the persistence of the diesel, we kept the reins in our hand,

steering the ship behind the mountain of petrified lava. Still, waves slammed *Trillium II* with abnormal force as if she were merely a piece of driftwood. But each time, the storm jib, that blessed piece of dacron, pulled her head on course again. We rounded a cape and maintained a westerly course, but frenzied waves and howling winds followed right along. Darkness set in and lights on the island winked.

Something uncanny was happening in this Devil's Passage. High above the raging sea stars shone peacefully in a dark sky. Foam swept over the decks. According to our sea chart, there must be a cape with a deep bay behind it. The likely haven was about four miles from our present position. Those four miles were a fore-taste of hell for us and our little nutshell. Wind and water round-ed the island from both sides and met together somewhere in the middle of the south shore. We were in that rendezvous of un-bridled, crushing forces of hell on earth. Why had we chosen this day to go for a weekend sail to Gomera? A few miserable American dollars? If so, those dollars were the most hard-earned dollars in our whole enterprise...ever.

We were thrown back and forth repeatedly. *Trillium II* could not distinguish between her front and rear end.

Finally we reached the bay behind the outcrop, but neither Harry nor I knew how we arrived. Our only thoughts were of sur-vival. We motored further into the bay. There the water was calmer. To throw an anchor overboard was useless. The ocean floor was much too deep to hold it. All the sails were taken down and the diesel set on dead slow ahead, bows toward the coast. Lights from the land became our beacons. Around and over the mountain the storm raged on. When the wind pushed us farther out to sea, Ethel was given more power, until we were under the protection of the coast again.

It was a long, long night watch. Harry and I switched wheel-watches every hour. How our guests were doing, we didn't know and we didn't have time to care. We could see the lights ashore, and were envious of the people sleeping peacefully in their soft beds, unaware that a storm raged around their beloved island. Later we were informed that the houses had been shaking on their foundations and no one had gone to bed.

The morning sun, peeping over the eastern horizon, was a very welcome sight. Also, the wind seemed to abate. Harry and I both had severe headaches from tension and a sleepless night. We motored out of the bay that had been our refuge, and set an easterly course back to Tenerife and lovely Los Christianos. From under the lee of Gomera the wind grabbed us again, making it impossible to set course to San Sebastian.

After four hours of motoring, we glimpsed Tenerife coming up out of the horizon. Soon, we were back in the bay. We made fast at the pier and then our guests appeared on deck.

Ho ho, boys, no disembarking yet. You have to clean your cabins first. Here is water and soap, and do not complain....
Scrambling ashore with their backpacks, they left without saying goodbye, still shaking in their shoes. Later, we talked to our fellow yachtsmen. There had been no bad weather there at all. It had been just fine.

We looked up at Pico da Teide, the Peak of Hell, as the natives call the 12,480-foot mountain because they believe the devil lives inside it.

Whatever it is...her cloud-cap had gone.

An Empty, Empty Ocean

From the Canary Islands to the West Indies

We anchored in Carlisle Bay, Barbados, after 21 days of sea, sky, and tradewinds. The emptiness of the ocean was broken only once when a yacht from Germany passed us at mid-point, the point of no return.

That Western Ocean, as it was referred to by sailors of old, was immeasurably vast and empty. The ship sailed inside an enormous disc of water, the horizon always in the distance, the sky a forget-me-not blue. White, fluffy tradewind clouds sailed along with us toward an unchanging skyline. At night, that blue sky became a velvety darkness, sparkling with stardust. Stars twinkled, and deep in space shone planets like candles in a window. A starlit night at sea is awesome and beautiful.

The tradewinds continued to blow from east to west, with Beaufort 4 or 5, as they had since time began. Waves rolled with the wind in an endless procession toward the far islands, and then broke on rocky shores. They lifted *Trillium II* on their foamy backs and carried her along. The bows rose and fell, rose and fell. The constant motion made the landlubber seasick.

At night, the wheelhouse was faintly lit by the lights on the instrument panel. A red light shone within the compass bowl. The doors were left open to let in the cool, refreshing sea air. Now and then the sails flapped as the helmsman allowed the ship to wander off course. Startled out of his nocturnal musings, he corrected it by turning the wheel a few degrees. The sails pulled again and tugged the ship along the same route as our forefathers had sailed in their wind-jammers.

Twenty-eight hundred sea miles separated the Canaries from Barbados. Five hundred years before, Christopher Columbus had embarked from Spain, across the Sea of Darkness, on a quest to discover a land of gold. Feeling like explorers, we followed his trail, knowing we would not find gold but a rich kingdom of lush, emerald-green tropical islands.

Much could happen on that lonely part of the ocean, the restless sea. Ships had disappeared without a trace, but ships had also been found drifting aimlessly with no crew. Such was the case of the *Marie Celeste*, the most talked-of mystery ship in the world. It was November 1872. She had loaded a cargo of 1,700 casks of commercial alcohol in New York and set sail for the Mediterranean. On December 5, she was sighted between the Azores and Portugal, not a single soul aboard, ship and cargo intact. She was yawing erratically. A boarding party found the ship's journal in which the last entry had been written on November 24. Its position was recorded at 100 miles southwest of San Miguel, in the Azores. It seemed the crew had abandoned the ship in a great hurry, with all sails set, but no trace of the missing persons was ever found.

We had stayed quite a while in the beautiful bay of Los Cristianos in the Canaries. Winter lay ahead, and Harry and I pondered whether to stay and see how long our kitty would hold out. Sailing around all the islands did not attract us. Most of them were bare and dry with dormant volcanoes. We had already climbed them and found that their parched slopes were all the same. In the village of Los Christianos we had made friends among the European "snowbirds." A German couple, who had rented an apartment, often invited us to dinner.

In the meantime, Hetty had flown from Holland to join us and to escape the long, dreary winter in the Lowlands. Every morning we went ashore to drink our sweet, black coffee on the terrace under the palm trees. It was there we met a young couple from Sweden and two Canadian graduates from a university in British Columbia. As they spoke about going to the West Indies, Harry and I perked up. Here was a golden opportunity to leave the

Canaries and get paid for taking these four people across the Western Ocean to the islands off the leeward bow. After some chatter, we installed them aboard ship, cashed their traveller's cheques, bunkered, and filled our water tanks. The new crew was sent out to buy their own drinks and victuals. On previous trips, meals had been included with the fee, but Harry and I found it very inconvenient. Now our paying guests bought food for themselves, and also for us. It was a satisfactory arrangement, and worked very well for us.

Hetty had stored her winter coat and donned her polka-dot bikini. We were ready for takeoff. Up went the sails. But there was a sirocco blowing that hit us when we came from under the lee of the island. It heralded itself by mean, red skies and fierce gusts of easterly winds. The phenomenon originated above the western Sahara, where, during the day, hot air rose sucking up fine particles of sand. Then it blew for hundreds of miles out over the ocean, far past the Canary Islands. There it descended slowly, and in no time we were covered with red dust. It penetrated the sails and spirals of the stainless steel rigging. On the decks, it formed a film that was difficult to scrub off the surface. It clung tenaciously to the ship, and worst of all, the dust entered the cabins, wheelhouse, and saloon. We were forced to breathe in the foul air and powdery dust.

We had planned to sail back from Los Cristianos to Puerto Rico on Grand Canaria. It was 36 hours before we turned into the piers of the harbour at 2:00 A.M. After throwing our lines around bollards in front of a large factory, we tried to get some sleep.

When daylight arrived, we transferred *Trillium II* to the visitors parking of the local yacht club. There we were greeted by members of the club. We were able to top up our water tanks and do some last-minute shopping. The weather report informed us that the sirocco was still blowing. We were warned to wait one more day.

That we did. At 9:00 the following morning, December 2, we were once again on the great waters of the Atlantic Ocean. Then, free of the island, the wind grabbed us and within 24 hours we were abeam of Hierro, the most western island of the Archipelago. We had sailed like greased lightening. *Trillium II* had nibbled 200 sea miles of the total of 2,800 nautical miles to Barbados, our destination in the West Indies.

When I took my place at the navigation tables to chart our

courses from Hierro to Barbados, our new crew stood around me. They seemed a bit subdued, most likely from the realization of the distance we had yet to sail, and in awe of the might and vastness of the Atlantic.

As we were nearly sailing along a parallel, I chose the composite sailing method, so we were able to use the same compass course for most of the way. In case we should become becalmed in the Horse Latitudes, I could change to a more southerly course to pick up the tradewinds.

For one more day, *Trillium II* continued to travel with the wind in a perfect corner. She proudly showed nine to ten knots on the log. We pressed on under full sail and felt assured we would be in Barbados in record time.

The next day it was over. The wind disappeared completely and the sea was a smooth, glassy, blue-green surface. We were in the Horse Lats, the dreaded latitudes of little or no airs.

Trillium's sails hung listlessly like a wet dishcloth. Harry and the crew furled them around the booms. We had no desire to waste precious days or weeks in those hot latitudes. We considered setting course to the Cape Verde Archipelago and pick up the tradewinds along that south-sou'westerly course. Our paying crew didn't mind at all. They enjoyed being on a calm ocean with no seasickness, no heaving ship, just sunbathing and jumping overboard to cool off.

I was concerned about the water supply. We had enough food to last for at least three months, but water was always uppermost on a mariner's mind. Making a landfall on one of the green islands, Cape Verdes, seemed like a sensible idea.

To our guests, it was paradise, this life without a care in the world. They hoped it would last forever. But alas, Harry turned the key and the diesel sprang to life. They were forced to listen to the deep, throaty roar of Ethel. Because of their disappointment, Harry promised to stop the ship twice a day so they could have their swim.

The weather chart indicated tradewinds at a latitude of approximately 22 degrees north and, as expected, it had proven to be correct. First, the usual cats' paws made their debut. Then came the wind and the friendly, white-capped waves to carry us along toward the western skyline. Harry roused the lazy bums from their deck mattresses. There was work to be done. Up went the sails. The mains'l all the way out to port and the boom was secured so as not to slam back into any unsuspecting people. Our good old ship picked up speed in no time and even doubled that when Harry supervised the crew on the lightweight genoa, paying her out like a balloon. The bows dipped and rose in cadence with the combers passing underneath the ship. Spray flew over the foredecks. Now, this was sailing! Ethel was shut off. Her services were no longer needed. We would probably put her into action once we reached the islands of the West Indies.

One morning, Harry, *Trillium*'s first mate, bosun, engineer, and jack-of-all-trades, reported something very unpleasant. He had checked the water level in each tank and discovered that during the last few days more than 300 litres of drinking water had been used. That was far too much, so we called our crew to the fore. There were innocent faces all around. Nobody had used water for laundry, nobody had rinsed salt out of their hair, and definitely nobody had left a tap dripping in his cabin. The mystery of the missing water was never solved.

Harry installed a concealed switch on the electrical pump that saved us from running dry. Now only Harry and I controlled the flow of our precious water. Upon arrival at Barbados, we had 200 litres to spare. A ship without water in tropical waters is like a floating coffin. So many things could go wrong when sailing in the middle of nowhere, weeks away from the nearest land: illness, accidents, even mutiny of unhappy guests or crew. Harry was excellent at pacifying frayed nerves and restoring peace on board. In case of injuries, I was a pretty good doctor. I had taken a course in first aid.

Quite often, at the beginning of a long ocean crossing, people who were not accustomed to seafaring would ask, "Skipper, what happens if one of us gets seriously ill in the middle of the ocean?" My reply, though insensitive, was, "If you die, we will sew you into a canvas bag and throw you overboard." If they reflected on it long enough, I consoled them and said, "Come, come. It is not that bad. Young healthy people like you don't become ill too easily. You breathe clean, fresh air. You eat a proper diet, no meat, but fish when we catch it. We have lots of oranges and lemons on board for your vitamin supply. I would not trade this life for living in a polluted city, would you?" That perked them up and they commenced scrubbing the decks, singing a sea chant that Harry had taught them.

Crossing the Atlantic Ocean from the Canaries to Barbados was a long and lonely journey. The sun shone relentlessly day after lonely day. Starlit nights alternated in eternal rhythm with nights when moonbeams drew a silvery path across a calm sea. Sun, moon, and stars were our guiding lights. We needed them to find our way over that giant body of water. Sometimes we wondered what we had gotten ourselves into. Week after week there was nothing but water and sky and only one inch of wood to keep the brine outside our floating home. We understood that we could not compete with the forces of the sea; we could only respect them. Then what in the world were we doing here? Of course, there was a reasonable explanation. Mankind is constantly searching for knowledge, therefore he explores the unknown and at the same time he seeks adventures.

One ordinary day, we noticed a break in the skyline—a tiny white triangle. It was a ship under full sail following the same route as we were. Such a sighting broke the monotony on board. Everyone was very excited. Within two hours she was abeam of us. She was a little faster than our ship. She drew close and we were able to converse across the gap. We told them a little about ourselves and our ship and also compared our last positions. She was the 25-metre yacht *Happy Taurus*, from Hamburg, Germany, on her way to St. Vincent. With farewells, *Happy Taurus* stormed past us, but her white sails stayed visible for a long time.

The ocean was not as empty or lonely as we had thought. Dolphins showed up frequently in front of our bows and played tag with the ship. Sometimes they stayed for hours demonstrating their swimming abilities. Their performances were awe-inspiring. During the day, we saw schools of flying fish emerge from a wave, fly a few metres, and then dive into the next one. At night they flew right on deck. When there were enough, we fried them up for breakfast, nice and crisp. An albatross glided toward us, circling the tops of the masts and glaring at us with sharp, black eyes. What was he doing so far from his usual haunt, the waters of the southern seas? Sometimes those artists of the wind would soar high in the sky without even moving their wings a fraction of an inch. Then they would swoop down and catch a flying fish. Our friends, the dolphins, birds and fish, provided us with many days of entertainment.

On this particular voyage, we had a pleasant crew. Watches were run without any grumbling, and cooking and cleaning posed no problems. I took sun sights only in the morning, at noon, and again in the evening to determine our position and progress. Day after day we ran under full sail. By day we made seven to eight knots. By night, when the wind had subsided, we made 5 knots or under. Our daily average remained at approximately 130 sea miles. For *Trillium II* it was no record.

At 5:00 P.M., when the sun was over the yard-arm, we split the mainbrace. Hetty and I occupied the bench seats at the starboard side and Harry kept the other crew company wherever they had found a place. We chatted and mused about the day gone by. I enjoyed my rum-cola and Hetty sipped something less powerful. The cook-of-the-day excused himself and disappeared into the galley. We all stayed on deck and watched the sun slanting toward the western horizon. None of us ever tired of that spectacle.

The boys had discovered a way to break the boredom of the lonely days. They strapped on a safety harness, secured a line onto the musketon hook, jumped overboard, and let *Trillium II* pull them through the water. They dragged along more underwater than above, so they improved on the invention and took a floorboard, put the line through the finger-hole of the plank, and presto, they had a surfboard. Their fun was short-lived. A shark had taken position next to the ship, its triangular fin acting as a sentry. The boys wisely decided to stay aboard. Their zest for surfing had dissolved. That old shark kept us company until we were 100 sea miles from Barbados, then it vanished just as suddenly as it had appeared.

Every evening, just before dinner, I plotted our new position on the chart and gave the helmsman a new course. I also scribbled down the day's run, and our crew took notice of the results of my mysterious actions with sextant and calculators. They learned to read the chart. The course line crept slowly across, every day two degrees longitude toward the west, as regular as clockwork. At 40 degrees west and 20 degrees north, we were at the halfway point— the Point of No Return. Whatever happened to the ship or crew, we could not go back. We must press onward on our westerly course.

Under Hetty's supervision, a special dinner was prepared. The table was decorated with bottles of wine. When they were empty, messages were written and inserted into the bottles. Then they were corked and thrown overboard. The sea current would taken them along and we hoped they would wash ashore and be discovered by someone on a distant island. The party continued deep into the night, and everyone had a jolly time. Outside, the tropical sky domed over the ship. Waves in endless procession lifted *Trillium II* on their foamy backs. It was so idyllic, we all wanted to sail on and on forever.

Once in a while, we would have a day when line squalls would surround us. Those dark cloud formations would send down sheets of rain slanting in heavy gusts of wind. We tried to avoid them, but when we were not able to steer clear in time, we dropped all sails and secured everything on deck. The next day, the sky would be bright again.

I had explained to the crew that if the Polestar were 12 degrees above the skyline, we were then on the same latitude as Barbados. That meant we were near our destination. I allowed them to use the sextant, and evening after evening they "shot" Polaris.

Long ago we had left the "Azores High," a huge part of the ocean with a high barometric pressure. We were now in a tropical flow. The temperature had risen, and even at night it did not cool off. Our crew had taken to sleeping on deck. They had lugged the mattresses from their bunks, and with a line around their waists, had tied themselves to the masts or rigging just in case *Trillium II* made a sudden lurch when they were asleep.

In time, Polaris had dipped to 12 degrees above the horizon. I happily announced that we had only 500 more sea miles to go. At Christmas, we would be in Barbados. My crew slapped my shoulder, "Well done, Skipper." The sea miles rolled away under the ship's keel, and at 100 miles from Barbados, not only our friend, the shark, disappeared, but also the wind died down completely. We had to call on the assistance of our diesel.

Harry put the crew to work. The sails were furled, and the blue covers put in place. The decks were scrubbed, and the cabins cleaned. Hetty busied herself in the galley and Ethel rumbled in her engine room. Everyone was in a good mood.

On Christmas Eve, just before sunset, we dropped our anchors in Carlisle Bay, Barbados.

It was a happy ending to a very long voyage.

New Year's Eve on Barbados

On a tropical evening, at 8 o'clock, there were only four hours to go before we entered a new decade. Our crew, under the leadership of Harry, had gone ashore to the Barbados Cruising Club for a dinner and dance. Young people belonged there on such a special occasion. We had given them our blessing, and Hetty and

Carlisle Bay, Bridgetown

I stayed to keep watch on board.

Our guests, who had joined us in the Canary Islands and crossed the Atlantic Ocean with us, had left to find their own way around the Caribbean. A new crew had already taken their place to explore with us the Lesser Antilles. There was Monica, very young and very blonde, and her friend, a nice young man with a swarthy complexion. Two American boys had also come aboard and paid in advance for a four-week stay. Our kitty was doing well. Diana was still with us since embarking in Holland. Even though she was Harry's girlfriend, she paid as she went like everyone else.

In the Lesser Antilles, the dead are buried above ground in tombs of concrete blocks. The corpse is covered with coral sand.

Our young people slipped away in the sloop before the tropical dusk set in. Hetty and I made ourselves comfortable in the cockpit on the starboard side where we had a view of the beach. In the distance we could see the clubhouse still festooned in Christmas lights, and hear wafts of the rhythmic beat of Goombay drums. The yachts around us turned on their deck and mast lights as soon as darkness arrived. We followed suit. The trade winds had diminished to a whisper, the seas were flat, and the bay lay calm. The moon had risen from behind the island, big, round, and rosy.

We heard the laughter of happy young people, and the murmuring of the hissing surf on shore. A tropical island is a paradise for both young and old, for those in love. It was an enchanting evening. Hetty and I held hands and drank in not only our rum-colas, but the captivating atmosphere as well. Long ago, in the years of planning sea voyages and building my ship, I had dreamed of times like this. I had been like a schoolboy with an all-consuming desire to become a ship's captain and visit faraway lands. Not only had I fulfilled my

A relic out of times when England ruled the waves. Viscount Horatio Nelson, English Admiral, built fortifications around English Harbour in Antigua. Buildings in the fort have been restored and the harbour is a yachtman's

wishes, but I had the gratification of sharing them with my wife and youngest son, Harry.

The moon's path of burnished copper reached out toward Hetty and me as we enjoyed the unbelievable loveliness of the night. A slight, lazy swell entering the bay rocked the ship slowly, sometimes splashing against the hulls. We were in harmony with the world and with the universe in which our ship was a mere speck. Tomorrow would be another day of sun, water, and wind. We had the freedom to come or go as we pleased. No landlubber had such an opportunity.

With a start, we roused from our reverie. It was midnight. The old year had made a place for the new. Fireworks at the yacht club crackled and banged. From the other side of the bay, above the palm trees, Bridgetown let loose a feast of sparkles and colours against the night sky. There was activity on some of the yachts as well. They used their Very pistols to shoot some red, green, and white magnesium flares, a few with parachutes to slow the descent. The colours were reflected in the sea. Refusing to be left out, I chose a number of flares without parachutes (they were too expensive to use for fun). Our Very pistol resembled a miniature cannon, and the flares soared skyward with a loud, hissing sound. I am positive I heard applause from the shore. Could it have been our young people?

The last bang died away and it was Happy New Year to everyone. I gave Hetty a big traditional New Year's kiss and then we went down below. It was bunk time for us oldies. We did not expect our crew to return for a few more hours. I turned on the shortwave radio and tuned in to the world broadcast of "Radio Nederland." It came through loud and clear. The first thing we heard was Marlene Dietrich singing, "Ich Kusse Ihre Hand, Madam," ("I Kiss Your Hand, Madame"). I would rather have listened to "Moonlight and Roses," so I snapped the radio off.

A ship is never without noise. Lying in our bunk, we heard the usual creaking of masts and rigging. Soon Morpheus transported us to the Land of Dreams. The sleep of a mariner is different from others. I remained aware of the ship's movements and sounds, my inner ear constantly on guard. That is how I heard the bumping of the sloop against *Trillium II*. It was early morning, but still dark, when the young people quietly climbed on board. One of them whispered, "Shhhh, the skipper is asleep." But the skipper immediately returned to dreamland, with a smile, satisfied that his crew was back aboard.

Did Hetty swim all the way from the ship to the beach?

The Bermuda Triangle

**Mysteries of
the sea**

The Bermuda Triangle, also called the Hoodoo Sea or the Devil's Triangle, is the graveyard of the Atlantic Ocean. In the stretch of the Western Sea, between Florida and the Bermuda Islands, lies the Sargasso Sea. Sailors of old told eerie tales, and even Christopher Columbus wrote in his ship's journal about the white seas, the mysterious disturbances of the ocean's surface. Through unknown causes, a calm, smooth sea would suddenly change into a witch's cauldron of foam and swirling mists.

Since 1945, more than a hundred ships and planes and thousands of people have disappeared into this realm of horror. In 1908, a Dutch steamer from Amsterdam bound for Paramaribo in Surinam never arrived. This ship had reported a tornado west of the Azores, and was never heard of again. The Danish bark, *Kobenhavn*, a five-masted training ship, left Copenhagen on December 14, 1928. Her destination was Freemantle, Australia, and she would sail via The Horn. This ship, with a crew of 60, was equipped with an auxiliary steam engine and radio. On Christmas Eve, it exchanged greetings with a ship from Norway, reporting her position as south of the Azores. It did not arrive. No distress call was ever heard.

The year 1921 saw, in the first three months, a record number of vessels that vanished without a trace. Some had entered the Hoodoo Sea. Some had skirted around it, most to the north of the Azores. After World War II, the list of missing ships and planes grew longer. In most cases, the results of investigation were the same—no trace.

One of the 39 vessels that took part in the Trans-Atlantic sailing race was the *Marques*, a beautiful three-masted ship almost 40 metres long. On June 3, 1984, a heavy storm from the nor'west hit the ship, and at sunrise sails were furled. Her position at the time was north of the Azores. The 48-year-old captain was an old hand at sail racing and was experienced in the handling of ships in those circumstances. Unexpectedly, an abnormally strong gust of wind forced the ship over to starboard, as later told by the helmsman, Philip Sefton. Immediately after, an enormous wave rose up behind the stern and broke right on top of her. The ship sank quickly, taking with her 19 of the 28 crew members. The *Marques* became the victim of a rogue or mammoth wave.

A rogue wave is a wall of water which emerges from nowhere, suddenly and deadly. The highest one ever recorded with a certain measure of reliability was 40 metres. In many sailors' tales about mammoth waves, the height seemed always to be exaggerated and they were considered imagination or flights of fancy.

It has become clear that these waves really do exist. They have been given several different names: spook waves, freak waves, killer waves, mammoth waves, and even the waves from nowhere. The question is, where do they come from, and how frequently? Were the spook waves always responsible for the disasters such as the *Marques* and the other lost ships?

They have been accepted as an existing phenomenon. Some guesswork has also been done concerning their recurrences. Based on incoming reports, one in 23 waves is twice as high as the average wave with a given wind force of Beaufort 8. One in 1,175 is more than three times as high, and one in 300,000 waves reaches four to five times higher, which means a wave of plus or minus 40 metres. Probable cause of the giants could be interference. A leading, large wave is slower than the following waves. The apex of each succeeding wave builds up the height of the slow one ahead of it, and the resulting energy contained in that mountain of water is awesome. When the crest breaks on top of a ship, it means total disaster, and may God help the mariners who are in the wrong place at the wrong time.

A SECTION of the Western Ocean, called the Devil's Triangle, has a reputation of being jinxed. The angles between the meeting lines are situated at the Bermuda Archipelago, Florida, and Barbados, encompassing the Bahamas, Greater Antilles, and the Sargasso Sea. However, the infamous site where many ships and planes have met their fate is not actually a triangle but a trapezoid. The first four letters of the word describe it well. It is a trap. Mark Twain once wrote, "Bermuda is a paradise, but to get there, one must go through hell."

We had arrived at Barbados after a three-week crossing of the Atlantic from east to west. In January and February we had done some island hopping in the Greater Antilles. Picking up paying passengers at one port and dropping them off at another kept our kitty full.

For a week we had stayed at Charlotte Amalie on St. Thomas in the American Virgin Islands. Time pressed on. I had assured our agent in Harlingen, Holland, that we would return in May for a summer of chartering on the North Sea. Departure day was set for February 23. We intended to sail along the Atlantic side of the

Trillium II in the Triangle

Bahamas to Fort Lauderdale, not realizing that it coincided with one leg of the Bermuda Triangle.

Mooring in Charlotte Amalie at the Sheraton Marina had cost $25 a day. The rum sold for $1.25 per litre—tax free. We loaded up with Jamaican white rum (200 bottles) and started off with an amateur crew.

The direction of our first leg was northwest, from the straight between St. Thomas and San Juan to Grand Turk Island. By setting course along the Bahamas we suddenly realized we were following the southeast–northwest side of the Devil's Triangle. What on earth were we doing venturing into waters of bad reputation? There was no use in worrying, so we adopted a wait-and-see attitude. Sailing on that deep, blue ocean was marvelous. It was as smooth as glass, with no wind, and only the sound of Ethel rumbling the miles away while the sails hung listlessly down the masts.

Pascal Joseph—an adorable boy who could speak fluent French, English, and Papiamento, an old language spoken by the black people of the West Indies. His father made a new oar for us.

The second leg was from the Turks and Caicos Islands to San Salvador, or Watling Island. Closing in toward the dazzling beaches of the island, we paid our respects to an enormous cross. It had been erected to commemorate the landing of Columbus in the West Indies early on Friday morning, October 12, 1492.

From Watling to Eleuthera was the third leg. There we would change to a westerly course for the Biminis. We had enjoyed eight days of enchanted sailing. To our port, the dream islands of the Bahamas, to starboard, the Atlantic Ocean, friendly now in all its grandeur and vastness. Was that all there was to it? Sailing along the periphery of the Hoodoo Sea in the Western Ocean seemed no more hazardous than sailing on Lake Simcoe on a sunny afternoon.

But the weather changed. Between Eleuthera and Bimini, a storm from the west hit us full force. We hove to for two days and were set back 40 miles toward the Atlantic Ocean. It was a serious upset to our time schedule and that of our paying crew.

In St. Thomas new passengers had come aboard. Among them was Pearl Ong. She was a rare beauty of Eurasian descent with a creamy complexion and sported a man's old-fashioned hat. Then there was Elaine Sabina, with Italian blood in her veins. She could have competed in the Miss World contest and won. The quiet Thomas came from Kitzbühel in Austria. He was a willing worker and was not afraid to go on deck in inclement weather. The last was Anthony, an American. All of them had booked for Fort Lauderdale, and all of them had to be there by a certain date. A deadline is an absurdity on board a ship that roams the Seven Seas. I always made it very clear to new passengers that a specific date of arrival could not be guaranteed.

The two-day storm slowly abated, so Harry, Hetty, and I decided to set course for Nassau on New Providence. It was well with our crew. They had seen enough of raging masses of water slamming across the decks. They were weary of wind and waves. In Nassau, they left ship and flew to their respective destinations. The four of us took a few days of rest to dry out *Trillium II* and also ourselves.

Close-up of the village. In spite of the omnipresence of Roman Catholicism, voodoo is practised with enthusiasm by the men of the village. For the sessions they retreat into the jungle.

At the marketplace in town, we were amused by the friendly women who sold a variety of tropical delectables for the table. We bought some beautiful conch shells as gifts for our friends in Holland, and also a crate of coconuts for ourselves.

Early in the morning we departed, sailing along the northern part of San Andros at a safe distance so as to avoid the dangerous coral reefs lying offshore. We passed Great Stirrup Light, and 60 miles later we rounded North Bimini and Great Isaac Light. There the strong gulf stream gripped our ship. With sails set for the trade winds, aided by the diesel power of Ethel, we headed for Fort Lauderdale with a course correction of 25 degrees against the current. We seemed to skate across the Florida Strait.

Johanna and her friend, Flap, waited anxiously for us in the local marina. They had booked for the Atlantic crossing from Fort Lauderdale to Holland. We had informed them of the landfalls in the Bermudas and the Azores. They were bursting with energy and impatient to set the canvas, but we had to wait for Adrian, who still had not arrived from Holland. When we heard that he had arrived at Miami Airport, we went to pick him up. At the same time, we dropped Hetty off to board a plane back to Canada and her job.

Cruise ship tourism in the West Indies—they sail at night and in daytime drop the passengers off at islands for sightseeing and shopping.

If everything went well, we could be in St. George, the harbour town of Bermuda, in eight days. A perusal of the navigators' bible, the *Pilot*, pointed out that we could not expect good weather this time of the year (March/April). Winds could vary between Beaufort 5–9, mostly from the northwest. We hoped to meet Beaufort 5, but prepared and settled for a Beaufort 8.

It did not go well. First, after rounding the coral reefs of Great Abaco, the Atlantic lay calmly before us with a slight swell. The wind was no more than the recorded Beaufort 5, a mere fresh breeze of twenty knots or so. Our new crew, with faces beaming, hoisted with pleasure all the sails *Trillium II* could carry. Our ship danced over the waves. Now and then water sprayed over the bows as she dipped her nose into the next wave. This was pleasant sailing.

When the sun is over the yardarm (sun going down towards the west horizon), it is time for a tod of good West Indian rum. When the sea was calm and the sails pulling, Harry and I loved to sit in the open cockpit watching sunsets. We never could get enough of this spectacle. This was the supreme moment—when the sun touched the skyline.

But before evening, the wind veered to the north-nor'west and increased in strength. Surging waves ran under the ship in a diagonal direction, yet *Trillium II* stormed on into the night. All the canvas was left up and Harry and I enjoyed it immensely. This was the real thing, the very reason we had gone to sea.

Inevitably, our crew became quiet and wan. Then they turned greenish, and not long after that they joined each other at the railing to feed the fishes. Harry and I were used to such views and were not worried. We could handle the ship with just the two of us.

For some people seasickness lasts only a few hours. For others, a few days. Harry and I had never been seasick. In our family it is an unknown matter. Thus, we could not muster up much sympathy for the people affected. Harry assured them, "It will pass. Don't worry. Tomorrow you will have earned your sea legs." I smiled and they turned their backs on us. "Let us die," they moaned. They were all advised to go to their bunks.

On the third day out we noticed the barometer had fallen and a halo had formed around the sun. These were signs of heavy weather coming our way within 24 hours. We also noticed that the ship lurched strangely and sheets of spray flew across the decks. As our crew was feeling better, Harry took them up and changed the foresail to stormjib, and they reefed main and mizzen. The deck was cleared of anything that could go overboard. The sloop on the aft deck was firmly secured with heavy lines. Let the blow come; we were ready for it!

It did not wait 24 hours. That afternoon the wind backed to nor'west and brought sleet and hail, winter on the Atlantic. Huge waves clawed at *Trillium II*. Still we kept on course. As the monsters of water and foam came in from the port quarter, steering became difficult. We changed the watches on the helm every hour. When I had built *Trillium II*, I had added an enclosed wheelhouse with windows providing a 360-degree view. In the original plans there was only a windshield and half a roof, leaving the sides wide open. Under our present circumstances, my idea paid dividends. It was warm and dry inside the wheelhouse, which also seemed to have a psychological effect: the tempest raging outside looked less awesome and dangerous to the helmsman who felt protected.

Even under reduced sail we made good time. Wind and waves were with us. Sometimes on large waves we planed and then surged down a long slope. As the crests caught up with us, we dropped, the stern downward and the bows pointing skyward. It was a wild storm. Never before had we been confronted with such dreadful seas. The North Atlantic had kicked up her heels.

Low-hanging clouds scudded overhead. Their ragged edges seemed to touch the waves. The barometer showed 960 millibars, which was low, and it remained steady. Darkness fell early and at dinner time we opened a few cans of beans. Cooking was impossible in a ship being tossed up and down like an orange crate. With masts creaking and hulls groaning, it crashed and pounded into the Atlantic. Why had we dared to travel this wilderness of mountainous seas and screaming winds? We should have stayed in the warm West Indies for another month or so.

The night passed and in the morning a watery sun shone for a moment through a hole in the storm clouds. It was not enough time to take a sighting, so we were still running under dead reckoning. Our crew showed up only to take their wheelwatch or have a bite to eat down below, with fear in their eyes.

That afternoon I took my turn at the wheel. Harry chose a watch in his bunk, and Johanna and Flap attempted to play cards in the saloon. The weather had not abated at all. *Trillium II* was continually pounded in her rear by colossal waves.

Sitting behind the wheel, I suddenly felt a great uneasiness. What was happening? This was not a regular storm. The waves were unrelenting. They wanted the ship and they wanted me. My

The rogue wave

body became rigid and my mind did the same. We were going to die right there and then. At that moment a strange sensation overcame me. I felt a reassuring presence and a voice warned, "Look behind you!"

There it was, the mammoth killer wave. Slowly and menacingly she rose. A steep wall of dark, green water sneaked closer and closer. Water filled my mouth. This was the end of the ship and the crew. I gripped the wheel as though I were able to outrun the approaching demon, but then came that feeling again. It was not I who held the wheel, but someone grasped the spokes and steadied us on an unerring course. Suddenly I could not hear the wind, and an eerie, green gloom replaced the daylight. We were inside the monster wave. The ship, unable to rise on the steep foreslope of that mountain of water, protested loudly with cracking sounds. How many thousand tons of water pressed her down? I felt the ship sinking toward her watery grave. Strange as it may sound, I did not think of myself or even the others on board. I thought about the ship, our trustworthy, lovable *Trillium II*. Would she rise again? Could she cope with the tremendous pressures inflicted on her. Would she break up under me?

Then the darkness was replaced with a green glow that became lighter and lighter. *Trillium II* had fought her way back to the surface. The wave had passed, and the ship had emerged from the briny. In front of her bows the giant wave broke in thunderous violence.

We would live and sail on.

We had survived where the unfortunate *Marques* had gone down with so many hands.

Had it been the Omnipresence, the Omnipotence of an essence that had saved our ship and all those on board?

Or had it been the indomitable spirit of the ship that had refused to yield to destructive forces of nature?

Water had poured inside through all the doorslits and hatches and anywhere it could find an opening. Harry, in his bunk, had had the deck hatch ajar. The rushing waters had thrown it wide open and he had floated on his mattress out of his bunk. Dripping and shivering, he stood in the wheelhouse. Johanna and Flap, in the saloon, had noticed the daylight growing dark and had felt the ship shaking and shuddering. They had clung to the edge of the

Rogue waves— they loom up without warning, as tall as buildings, overpowering ships in their paths. These enormous waves remain one of the great unsolved mysteries of the sea.

table as if it could save them. With terror in their eyes, they stood in the doorway staring up at me. "Wha...wha...what has happened, Skipper?" stuttered Johanna. Still half-dazed, I tried to joke. "We almost danced with the mermaids down where the seaweed grows, Johanna."

Oh, great miracle, the masts stood erect, and the sails pulled as if nothing had happened. *Trillium II* sailed on as though we had not been in any danger and so close to death. Nothing had broken, no one was hurt, and there had been no cave-ins. But all the electrical bilge pumps had to work for hours to pump away all the water inside the ship.

WE CONTINUED on our way to Bermuda. The storm followed us with rain, hail, and shine. It was still winter on the North Atlantic. Our crew had earned their sea legs, so Harry and I could catch up on sleep and leave the ship to our newfangled mariners.

Bermuda A'hoy!

Since the killer wave had struck, the atmosphere on board had changed. It was hard to explain. There was something untouchable but ever-present that depressed us. We had no zest, no love of life, no pleasure in doing our usual duties. Watches were done out of necessity. I had to force myself to make up the daily position and bring it in chart. The young people performed their tasks without enthusiasm. Only *Trillium II* plowed on and on, indifferent to what had happened. Her strength and undauntedness would carry us to our destination, we were sure about that. But what's next...?

Was a malicious ghost hovering over the Hoodoo Sea casting a spell on us? I had read that others who had sailed here before us had encountered the same wretched feelings.

What was it?

By making the daily reckoning, I had to assign a different compass course each time. We were not where we were supposed to be. I suspected the crew had steered a sloppy course but could not prove it. The same had happened when Harry and I had wheelwatch. There could only be one conclusion—a persistent compass aberration. If I could not obtain a sun, moon, or star sight, we would, in all probability, bypass the Bermudas and find ourselves in the middle of nowhere. We prayed for a break in the cloud formations. According to the sea charts, we were approaching shipping lanes, a route for freighters and container ships. If we saw one, we could ask for a position to verify our own.

It was also routine, when crossing a shipping lane, to turn on the radar. A vessel within a 16-mile radius would show up on the screen as a moving white dot. Radar was our third eye. Harry switched it on and we heard the humming of the antenna, but the screen remained as black as the night into which we were sailing. We had no radar at a time when we needed it most. At that moment, nothing could have been worse.

While I was seated at the navigation table figuring out our position, the crew mingled around and asked, "When will we arrive in Bermuda, Skipper?" Invariably I answered, "Wait and see." A dead reckoning was not the most accurate method of determining one's exact position, and I did not want to raise false hope. We certainly hadn't lost any time. The storm had pushed us at top speed eastward. On the sixth day, the weather had cleared, the barometer had risen, and the wind ceased its howling. No more waves climbed the decks. Now and again the sun broke through the clouds and I was able to use the sextant for a morning shot to resolve our ship's longitude. At noon I did the same. When the sun was at its highest point, I had a latitude, and combined with the morning sight, I had a reasonable fix.

After some figuring, talking to myself, and scratching my head, I informed the group around me, "In a couple of hours, you will see Bermuda." They bolted out and took position on top of the wheelhouse. Each of them wanted to be the first to shout, "I see land!" However, it was difficult to distinguish between sea and sky in the haze and I hoped it would clear in time. I did not want to disappoint my crew.

Our radio was on standby, and suddenly we heard voices. Harry grabbed the mike and called Bermuda Harbour Control. He received an answer immediately, loud and clear. Not much could go wrong now, but the horizon stayed hazy. The islands are only a few metres above the sea surface and, in good visibility, can only be seen at a distance of about three miles. Then I heard dancing on the roof of the wheelhouse and Johanna shouted excitedly, "Land! Laaaand!" What they saw was Gibb's Hill Lighthouse appearing out of the fog. But as we entered St. George's harbour the sun shone brightly and warmly. It was Easter Sunday.

The next day, Harry and I paid the captain of the Bermuda Coast Guard a visit and reported to him our experiences in the Bermuda Triangle: the unreliable compass; the defective radar that worked normally again when we were in the harbour; our depression; the mammoth wave into which we had disappeared completely and had come through at the other end without so much as a scratch. Besides all that, Harry and I, who had never been seasick before, had also helped to feed the fishes. The captain was not surprised or moved by our adventures.

"You have not told me anything new," he said matter-of-factly. "You sailed through a part of the ocean that has a bad reputation. And," he added after a moment, "if that wave had broken a few seconds earlier, it would have left nothing but splinters of your ship. You would have been just another statistic along with the other ships and their crews that vanished without a trace."

Harry and I paused to reflect on his words. Had we crawled through the eye of a needle? Had it been pure luck that we were still alive, or had it been the indomitable *Trillium II* that had carried us safely through the perilous seas? Or...had an unseen hand protected our ship?

A few days later, Johanna and Flap presented me with a very appropriate book called *The Bermuda Triangle*, by Charles Berlitz. On the title page they had inscribed:

> *For Captain Heutink, so you can be scared again.*
> *Thank you for saving us.*
> Bermuda, 27/3/80. Johanna and Flap

I WAS STILL CURIOUS about the white seas. We had encountered the freak wave and a mighty, prolonged gale with winds up to 45 knots or more. We had been surrounded by waves with white, foamy crests but pure white seas we had not seen. Columbus had reported this over 500 years ago. Also, on December 4, 1945, five Navy Avenger planes on a training flight from Fort Lauderdale, winging out over the Atlantic, radioed: "We can't tell which way is west. We don't know where we are. Something is very wrong...strange. We can't be sure of any direction. Even the ocean does not look as it should." Shortly after, the base heard the frantic voice of the flight leader: "We don't know where we are," (then some static). "It looks as though we're entering...white water." His voice broke. "We are lost." That was the last message from the Avengers. They were never seen or heard of again.

In January 1977, two clairvoyants from the Netherlands, under the supervision of a professor of the Netherlands Institute of Parapsychology, conducted some experiments in order to lift a tip of the mysterious veil over the Devil's Triangle. They concluded that it was a natural phenomena, natural causes.

A Russian expedition returned from the Bermuda Triangle in October of that same year. One scientist stated, "A close study of the structures beneath the ocean, and the atmosphere of the area revealed to me that nothing supernatural is occurring." One of his colleagues added, "Accidents in the Triangle can be traced to any natural factor or complicated meteorological conditions. Tides caused by the sun or moon may cause magnetic disturbances under the ocean floor, disrupting aircraft compasses and sweeping planes onto a fatal course."

Their statements were close, but what about the white seas? An article in the *Toronto Star*, dated March 4, 1990, may have had the answer. Donald Davidson, a Canadian scientist, proposed in 1984 a theory of how a thundering, hissing rush of methane gas breaking free through cracks in the rocky sea bottom could be the cause of ships disappearing from the face of the earth without a trace. Gas bubbles at first are greatly compressed by the enormous pressure of the sea, but by rising expand and at the surface they burst, causing the sea surface to take on a frothy, white appearance, as Columbus had reported.

Ships can only float on solid water. When it is suddenly replaced by air or gas bubbles of gigantic dimensions, the ship falls like a stone into the void without a chance to call for assistance. The impact at the sea bottom is so tremendous that the ship breaks up.

When the methane gas has reached the surface, it forms a cloud above the sea, nearly invisible. Planes flying through it could have their engines starved of oxygen, or worse yet, the hot engine or its exhaust flames could ignite the methane cloud and everything would instantly turn into a huge fireball.

Methane gas can be found under almost all ocean floors. People drill for it, because it has been estimated that it contains 100 times more energy than all other fossil fuels in the world.

The Bermuda Triangle is not the only mysterious area around the globe. In the West Pacific, bordering the East China Sea, is also a part of the ocean named the Triangle of the Dragon. The Japanese call it *Ma-no Umi*, or the Devil's Sea. It has the same reputation as its counterpart in the Atlantic—ships disappear without a hint of what has happened to them.

We, too, had sailed in a Devil's Triangle. We, too, had almost met our doom. For days we had fought galeforce winds. Only a mariner understands the meaning of endless rows of savage, towering waves slamming against the ship over and over again, like the deafening roar of cannon firing staccato rounds.

Much later, I entered into the ship's log: "Monster wave boarded ship from abaft the beam, no damage to ship, pumps all working, white horses everywhere. On course to Bermuda."

With a satisfied grin on my face, I leaned back into my captain's chair. My ship, the *Trillium II*, had survived the onslaught. And so had we.

The Ocean of Storms

St. George, Bermuda—March 29

Dearest Hetty,
We are docked in the harbour of St. George, waiting for the arrival of the *Peter-Peter*, the English catamaran. She departed from Fort Lauderdale a few hours after we did, and is long overdue. She is a swift sailor and I am worried about her and her crew. Did she disappear in the Diabolo, the Bermuda Triangle? We keep waiting, hoping for the best....

Excerpts from a captain's letter to his wife

300 Nautical Miles from the Azores—April 18

...On Tuesday, the *Peter-Peter* had arrived in St. George. John wanted to avoid the Bermuda Triangle, so he had taken a route far north of ours. In so doing, he had encountered weather worse than the conditions we had been sailing in. But, no, they had not met a killer wave.

On Wednesday morning, we took in our lines. We waved farewell to the crew of the *Peter-Peter* and to the Bermudas, and headed into the ocean where far, far out, the Azores and new adventures were waiting for us.

John, in his catamaran, could not follow us immediately. He had sent his crew ashore to pick up the needed supplies for the long haul to the Azores. One hour after we had left the harbour, we made radio contact. He was under way, too. We communicated all day, and they stayed right at our heels. The next day, radio contact was lost and the sea empty. There was no catamaran in sight.

180 Nautical Miles from Horta—April 19

...*Trillium* makes good time under full sail close to the wind. We have tried to make contact with the *Peter-Peter*, but to no avail. He does not answer our calls. What kind of wayward course is he following this time? At two o'clock in the morning, I woke up. Someone had started the diesel and revved her to full power. It was unusual. We were sailing under a stiff breeze, and there was no need for the diesel. I jumped out of my bunk and ran to the wheelhouse, where Flap held the spokes. He and Johanna, who was also present, gazed agitatedly out into the night. The diesel roared and when I switched on the deck lights, I saw the sails backed. Then Flap yelled, "A collision, a near collision!"

Somewhere in this darkness ahead of us shone a feeble light against a sail. I asked Flap if it was a fishing boat. "I don't know," he answered. "Suddenly, I saw a shadow looming up in front of me. With the diesel under full power, I could change course in time. But I don't know who it is." I patted Flap on the shoulder and said, "Well done, my boy, well done," as I took back the gas handle. I sent him and Johanna on deck to lower the sails. Then I tried the radio which is always on standby on the distress frequency.

I grabbed the mike and hollered, "This is Canadian yacht, *Trillium II*. Unknown vessel without lights, please identify yourself. Do you read me?" There came an answer, unclear and garbled at first. Then we heard, "Peter-Peter—Hello, Jerry, is that you? This is John on the *Peter-Peter*. How are you doing, you son-of-a-gun? You almost hit me!"

"Yes, yes, we almost rammed you," I replied. "We didn't see you; you have no running lights." It turned out that the starter motor of his diesel had given up the ghost, and he could not charge the batteries. Therefore, he had used no lights at night and also turned the radio off most of the time.

We were glad to hear from him, and the feeling was mutual. He had been fortunate not to have been hit, thanks to a very alert Flap. Here we were, two small, wooden vessels on an immensely vast ocean, sailing through storms and cross winds, becalmed in doldrums, navigating on dead reckoning most of the time, meeting each other after twenty days at sea. I shook my head in disbelief. It had been a chance in a million.

Your bewildered and flabbergasted,

Jerry

P.S. During a storm, I went on deck to help fold some sails, and I tripped over a deck fitting. I fell on my tailbone and I must have broken it, because the pain was so intense I almost fainted. I still cannot sit without feeling the hurt.

South of the Island of Flores—April 20

...This morning, the huge, dead volcano on the island of Flores loomed up from a hazy horizon. The island itself was still below the rim. In the afternoon, we had reached the general latitude of Flores and had to change to an easterly course. Flores is the most westerly island of the Azores Archipelago. Since our encounter with the *Peter-Peter*, they have been travelling in our wake. During the night, they were able to follow us by keeping an eye on our mast-head light. In late afternoon, the wind dropped, and we rafted up beside each other.

At a cable-length's distance, a small freighter passed us. She was sleek and white, without a rust spot on her sides. She changed course toward us and over the radio her captain hailed us and offered his assistance. He asked if we had enough provisions and water. We thanked him profusely for his kindness and could not resist complimenting him on his fine ship. As we chatted, he informed us they were Russians from the Baltic Sea destined for Cuba. We wished him Godspeed as he turned with rumbling diesels. Such an act of kindness is always heartwarming, especially when it is unexpected.

Anchored in a bay, two miles north of Santa Cruz—April 22

...Two days have passed since I wrote last, my dear Hetty, and we are not in the harbour yet. When we rounded that southern point of the island, we were met by enormous swell coming from the north. They are the same type of conditions we had when we were here a few years back. As darkness fell, the weather deteriorated quickly. We gave John back his tow lines, and we both put up some sail. The only thing we could do was to look for deep water. Soon the lights of Santa Cruz disappeared. Where was John? The catamaran had also vanished from sight. We turned the radar on, but we could not see a blip. However, that was not surprising. John's boat was made completely from wood, and wood does not reflect radar beams, thus there was no echo on the screen. We called him over the radio and he answered immediately. He told us he could see our top lights clearly and estimated his position as 300 metres ahead of us. We thought that was a little too close for comfort in this darkness and bad weather with fierce winds. None of the crew went to their bunks, but kept an eye open for John's ship.

Where on earth was he?

John was not 300 metres ahead of us. We were on top of him! Adrian had the wheel, and Harry was beside him. Both of them screamed when *Trillium*'s bow bored into the side of the catamaran. This time we had really hit him. Harry took over the wheel, turned the diesel on and put her in reverse. With a splintering sound, we freed our ship, scraped along the sides of the *Peter-Peter*, and then kept our distance. Harry turned the floodlight on the other ship which was wallowing in the seas with its sails dropped on deck. The hole was the size of a horse's head, but luckily, it was above the water line. Our bow was not damaged, and the hole in John's ship could be repaired.

Santa Cruz, Flores—April 24

...After the collision with the *Peter-Peter*, I did not return to my bunk. It was four in the morning, and I was still keyed up. Under furled sails, we waited for daylight. Dawn came, grey and bleak. John still had some juice in his batteries, and we were able to keep in touch by radio. We decided to go back to Santa Cruz to find out what the conditions were there. After a couple of hours of sailing, the island showed up again. When approaching Santa Cruz, we saw sky-high geysers of water at the harbour entrance. This was too much for us, so we sailed northward along the coast and found a sheltered cove in which an American yacht had already sought refuge. By after-noon, wind and seas calmed, and we lifted anchor. But, oh my, that harbour was still pounded by a huge swell, so we cruised back and forth about a mile from shore. John, in his catamaran, stayed away at a safe distance. One hole in his boat was enough, he thought. After a short while, I men-tioned to Harry that I thought I saw a ship coming out of the harbour. Harry thought it was the water geysers. But, indeed, after some time, a launch danced her way toward us. In it were our old friends, Augusto and Umberto, smiling and waving at us. They maneuvered the launch so we rose and dropped simultaneously, and Umberto jumped over. He took the wheel without much ado, just like the first time we were here. I told him that the *Peter-Peter* would like to come inside too, but was without diesel power. Umberto replied, "No problemo, Capitano, no problemo. We will take you in first. Tell him to stay where he is until we come back for him."

The entrance was the usual witch's cauldron of turbulent waters breaking over the rocks, but Umberto steered *Trillium* inside the harbour works as though it were his daily job. After they had secured our lines to rings in the rocks, they left to pick up John.

At the quay, people had gathered to wave at us. We yelled, "Hello, Hello, how is everything?" But they did not hear. The wind snatched our voices and drowned out the shouting.

When Umberto brought us in, we had passed a small freighter anchored offshore. They had been unloading this ship with their launch, but as soon as they had seen us rolling and heaving on that rough sea, they had stopped working. That freighter could wait. Were we not old friends? After the *Peter-Peter* had been towed in and secured, we left one man on each ship as deck watch, and the others went ashore. With Umberto leading the way, we headed for the police station to register. When that was done, the friendly policeman closed his office and, in procession, we walked to the customs office.

The customs officer stamped our passports, and believe it or not, my dear Hetty, he also locked the doors.

Together, we all went to the pub. We were the first yacht that year to call, and such an event had to be celebrated. Oh, I forgot to tell you. That American yacht we met in the cove left at the same time as we did but he sailed on, perhaps to Horta.

The atmosphere in the pub was lively. The bartender kept bringing bottles of heavy port wine to our tables. We toasted "A votre santée [sic]!" to Umberto, the policeman, the customs officer, and to all the men who had helped unload that freighter waiting out there in those rough seas. They all understood what we meant, even though it was not Portuguese.

Silently, I tried to figure out how many American dollars I had in my pocket. Would it be enough to pay the bill? We had not eaten before we left the ship, and that port wine on our empty stomachs didn't feel good. We were beginning to see stars. I asked Umberto if food was sold at this establishment, and in no time plates of hash were set before us. That did the trick. We soon felt better. But now I knew I did not have enough money. While we were eating, Umberto and his crew left. The police and customs officers kept us company and ordered fresh bottles of wine. Who would pay the bill, I wondered? I broke out in a cold sweat.

The village telegraph must have been working overtime. The local doctor and a few other people showed up, and took the seats left by Umberto and his gang. The good doctor enjoyed the port and invited us to a party at his home that night.

It was high time for us to leave. Reluctantly, I walked up to the bar and asked the man behind it in my best Portuguese, "Quanta costa, quanta costa?" His reply was, "No, no, sig-nores, Umberto pay all!"

...There is something else to tell you that is worth a good laugh. When Umberto and his men were busy securing the lines to our ship, Adrian stood at the forward deck. He had not yet cleated the line he held in his hand. Suddenly, a huge swell entered the harbour and lifted the ship up, up, up. Instead of paying out the line, Adrian held it in a crampy way and was pulled overboard. It was our first 'fish' that day. The people on shore watched with interest as Adrian climbed back on board, dripping wet.

Adrian was not the only fish that day. Two more would follow. After we returned to the quay from our merry party at the pub, we hollered for the dinghies to pick us up. Harry had remained aboard and came rowing over immediately. But young Charley, the navigator of the *Peter-Peter*, fiddled with the painters that held their sloop to the catamaran. By giving a hard push with a paddle, the dinghy turned turtle and Charley was caught underneath. Again, the Santa Cruzians looked on in fascination. Luckily the water was not cold, and Charley popped up and somehow righted the sloop. From the shore he received applause and also from us.

And now, about the third fish. Flap did not like going back

and forth with the sloop between the ship and the wall. He
dug up an inch-thick nylon line from the storage space, and
fastened one end to the main mast. The other end, he took
ashore and knotted it around an iron post. Curiously, we
watched him, but he wouldn't tell us what his plans were.
Then he slung the bosun's chair with a block to the heavy
cable. Presto! He pulled himself over to the other side in no
time at all. All of us, including those on shore, looked on in
admiration. Even Augusto, the most important man on the
island, came to see Flap's invention. Of course, Flap had to
demonstrate it for him. When he was halfway between ship
and shore, the knot around the mast let go and good old Flap
dunked in to the murky waters below him. He didn't get an
applause, the men on the shore roared and even Augusto,
who was usually a quiet man, was bent over in laughter,
wiping the tears from his eyes.

Harry went to Flap's rescue and rowed over to fish him
and the bosun's chair out of the water. Flap dove straight for
his cabin, madder than ever, because everyone had a laugh at
his expense. For a long time to come, the story must have
been told and retold in the fishermen's pub of Santa Cruz das
Flores.

...Going out in the evening never starts early in Latin
countries. At 9:30, Umberto waited for us at the quay. The
doctor's house was large, with an impressive and heavy front
door. The ceiling of the hallway disappeared in dark shadows.
There were many rooms with oak wainscotting, sparingly lit
with chandeliers. Except for chairs, there was not much furni-
ture. As soon as we were seated, we received a goblet of sweet
red wine with good body. More guests arrived and we were
asked to tell about our travels. Most of the people (only men
were invited, but our girls were welcome) spoke English to a
certain extent, and made conversation easily. There was
music and singing, and in the long, dark hall one could try
his hand at air rifles and guns. I did not want to drink too
much wine because I intended to take a couple of aspirins
before going to my bunk. My broken tailbone was hurting
very much. Aspirin and wine is not a good combination.

he islanders sang melancholy folk songs accompanied by
an accordion, mouth organs and a guitar. One fellow had
such a beautiful voice that everyone was silent long after he

had finished his song. We all enjoyed the evening given in our honour, but I had felt uneasy all the time. One does not know what it is or where it comes from.

After we had left the restaurant earlier in the evening, I had noticed that the wind had increased, but when Umberto picked us up, he had said nothing. I thought, if he, a fisherman does not worry about it, why should I. We had left our ships without a watchman on board, and that was certainly not good seamanship.

After midnight the party ended, and fifteen minutes later we stood at the quay gazing at our ships over an abyss of whirling, boiling waters. The wind had reached storm proportions, and it was so cold that my wind jacket gave no protection at all. It felt as though I were standing naked in the turmoil of wind and water. The ships danced and pranced only twenty metres away, but it might as well have been 200 miles. It would be suicide to try to cross. Still, we had to get back aboard somehow. Our sloops were high and dry on the quay, and we let the more stable one of the *Peter-Peter* in the water. Charley volunteered to go first. He rowed over and managed to climb onto the heaving ship. We saw him fasten a line around the mast, drop back into the sloop and bring the line back to the quay where we slung it around a bollard. Now we had something to hang on to, like Flap and his bosun's chair. Hand over hand we palmed the sloop back and forth and within a quarter of an hour, we were all standing on deck of John's boat. With the last crossing, we had dragged our own sloop with us and used it to make a line connection with *Trillium*. All went well. We were soaked, of course, but that, we ignored. The main thing was that we were back on our ship, which shook and pulled on the mooring lines like a rabid dog. The much lighter catamaran took a real beating, catching the full impact of the waves smashing over the rocks. It became a wild night. None of us went to our bunks.

By morning, it was a full blown gale. The seas smashed higher and higher over the concrete walls and rocks. That freighter had disappeared over the horizon searching for sea room. It was empty, having been unable to load the hundreds and hundreds of propane bottles stacked up on shore. They were piled up on their sides, six high in a long endless row, sloping toward the harbour. If the bottom one were pulled from under, the rest would come tumbling down like an avalanche. People stood on the quay shivering in their jackets and coats, watching the forces of nature with frightened eyes. They pointed at us and shouted something, but their voices were drowned by the thundering noises of wind and water.

We were caught in a trap with nowhere to turn. If we were freed from the mooring lines, we would be crushed and splintered to pieces before we could get enough headway to reach the entrance. This was not a harbour to be in when gale force winds roughened the ocean this way.

What we had feared actually happened. The wind got hold of the propane bottles, ripped the first ones from the row, and in minutes, hundreds of them came rolling down the quay and plunged into the harbour. The people on shore had to run for their lives. All that steel came down the slope with awesome speed.

The empty tanks bobbed on the waves, and soon we were surrounded by those raging missiles banging and clanking against each other. With all hands on deck, we tried to push them away with our boat hooks, but to no avail. There were too many of them. Some we were able to hoist aboard and pile into the cockpits, but soon we had to stop that futile monkey business. But help was on the way. That wind, the source of the calamity, forced the bottles toward the entrance of the harbour, to open water where they could not do any more harm to our ships. It was catastrophic, for thousands of dollars worth of bottles were lost in the sea. Perhaps, a long time from now, they would wash ashore as rusty, unusable cylinders of steel on some faraway coast.

Then who came swinging into the harbour, sputtering and pitching in his pilot boat? It was Augusto, unperturbed at the helm, just like Skipper Van Der Decker, of the *Flying Dutchman*. Had he been at sea all night? Where had he come from? Skipper Augusto to the rescue. First, he took the *Peter-Peter* in tow, and brought her out into deep water. In one hour he was back. It was our turn. Harry had the whole crew at the lines which held us to the embankments. In a second, they could let them go, when Augusto had thrown us his tow line and pulled it taut. Later, we could retrieve the lines, and if not, Augusto could keep them for all his troubles.

In no time we were outside, and there, our own diesel could take over. Augusto came alongside and hollered that we should go to the other side of the island where we could safely throw our anchors into a deep bay. When we got there, the *Peter-Peter* was waiting for us, bobbing peacefully. Then, guess who drove over the hill in an old truck? Augusto and Umberto playing Santa Claus. They had brought a 200-litre drum of diesel fuel and plenty of groceries for us to share. Augusto adamantly refused any payment for his help, but he did accept reimbursement for the fuel and provisions. And all that for a bargain price.

We had a quiet night in that secluded bay. Some rain had fallen, but in the morning the sun shone bright and warm. The crews hung all the bedding on deck for a good airing, and later we had a pow-wow about what to do next.

The provisions Augusto had brought were not enough to last over the long haul to Plymouth, so we delegated the girls to go ashore to see what they could buy in the nearest village just over the hill. John and Harry would stay aboard as deck-watchers, and I and the other boys would accompany the girls to carry the stuff.

I had our working jib with me, which had been torn in two, and John also had his genoa badly ripped. In the centre of the village, I located a tailor who worked from his front room, and showed him our sails. With a stream of gibberish, and wild arm movements, he pulled an old Singer sewing machine out of a corner, planted it in the middle of the room and commenced sewing. His wife made coffee and bade me sit down while the tailor treadled away on that machine. To wait for the tailor would take too long, so after I thanked the lady for the good cup of coffee, I went into the village in search of the rest of the crew.

Later in the afternoon, I returned to the tailor, and the sails were ready. They may not have been professionally done, but they were good enough to use again. The bill came to 200 escudos, equivalent to four American dollars. For that little money, the tailor and his wife had worked the entire after-noon. As a parting gift, they offered me a glass of port wine and a series of Portuguese postage stamps. I felt a bit like a swindler, so I secretly left a 100 escudos bank note at the door. Later I shared the bill with John. Still it was a bargain.

Unbelievably, the village owned a taxi—an old American rattle-trap. We crowded into it and drove from store to store to pick up our groceries. It was past closing time, but the store-keepers were waiting for us with broad smiles on their brown faces. The taxi brought us to the old pier, where offshore our ships waited calmly and quietly for our return.

Later in the evening, we rowed over to the *Peter-Peter* to have a meeting with John and his crew. The wind had turned north and was bone-chilling cold, so we decided to leave in the morning. We had to say good-bye to Flores and its friendly people who had made us feel so welcome.

I haven't the slightest idea what the weather is going to do. The barometer is still high and steady–the Azores High–but the weather pattern is not right. The wind is screeching through the rigging, and *Trillium II* is rocking and pulling at her anchor rope. According to the weather and pilot chart, we should have nice settled weather. Tomorrow we leave, but if the wind does not change, we will have it right on the nose all the way to good old England. Since Bimini, we have had no luck. What lies ahead for us? The sea is no longer our friend.

Yesterday, I had planned to mail this long letter to you, but somehow it was not possible. In these letters I am talking to you, but alas, I don't get a reply...

90 Sea miles north of Flores—April 26

When we were ready to leave that little bay of Faya Grande, Harry pushed the starter button of the diesel, and nothing happened. There was no grumbling from Ethel in her engine room. We looked at each other. What was it this time? It was not as bad as we had thought. One of the bolts that connected the battery cables to the starter had corroded. A new bolt did the trick. I gave an order to the boys in the cockpit to hoist the ground tackle. Harry checked all the indicators, the lights and metres on the dashboard, and noticed that the batteries were not charged. "Down with the anchor, boys!" was my next command. Again, Harry went into the engine room. This time it was the alternator, but luckily we had a spare one. As he installed it, he muttered to himself, "Why did I ever go to sea? Always something goes wrong at the wrong moments."
"Didn't I remind you about Murphy's Law?" I reminded him.
"If something *can* go wrong, it *will* go wrong."

In the meantime, hours had passed. The people on board the *Peter-Peter* were becoming impatient. "When are we leaving? When are we leaving?" John, who had waited long enough, lifted his anchors and told us he would first go to

Santa Cruz to pick up his lines. When he vanished from sight over the northern horizon, we lost radio contact. It was the last we ever saw of him, his crew, and his catamaran.

400 Nautical miles from Landsend—May 8

...We have finally left the Sea of Damnation behind us.

During the night, the wind died down to a zephyr and the sea is calm. When I woke up this morning and had a look on deck, it felt like spring in Holland. The light breeze is pulling *Trillium* in the right direction, eastwards to the shores of Europe. We were elated! Everyone got busy bringing their bedding on deck to dry out. When we were festooned with fluttering bed sheets like on Navy Day, a tanker passed us. What seldom happens, he called us. He told us he was bound for Rotterdam, and gave us a position to verify our own. Half an hour later, he called again to supply us with a weather report for the next twenty-four hours. It did not look good—winds from the south-east to south with Beaufort 7 to 8, occasionally gale-force 9.

The whole crew took advantage of the respite we got from the nice, sunny weather. The bedding dried out nicely. The wind picked up a bit and the speed we made was good—150 sea miles in 24 hours. Fine, fine, we couldn't have done any better. Within three days, we could raise the English Channel. Then all our struggles with wind and water would be over. But that dear little storm from the south did not wait three days. It started pounding us in the afternoon. Now, Harry is calling me on deck. A halyard has let go and the mains'l has come down.

Valentia on Valentia Island, Ireland—May 12

...We definitely had some problems before we arrived here. That gale actually blew from the south-south-east, and we did not get a chance to set sail to Landsend. It forced us far north past the Latitude of the Channel. This gale continued for three days on end. We were under water more than above it, and the ship groaned and cracked from the onslaught. So much for crossing the Atlantic in the early part of the year. It has been a lesson, a hard lesson. All the bedding which we had been able to dry in those few hours of sunshine, was soon damp again and sleep was difficult with this tossing and smacking up and down. We became very tired, and so did our good ship *Lollipop*.

Yet *Trillium II* endured until finally we saw the jagged line of a mountain chain looming above the horizon. It could be nothing else but Ireland. As we did not have charts of this part of the coast, we used an atlas and motored closer and closer until we came to an inlet. There was quiet water, so we dropped the hook. All we wanted now was sleep, sleep and more sleep. To make a long story short, the inlet was the mouth of the river Shannon. We had survived a nightmare of howling winds and savage seas.

Valentia on Valentia Island, with the hotel as centrepiece. To the right of the hotel is the the only street.

The next morning, we lifted anchor and followed the coast south, crossed Tralee and Brandon Bay, and then we saw a fisherman heading east, perhaps to his home harbour. We followed him and arrived at Valentia Harbour on Valentia Island. With landfalls in Bermuda and the Azores we had been at sea for 53 days, a long time for an Atlantic crossing, a long, long time. Easing in towards the quay, the boys stood ready with the lines. Adrian was the first one to jump ashore, and he promptly smacked down on the concrete floor of the jetty. His sea-legs were not used to terra firma anymore and his legs had buckled under him. Poor Adrian, shaking, half dazed, he rose on all fours and then with feeble legs he stood on his feet again. Fishermen from neighbouring ships looked on with grinning faces...

Valentia is a small fishing village with only one street that runs up a hill. The focal point is a large hotel with a pub. Once we secured *Trillium II* on the quay, someone who must have been an angel offered us a free room at the hotel for as long as we stayed. A room, and a bathroom! We could have a bath, a shower, and rest on a real bed. From that moment on, the Irish were our friends for life.

Presently, we stampeded to the hotel and met the management in the lounge. A very friendly young couple informed us that they had taken over the hotel not too long ago. They showed us to our room, and gallantly we proffered the first fling at all the nice, sweet water in the tub to the girls. I stretched myself out on the bed and fell asleep immediately.

After everyone had a chance to wash the salt off their skin, and the girls made sure we left the room tidy, we made our way to the pub. Upon entering, we were greeted with an Irish sing-song. Word had spread about our arrival. In the middle of the pub stood a large pot-bellied stove with fishermen sitting around it. They made room for us, and soon we had a pint of Guinness in our hands. I was seated next to an old sailor who must have bid his farewell to the sea long ago. He was bent over with rheumatism, but tended the stove by pushing large logs into it. Of course we were expected to share our adventures of what had happened on the ocean.

Adrian had had enough of the sea. He inquired of the men if there was a ferry to the mainland. There was, on the other side of the island. Soon after we were back aboard, Adrian packed his belongings, said good-bye, and took off. He had a walk of two hours ahead of him, a good exercise to lose his sea legs. We watched as he disappeared into the green yonder. The hills of the island were so green. Beautiful Ireland, the Emerald Island.

We never heard from Adrian again. That is the way things go.

Valentia Harbour—May 14

...The BBC weather forecast does not give us any hope of leaving this harbour within the foreseeable future. They call for storms and more storms. We will stay in Valentia until we have more favourable forecasts.

I have explored the village and found the ruins of the building from which Marconi sent the first radio message to Newfoundland in December 1901. Other than that, we do as the Irish fishermen do, putter around on the ship. We go together to the pub, treat each other to a pint, and chew the rag. We always bring the girls with us. They are not only tolerated but most welcome. Those men are not accustomed to having women in the pub. We have asked ourselves when are these fishermen ever at home? They are either on board or in the pub, drinking and singing those haunting Irish songs. In the meantime, hanging around here is costing me handfuls of money. I can see you frowning, saying, "Can't you be a bit more frugal, then?" No, that is impossible. Ireland is by no means a cheap place to stay. The Irish pound is more expensive than the English one. We exchange money at the hotel.

There is no bank here.

You have probably noticed that the local fishermen have accepted us as their own. We are also men from the sea. However, we just learned not all of them are honest.

Diana and Harry had gone for a day to roam around the island, their knapsacks filled with food and drink. Johanna and I were alone on board. Some fishermen came over in the morning to inform us that it would be very low tide today, so low that we would be grounded. It was neap tide, and ebb would dry part of the harbour. They showed us a place more in the middle where we could anchor and wait for the upcoming flood.

Johanna took the wheel and I threw our new nylon lines ashore, flemished them there, and thought, "We will be back in a few hours. The lines are safe where they are." I jumped back on the ship, and we anchored in deeper water.

After a few hours, the flood came in and we returned to our spot on the quay. There were no clean, white lines at the bollards. In a rage, I ran along the row of fishing vessels yelling at the men, "Who stole our lines? Was it you, or you?" I saw only smirking faces and heard that no one had seen our mooring lines.

Evening after evening we sat with those guys in the pub, singing a song or treating each other to a pint of Guinness, but when the coast was clear, they stole and played innocent, the scoundrels. I hardly dared to tell Harry when the two returned from their outing. In the pub that evening, Harry went around the tables and asked every one of them, "Did you take our lines?" The weathered faces looked like newborn babies. They shook their heads and whispered in their dialect with knowing smiles. We left the place. Fun in Valentia was over.

The next morning, sunny and calm for a change, we took off, still with a bad taste in our mouths.

Again, and because of our hasty departure from Valentia, I was unable to mail this letter. But Holland is just over the horizon and I will give you the lot on our arrival. It is raining, sort of drizzly weather, with no wind. Ethel, our faithful, old diesel, does the work.

After leaving the harbour, we set course to the Fastnet rock. Two days later, we passed the Scillies and Bishop Rock on the south-west point of England. ...The people at the

Mayflower Marina in Plymouth recognized us from earlier stays. We were bid welcome at the usual fee, of course. Here ended our Atlantic crossing and we have only 250 more miles to go to reach Holland. Tomorrow evening, when we pass Dover, it is only 170 miles to Texel and the marina in Oudeschildt.

From Plymouth to Dover, we joined the heavy ships' traffic—freighters, container ships, and what have you. Our radar was constantly on, and we watched the blips on the

The white cliffs of Dover—a hovercraft has given us the right-of-way. We were under sail.

screen with Argus eyes. It is said that more than 800 ships pass through the Channel in 24 hours...more than ten per minute, stem to stern. Unbelievable! One night it became foggy, too. None of us went down for sleep. We held watch not only with the radar going, but also with four pair of eyes. In the morning, we broke out of the line of ships and motored into Newhaven to get some sleep. In the afternoon, we walked in rain to a pub on the quayside, had a drink, and later ordered a bite to eat. There was not much entertainment in Newhaven, and the streets were deserted. The drizzle kept people inside.

We had another night of unbroken sleep, and in the morning, we went out with the tide. A moist west wind pushed us eastward. We had paid the mains'l all the way out to starboard and the genoa to port. For safety, we stayed under the English coast until we raised the White Cliffs of Dover. Here, we crossed the shipping channel and set course to Sandettié lightship. Once it loomed up into the grey day, we changed course to the Hook of Holland, which we passed about five miles out. The wind remained favourable, and at a good clip, we saw the dunes of the coast of the Netherlands passing by. This was the sight we had been waiting for anxiously since leaving Fort Lauderdale. We kept our watches now with two hours on and two hours off. We did a little cooking, but no one went to their bunks. All were excited now that the end was in sight. Finally, we saw the lighthouse of Den Helder and Mars Deep, where a flood current dragged *Trillium* toward Oudeschildt.

Late in the afternoon, we were at the dock of the marina from which we had left eight months, eleven days, and three hours before for a cruise to the West Indies. More than 11,000 sea miles have passed beneath our keel.

Johanna stayed one more night, and the next morning she had a very hard time saying goodbye. She clung to me, her arms around my neck. Johanna, that vixen from Amsterdam, could not let me go. She kissed me over and over again. Countless games of Double Patience we had played. Countless times we had bickered and quarreled. Together, we had watch on the bridge, one on the bridge, the other standing by the radar. She had been seasick, but it had not held her back from assisting on deck in heavy weather. Flap had left her, but Johanna carried on. Now, many anchor chains bound her to our ship and to us, chains of shared pleasures, memories of adventures and, above all, the sea, the ocean. Yes, the sea pulls and pulls. It is not easy to break that chain. That is how it was with Johanna. Tears streamed down her cheeks, sadness in her beautiful eyes because of the inevitable farewell.

Harry and Diana planned to take her to the ferry. Harry softly said, "Come, Johanna, the ferry does not wait." Once more she clung to me, and then she jumped ashore. Between Harry and Diana, she walked away. Then they disappeared around a bend. Johanna was gone. Resigned to this parting, and with loneliness in my heart, I went below. This is part of the seaman's life, but I will never get used to it....

Harlingen, Holland—May 26

...As you see, we are in Holland. Johanna and Diana parted from us in Oudeschildt on the island of Texel. Just the two of us were left. We sailed *Trillium II* over the Wad Sea to Harlingen. The agent and his wife bade us welcome at the dock of the marina.

You were not there. Ach, it had been one of my dreams to see you on our arrival. You are still in Canada.

When you return to Holland, I'll give you this long, long letter as a present.

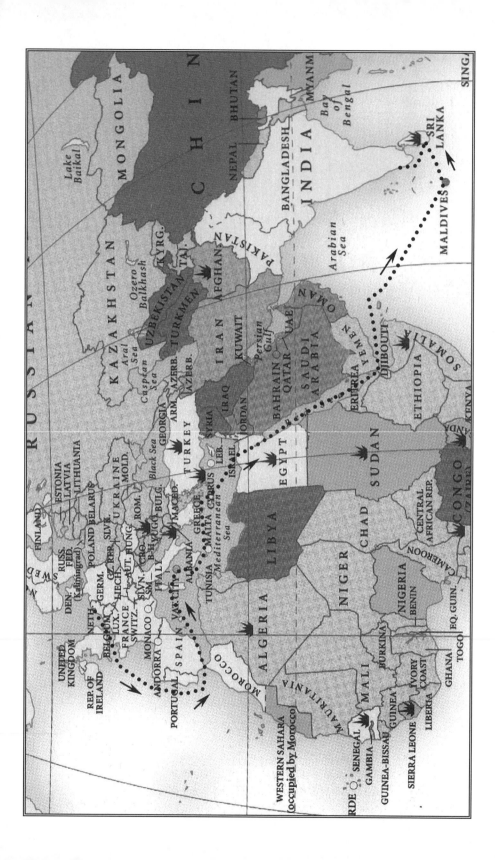

From Holland to Sri Lanka

Chaos at Departure Time

Once again we plied the briny. We were somewhere between the lightships *Noord Hinder*, twenty miles west of the Hook of Holland, and Sandettié, just before the entrance of the English Channel.

The weather had been calm all day long. The North Sea was as smooth as glass, with hardly a trace of wind.

When we passed the *Noord Hinder* at close range, we called her and were given an updated weather report. A small depression was approaching from Ireland. We should expect some rain, thunder on the horizon, and a slight breeze on the bow. It was nothing to get excited about.

THE WEEKS before our departure from Harlingen were a complete shambles. *Trillium II* had been on shore for repairs most of the winter. In January, I had given the wharf manager a list of repairs to be done. Four weeks before a departure scheduled for the middle of May, they had yet to begin. Nothing seemed to be ready for our new adventure, a 10,000-sea-mile trek to Sri Lanka in the Indian Ocean. According to the wharf manager, there was no problem, but according to me, we were drowning in problems.

During that winter, Harry had a job with an electrical firm not far from Harlingen. That had to end. There was work to be done on our ship. We had only thirty days left, as the agent wanted us at sea by May 19. He had rounded up a paying crew who waited impatiently to hear, "Come aboard. We go."

The first thing Harry and I did was wrench Ethel, our old diesel, from her engine room. A new Volvo-Penta, with significantly more power, had been ordered, as well as a diesel-driven converter to supply us with sufficient electrical energy (10 kilowatts at 110 and 220 volts) to keep the refrigerator running in

Trillium II gets a new diesel

tropical climates. The decks and hulls were scraped and burned to remove the old paint. Carpenters from the wharf were busy renovating the cabins. Provision lists were made up. Hundreds of kilos of tinned goods and dried foods were purchased and would be delivered on time. And to please our future guests, many crates of Heineken beer were loaded.

Trillium's buoyancy was sorely tested.

Days turned into weeks, and the new diesel and converter were nowhere in sight. The carpenters worked irritatingly slowly. Tempers flared like greased lightning. Many heated, angry discussions arose between Harry and me and the wharf boss, the agent and suppliers. Harry and I saw nothing but problems. We were so fed up with all the bungling and fumbling on the wharf that I suggested, "Come, Harry. Let's go into town and tie one on. Let the people here jump into the deep six. We won't be ready in time, anyway."

Four days before the set departure time the diesel arrived, but no electrical aggregate. The first paying guest had arrived with a kit bag over his shoulder, and looked on in amazement at all the commotion. He donned a coverall, found a paintbrush, and lent a hand even before anyone had greeted or welcomed him. One does not meet people like that too often. His name was Frank Schutten, a Swiss of Dutch descent. He was 67 years old and could speak four languages fluently. "Welcome aboard *Trillium II*, Frank." He joined us for 18 hours a day of hard work to prepare the ship for sea. Two days later, Gunther came. He was a German businessman who had booked to sail with us as far as Gibraltar. Frank and Gunther were a perfect team who knew by instinct what needed to be done. Hats off to them.

Victim of Progress—Our good friend the Noord Hinder is now laid up in the Dutch harbour of Hellevoetsluis. The lightship is replaced by an electronic beacon. Many times we had radio-contact with her crew when we passed her in the southern part of the North Sea and reported our sail plan. Now silent, she awaits her fate (1994).

Trillium II was launched. We had 48 hours to go. The mechanic wanted to try the new diesel immediately, so we made fast to the dock with heavy lines. Howling and roaring like a ferocious tiger, the engine came to life, and the propeller threw foaming water high over the quay. The lines were as taut as a bow string, and the bows of the ships rose skyward, the only direction they could go with all that power. Thank goodness it worked. There was no time to celebrate.

Soon two more guests showed up—a young Friesian man, and Abel Lang, a friend of Harry's from Canada. The crew was complete for the first trek, and they settled themselves aboard. There was still a lot to do. The Friesian man helped Gunther stow away the provisions, but Abel Lang vanished. We learned that work was not his favourite pastime.

Too soon, the day of departure was upon us. The remaining supplies on the quay were thrown on deck. They could be sorted out later, but the converter had not been delivered yet. The agent got active and shouted into the mouthpiece of the telephone. Within an hour, it arrived still in a crate. It was hoisted aboard and secured on the aft deck. Later, when there was time, we would check it.

We were interviewed by the local media. They compared us to the old buccaneers of the East India Company. The article said, "Captain Heutink and his first mate, Harry, will follow the historic route from Holland to Ceylon and further to the spice islands of the Far East."

My daughter, Ellen, and her friend, Betsy, had come to say goodbye. Frieda, from Hamburg, and Diana, Harry's girlfriend, were also present to bid us farewell. They planned to stay aboard until we reached the TjerkHiddes locks, where they would go ashore. Frieda would join us in Lissabon to sail the Mediterranean leg with us, and Diana would muster again in Oudeschildt, on Texel.

At 4:00 P.M. we threw the lines. The new diesel had the honour of pulling us away from the quay and propelling *Trillium II* to the lock. There was still enough time to make it to the yacht harbour of Oudeschildt before darkness fell, and we hoped we could sail on the Wad Sea. We said our goodbyes to the agent, his wife, and the personnel of the wharf. It felt as though we would never again see Harlingen or the people we knew there. The lock-master had heard of our adventure, and immediately sluiced us through. We thanked him with a blast of the foghorn. The girls waved until we disappeared from view down in the lock-basin.

Our ship had sprung to life after a long winter high ashore. The Wad Sea lay ahead. Harry and I were elated to feel that fair movement under our feet once more. It was wonderful! I clapped Harry on the shoulder. His face radiated pleasure and happiness. We said, "Adieu, Harlingen. Auf niemals wiedersehen."

At the yacht harbour on Texel, we were also noted as the Old Salts. Because of the occasion, the harbour-master refused payment for our stay. We presented him with a Canadian flag, which he proudly hung from the ceiling of the canteen along with hundreds of others in his precious collection.

Diana arrived by ferry from the mainland. She had had enough time to arrange her finances and other business. Our relations with the customs officers in Harlingen had remained cordial throughout the years. We had always received their full cooperation. But this time, there was no time to have a calm, quiet drink with them. Quickly, they stamped our forms and wished us a safe voyage and a happy arrival in those far away lands. They stood at the quay with all the others until we had rounded the bend in the Old Frankeker Canal.

WE HAD PASSED the *Noord Hinder* lightship, and set course for Dover. As usual, the Strait of Dover was busy. Ferries scooted across, and the large vessels did not bulge an inch to miss you. We had to make sea room for them. The customary parade of tankers, container ships, and freighters steamed past us. For our own safety, we stayed sheltered under the White Cliffs of Dover.

Our new crew was eager to put up some sail, but the wind was over the bow, so it was no use. The new Volvo-Penta did a good job. We felt its power throb beneath our feet.

In Plymouth, we took our time installing the diesel converter. We hired a carpenter to build a sturdy foundation in the aft workshop. As the unit was positioned, and Harry was busy hooking it up to our electrical system, we noticed that it did not deliver 110 volts current. It had only 220 volts even though we had insisted on both. All our electronic equipment ran on 110 volts. That was why they had delivered it at the very last moment, so we would not notice. The supplier had cheated and deceived us.

After Plymouth, we made a short landfall at Falmouth. Our crew wanted to have a last bash ashore before crossing the Gulf of Biscayne. Harry had charted the course already—a straight pencil line from Falmouth to Cabo Finistère Light on the north-west point of Spain. The next day, May 28, at 10:15 A.M., we departed from Falmouth regardless of any concerns we may have felt. We had learned to respect the quirks of the weather in the notorious Gulf. It would be our sixth voyage across that body of water.

We had a long way to go....

Frieda and Mercédès

"Ein schiff, mein Gott, ein schiff! Um Gottes Willen was musz Ich tun?" Frieda Strauss, from Hamburg, was in a panic behind the wheel of *Trillium II*. 'Das schiff' was a tanker still three miles away on a westerly course and heading in our direction. I assured her, "Keep your course, Frieda, and don't get nervous. Our ship will pass that tanker at a safe distance."

A mermaid comes aboard

Frieda was the widow of a German marine officer, and was crazy about anything to do with the sea. We had met her at Helgoland, a rock in the German Bight. Several times, she had sailed with us on the North Sea. In Lisbon, in the Bay of Cascais, she had come aboard, and there a small drama had taken place. The Portuguese harbour-master informed us of a lady at the police station who was completely distraught and in tears. All they could understand was that she was waiting for a Canadian ship that had not come to pick her up.

We were anchored quite a way out in the bay and she had not seen us. I hurried to the police station and when she saw me, she flew into my arms, tears streaming down her face, but this time, tears of relief: we had not forgotten her after all. Before leaving, I was asked to sign an affidavit taking full responsibility for her. She had already caused enough confusion for the police authorities.

Very unseaman-like, she had brought two heavy suitcases with her, which I lugged to the beach of Baia do Cascais.

Trillium II lay out too far to hail anyone. It took half an hour before Harry noticed our waving arms. Back aboard, we installed Frieda into her cabin. After taking an aspirin, she crawled into her bunk.

WE TRAVELLED eastward on the short swells of the Mediterranean, Gibraltar far behind us. Harry had made up a schedule for the wheelwatches, but had thoughtfully omitted Frieda from the list. She was not young, and easily became upset. That had displeased her greatly. She wanted to be part of the working crew and run her watches like everyone else. It had been quite an undertaking for Harry to teach her the rudiments of holding on to a course. He had spent many hours beside her, keeping an eye on the always wavering compass card. Now, she sat rigidly behind the wheel, clutching the spokes, her knuckles white from the fierceness of her grip.

There was something else, too. When she sailed with us on the North Sea, we hadn't noticed, but here on the Mediterranean waters she was constantly seasick. Was it caused by the short dash of the waves, or the Levanter, a steady, easterly wind that was dry and unpleasant? Whatever it was, Frieda had to break off her wheelwatch many times and retreat to her bunk in misery. She was not alone. The rest of the crew had a turn too—stomach cramps, headaches, always queasy and listless. Harry and I pondered over it. Had we loaded contaminated water in Gibraltar? Neither of us had been affected, and that seemed strange. The Levanter droned on, using the rigging, the stainless steel wires that held the masts up, as a guitar. No one had an answer, least of all the skipper.

Trillium II struggled on against the head winds. We appreciated the powerful new diesel engine very much. Our first port of call would be Saint Antoni de Portmany, on Ibiza, the first island of the Balearics. Gradually, it became warmer and the Levanter diminished to a soft breeze. Our ailing crew perked up and started to enjoy themselves.

England rules the waves—as long as there are monkeys on the Rock of Gibraltar. Frieda gets molested by one of those ugly monsters. If you make them angry they pee all over you or pick your glasses off your nose and run off with them.

Two of our other guests were Hans and Elsie from Basel, Switzerland. I had a problem understanding their Swiss-German language, but our widow from Hamburg became good friends with them. The Swiss couple had also been seasick, but Elsie had persevered and kept her wheelwatches. Sometimes she did the watch for her husband as well. Elsie told us she had the least trouble with her stomach when she was sitting behind the wheel.

Hans was a 200-pounder, maybe more. He was a huge fellow and his belly hung far over his belt. He had arms that could lift a car, and a neck like a bull. His sea voyage was meant to trim some of his weight. He did not join us at mealtime. A cup of tea and a Dutch rusk sufficed. Just like Elsie, he was seasick most of the time. It seemed to us that people from mountainous countries were affected worse than others. At sea, there is always wind, but between mountains, only rarely. We thought that Swiss people should stick to a Sunday afternoon sail on one of their beautiful lakes.

Whenever I tried to put Hans to work, he would say "Ich, Kapitoin? Ich habe dao jao so keine ahnung van. Und wohin fahren wir heut', Kapitoin?" I did not persue the matter. It was a lost cause. Elsie, from her seat behind the wheel, gave me a wink and a smile. She did the work for two people, that girl.

Then there was Harry's friend, Abel Lang, from Canada. He had booked for the entire trip, from Holland to Sri Lanka. What he had expected from such a long voyage, I did not know. After a couple of wheelwatches, he had given up, refusing to take his turn. He disappeared into his cabin after mealtime and never offered to clean up or do dishes. Long stretches at sea were not to his liking, and he spent much time sulking in the open cockpit.

I asked him once what he would rather do. His reply was that he just wanted to sail for a day, find a nice little harbour in the evening, and sit on a terrace ashore with a glass of wine and a nice girl for company. I told him we still had 9,000 sea miles to go, and his dreams were very unrealistic. For Abel, the fun was over, and his friendship with Harry was on the lowest burner.

The trek between Gibraltar and Ibiza had been long due to constant head winds. With the harbour of San Antonio in sight, the mood on board improved greatly. On the decks, more bare skin was revealed. Seasickness was a thing of the past, but unfortunately, Frieda suffered a mild heart attack. She had neglected to inform us that she had a heart condition, in fear that we would not take her along. Luckily, she had the proper medication, and shortly she was well again. But it had been a warning that Frieda was a risk to have on board.

Frieda contemplates life at sea while the ocean is as flat as it can be.

At Ibiza, the temperature climbed and hot days followed. Frieda rested in her bunk and the deck lights were opened to the wind so she could feel the breeze blowing in. That harbour was not good for her condition, and soon we set sail for Palma, on Mallorca, where there was an airport with international connections.

When we sailed along the north coast of Ibiza, a beautiful, dreamy blue lagoon suddenly came into view. At the end, a hotel stood regally on a mull. There were no houses, just some low mountains in the background, and clean white beaches all around. It was too lovely to pass, and soon we dropped anchor in the middle of the lagoon. Frieda perked up, and Abel, for a change, was ready at the anchor line. Later, he helped Harry put the blue covers over the sails. There were no other ships, only *Trillium II.*

Guests from the hotel dove into the water and swam toward us. Harry hung the boarding ladder over the side, and our crew joined the swimmers. The water was unbelievably clear, with a deep blue shine. Harry, ever the salesman, was on his toes. He attached a poster to the railing with an invitation to come aboard. Who knows when a fish would bite?

In the crystal clear water, a dark figure swam closer, treading water as she read the poster. Harry and I held our breath. Did we have a nibble already? She swam to the ladder, and in proper English, she asked permission to come aboard. What rose out of the water could not have been a human being. It was a goddess of the deep, who had left her palace between the seaweeds to greet us earthlings. She was clad in a sky-blue bikini with white dots. From her raven black hair, water dripped down her sleek, tanned body. Unfathomable black eyes gazed at us.

Elsie, the smiling helmswoman. She does not mind holding the wheel.

Madre de Dios...Harry and I were knocked over at once. Frieda, resting on her deck mattress, turned her back on us, noisily snorting her nose.

The water nymph's name was Mercédès Rodrigues, from Madrid. She not only spoke Spanish but also fluent English. She informed us that she was a secretary in a business office. Hypnotized by her beauty, we allowed her to do something that no one else could do—sit on our new settee wearing a wet bikini. Och, that bit of salt water could be washed out later. Her black eyes darted around the saloon, observing everything. When Harry told her of our plans to sail to Sri Lanka, and that we still had a few vacant cabins, she became very enthusiastic. She swore like a trooper, in Spanish, of course, but that was also forgiven her: tomorrow was the last day of her vacation, and she had to return to her job in Madrid. She left us her address, and a promise: "Next year I will fly to Sri Lanka. I will stay with you the whole summer, do you hear?"

We definitely heard that, and we were already looking forward to next year. Mercédès dove gracefully into the water, splashing us in the face. She swam away from the ship, back to her palace beneath the sea.

"Vaya con Dios, my darling...."

Frieda, still lying on her mattress, turned and smiled at Harry and me. Was that mockery we saw in her eyes?

IN LAS PALMAS, four of our guests left the ship. Frieda could not stand the heat any longer, and Hans and Elsie were running out of time. Unfortunately, we had lost some nice people. It was a pleasure to have them on board. Abel Lang could not get used to the discipline, and we were glad that he left. We had the ship to ourselves again, Harry, Diana, and I. We would be able to manage.

The horizon beckoned. *Trillium II* had been tugging on the lines long enough, so we freed her from the restraints. Far toward the east, new landfalls waited—Corsica, Sardegna, Napoli in Italy, Capri...

We turned the page on one adventure, and anxiously started another.

Dance of the Lights

The masts of *Trillium II* swayed back and forth creating an arc across the night sky. Twinkling stars in the heavens seemed so close one could pick them off a velvety, black pillow like diamonds in a jewellery store. Masts and spreaders formed an enormous cross between a multitude of stars. Measurements and distances were unreal. The Master Jeweller had mounted His diamonds in constellations so man could give them a name.

Mysterious lights over the Med

Through the open door of the wheelhouse, I could see the Big Dipper low in the sky, Cassiopea, the Seven Sisters, Orion, and still much lower in the northern firmament, Polaris, the Polestar.

The course we steered was a bit south of east. We were on the way to Capri from the Strait of Bonifacio between the two islands of Corsica and Sardegna, in the Mediterranean. The night was splendid. There was enough wind to fill the genoa and we also put up the mizzen sail for balancing to ease on the steering. The ship sailed at a good clip, but every once in a while she would wander off the course steered when the wind came from aft. She was like a capricious mare, but would listen to the reigns. I had the wheel-watch from 8:00 P.M. until midnight. I was alone with my ship; Harry and Diana had withdrawn to their cabins.

There is nothing more satisfying than holding the wheel of your own ship, sailing on a quiet night while calm waves roll along toward a far destination. The light from the stars cast a glow on the water and the skyline was clearly visible. In the distance sailed the ferry from Sardegna to Genoa. Yellow streams of light emanated from that ship, reaching me as reflections over the sea surface.

Soft, hissing waves passed under *Trillium*'s wing decks making her bows go up and down in a rhythmic cadence. Such a night was a sailor's dream. Did not John Masefield in his poem, 'Sea Fever,' say,

> *I must go down to the seas again.*
> *To the lonely sea and the sky.*
> *And all I ask is a tall ship,*
> *And a star to steer her by.*

Suddenly, when looking out through the doorway, I noticed the red, green, and white flashing lights of a jet airplane en route to its destination to some far-away land. The night was so clear I could see the lighted portholes in the side of the plane. How many people were flying high above my head? Were they having dinner? Were they reading or trying to catch some sleep in an uncomfortable airplane seat?

A ship, a ferry, an airliner passing each other in the night. From down here, the tremendous roar of the engines was no more than a soft humming. I followed the twinkling lights, on, off, on, off, until they disappeared in the eastern sky.

After a few minutes, another airliner pursued the first, flying the same course as its predecessor. When it had vanished, only the stars remained. All at once, high in the northern sky, a bright light flashed three times. With that, the Dance of the Lights began.

This time it was definitely not an airplane. Again it flashed, much lower, followed by a broad ray of vivid light reflecting on the water. I did not have enough eyes to take it all in. The heavens came alive from east to west through the northern sky and from horizon to zenith. The strange lights flashed, shone and twinkled in groups of three but also individually. Excitedly, I called Harry and Diana from their bunks to enjoy the eerie, spectacular performance. Not a sound could be heard. Then, as though a switch had turned it off, the starlit sky returned to its former peacefulness.

While Harry held the wheel, I entered in the ship's log the whole event. It had lasted forty minutes.

Harry didn't bother going back to his bunk. In an hour's time he would have to take over the wheel.

But the performance was not yet over. It started anew, even more interesting than before. Double lights swung around each other. Playing catch me if you can, they turned and dashed to and fro. It was an incredible display and Harry, Diana, and I had front row centre. It brought to mind the light, playful melody of Tschaikovsky's "Dance of the Hours" from the opera, *The Queen of Spades*. We were witnessing the Dance of the Lights, just as playful and extraordinary in the night sky above the Middle Sea, the Sea of Antiquity.

For another half hour we enjoyed this mysterious play of lights between the constellations. Suddenly, the heavens came to rest once more. I stared skyward and asked, "Who? What? Why? How?" I did not receive an answer. The stars remained silent. I asked my ship but she merely sailed on, unmoved and indifferent as always.

It was midnight. My watch was over and Harry took the wheel.

Isola d'Ischia

After the adventure of the Ballet of Lights, we had made good sailing, exceptionally good, because the wind continued to blow from the right direction. In the early morning hours of July 1, we stormed under full sail past Isola Ponziane. Then, four hours later, we had Isola Ventotene on our port. In the afternoon, we were to reach Isola d'Ischia to enjoy a couple of days' rest in its harbour. We had been at sea since leaving the Balearic Islands, and with only three crew members, the three-hours-on and six-hours-off watches had become a tiring routine. In the six hours between two helm watches, there were many odd jobs to be done, and, of course, cooking meals was always necessary.

The little harbour slowly came into view. It was remarkably beautiful even though it was crammed full of big, awkward plea-sure cruisers of shiny plastic. They were owned by weekend sea-men from Naples, which was on the other side of the Bay. A rude bunch they were, too, for while we were bobbing around in the middle of the harbour watching for a spot to anchor, there came a huge pleasure cruiser roaring in toward the moored yachts. There was no vacancy, but he squeezed his bow between two boats and revved the engine. Creaking and tearing, they parted bit by bit. Fists were raised and abusive language flew everywhere. One more push and he had found his spot. He didn't give a damn about the fury of his fellow boaters. Satisfied, he shut down the throttles of his two diesel engines. He must have had a least two times 250

A skimpy bikini and a ship taking off into the wild blue yonder

HP under his feet, otherwise he never could have made it.

We had to deal with this sort of behaviour as well. Harry proposed we bunker first, then we could look around some more. The oil dock at the end of the small harbour was narrow with little room to manoeuvre. At an angle, I guided *Trillium II* toward it at half speed. Tow speedboats passed us at full throttle and turned toward the dock. I blew the foghorn loudly while Harry waved furiously from the foredeck. They pretended they didn't notice, and docked their plastic toys. There was only one thing for us to do—the same thing as the thoughtless skipper of the heavy cruiser had done. With the foghorn bellowing at full strength, I gave some throttle and headed straight for them. That was when the fools realized they were no match for the 30-ton *Trillium II*. They grabbed their mooring lines and dispersed like the wind. That's the way pirates like these deserve to be treated. We had learned this lesson well. The oilman stood waiting at the dock, grinning appreciatively. That day, we got our diesel oil five cents per litre cheaper...and tax free.

In a corner of the little harbour, we dropped bow and stern anchors. In case sudden whirlwinds developed, at least we'd be safe and not cause any damage in the crowded port. Tomorrow we would sail around the island to look for a more suitable spot.

We found a place on the south side of the bay San Antonio. San Antonio, too, had a small port but it was only made for small yachts and some fishing vessels. We were satisfied with our bay. The sandy bottom seemed to hold the anchor well, and we were sheltered from the northerly wind. If the sirocco were to start blowing, we'd have to be prepared. This warm southerly wind would carry sand along from the Sahara Desert, and we weren't sure if the anchor would hold if that were to happen.

Harry and Diana packed their backpacks, and I rowed them ashore. They planned to take a few days of shore leave in Rome to visit a friend of Diana's. In San Antonio, they would catch a bus to the ferry and cross over to Napoli. From there, they would travel to Rome by train.

**A few days,
and adventures,
on my own**

SAN ANTONIO, to my relief, was not a tourist trap. It was very quaint with benches in the town square that looked out over the seawall. Here, old fishermen dreamed away their final years, holding their walking sticks between their knees. In the distance, Capri loomed from an azure sea, and beyond that, somewhat hazily, the Vesuvius thrust its head into the clouds. I went ashore often and got to know the people. I struck up a friendship with the old men on the benches. I was the "Capitano Canadése." They told me long stories in Italian and I responded to them in English. Despite the language barrier, we understood each other. That is true friendship. I also became familiar with an Italian family who was vacationing on Ischia. When I informed the man about the misconduct of the sailors in the yacht harbour, tears filled his eyes. With many "scusares" and "pardonnares," he apologized for his countrymen.

The old retired fishermen sitting near the sea wall must be reminiscing about times long gone by.

During lunch on board ship one day, I was eating my soup when I heard the splashing of oars and someone calling. I saw a young woman with two children about three or four years old, in a small rubber dinghy. The children were little darlings, and mama was the biggest darling of all in her scanty bikini. She was one of the boat people, and her yacht was moored inside the piers of the fishing harbour. Her husband, a doctor in Austria, had left the day before, but she would stay on board a few more weeks with the children. She had to run errands in the village, but she didn't decline an invitation to come to dinner that night. I was glad that she accepted. It gave me something to do. I would go into town and buy a bottle of good table wine. Such charming company surely was worth that, I thought. I put spaghetti on the menu, a pre-eminent Italian dish, and considered serving a Dutch pudding with thick red current juice, especially for the children.

At 5:00 P.M. she rowed alongside, and I first helped the little ones on board. After that, I gallantly offered my hand while she mounted the steps. We sipped a pre-dinner drink in the cockpit and our conversation was held half in English, half in German. The dinner was a feast! I had forgotten to break the spaghetti in half, so we had a competition with the little ones to see who could slurp the longest noodle in the shortest time. Pop, there they went! The children burst with laughter. Mama and I didn't stand a chance.

A counter-invitation was inevitable—lunch on board her yacht the following day. For dinner at my place, Frau Doktor had been dressed very properly, and the children had been wearing dirndl outfits. I felt I should dress up, so in my best white pants, crisp white shirt, white shoes, and white cap decorated with gold sequins and tilted to one side, I rowed myself over to the inner

harbour where her little boat was moored. The children were playing on the quay in their beach clothes, and when they noticed me
they called out to their mother that Onkel Jerry was on his way.

Mama had been busy in her galley, but came to greet me in
the little cockpit. She was wearing her skimpy bikini. It was
unbearably hot and below deck one could stand it even less, what
with the cooking and so on. Onkel Jerry didn't mind and the
children wanted to ride horsey on his knees.

From the cockpit and over the sea wall I could keep an eye on
Trillium's masts. To glance elsewhere every so often was necessary,
because all that soft bosom and healthily tanned woman's body is
hard on one's eyeballs, especially if it's sitting straight across from
you so that your knees touch. Those undersized cockpits will
embarrass a man yet. But in that cockpit an excellent lunch was
served. There was no spaghetti, which was a disappointment to the
children. They had hoped we'd continue the slurping party.

After the meal the children were put into their bunks for their
siesta, and it was also time for me to say goodbye. Harry and Diana
would be back tomorrow, and I needed to buy provisions. When
many *wiedersehens* and *danke-schons* had been expressed, I rowed
my little sloop to the beach and pulled it above the water line.
Beyond, in the glistening bay, *Trillium II* lay. Had she turned?
Perhaps the wind had followed the sun in the afternoon. That had
happened more often. I would run my errands, and see about
things in a little while. I climbed the stairs in the seawall, and did
my marketing in the little shops around the village square. Fully
laden with supplies, I rested next to my old friends from the
village, who were sitting in their regular place, coughing and sputtering. Talking for an hour was nothing, particularly if the conversation is like a Babylonian hodgepodge.

I told them "*Ciao*," then with sudden haste I bolted toward
the beach. The sloop was where I had left it, but the bay was
empty. There was no familiar silhouette in the warm afternoon
sun. No *Trillium II*! Blue, glistening, and barren, the sea stretched
out before me. For a long time I felt empty under my sailing cap as
well. My brain refused to accept what my eyes were seeing. There
was no ship! I was a skipper without a ship, stranded on an Italian
island. Then my consciousness returned. I still had the sloop, so I
shoved it into the water. Pulling hard on the oars, I reached open
water where the skyline widened. I stood up in the sloop, and with
my hand shielding my eyes, I searched the horizon. Nothing,
nothing, but wait, far off to the south two matchsticks pointed

upward. Could it be two masts? It had to be *Trillium II*. The hull had already sunk below the horizon, and only the masts were still visible. I plunked back down on the seat and began rowing again. How could I ever catch up with her?

It was impossible. She was too far away. Soon she would disappear completely, dropping down below the borderline of air and water. Had someone stolen her? Had she gone adrift? My mind was full of questions, but luck comes to those who don't deserve it. A water-taxi came storming down the bay. I attracted his attention by shouting and pointing to the horizon. Before I could express myself in proper Italian, he grasped the situation and threw me a line. It took twenty minutes before we reached *Trillium II*. Five cruisers were sailing circles around her like some sort of cordon. An abandoned ship in the middle of the Med they had never experienced.

The stepladder still hung outboard and I climbed on deck. The water-taxi driver followed me, inquisitively. From the bow, the anchor chain swung aimlessly in the water. Together, we hoisted the anchor on board. A ship has a will of its own, and *Trillium II* had gradually worked herself loose from the anchoring spot in the bay and run off. The wind and the sea had been conspirators in her escapade. But now I was on her back again and had her under control. I settled with the water-taxi fellow. It cost 10,000 lira, but that was a bargain just to have my ship back. I handed him 15,000 lira with a "Grazie Signore, mille grazie." The water-taxi tore away and the honour guard around *Trillium II* disappeared as well, all going their own way. I could now sail my ship back to the bay.

The harbour of Capri in the Mediterranean. In the distance Isola d'Ischia from where Trillium II sailed away without any crew aboard.

I started the diesel engine, seized the wheel, and immediately sensed a problem. The wheel spun around and around freely. Frustrated, I wondered what could be wrong. Had the steering cable snapped? It wasn't as bad as that. On inspection, I discovered that the turn-buckles that hold the steering cable taut had worked themselves loose. How in heaven's name was this possible? I've already said it. A ship has a will of its own and *Trillium II* certainly did, that know-it-all imp. After an hour of sweating in the bilge, the problem was cleared up. Then, home to San Antonio Bay.

It had definitely been a memorable day. First, in gala uniform,

I had enjoyed lunch with a charming, half-naked woman. After that, I spent time chatting with the well-worn old fisherman on a bench in the village square. Finally, I had rescued a ship that thought it would take off without the skipper's permission. For the second time that day, my knees buckled with fright. If there had been only one intelligent man on board those cruisers, he could have put a price-crew on board *Trillium II*, even if it had only been a child. He could have thrown a line to that abandoned ship, towed her into Napoli, and had her chained in the harbour. I would then have had to ransom my ship for half her estimated value, the price for salvaging her. Fortunately, there were enough fools who didn't know the laws of the sea. Otherwise, I could have filed for bankruptcy.

Tomorrow, Harry and Diana would return from Rome. I really had a story to tell them.

Dominique and Catherine— two Parisiennes

A hair-raising adventure on a Greek island

What an adventure we had with these two charming Parisiennes. From Capri to the Strait of Messina was a two-day sail, though it didn't seem that far on the chart. When we left Capri, it was windstill. We were delighted with our new diesel, which we could depend on to get us to every destination.

In the *Pilot*, the sailors' bible, we read that heavy currents in the strait could be expected. They could cause us to be dragged along uncontrollably. Fortunately, that turned out to be an unfounded fable. In the middle of the strait, between Sicily and the mainland of Italy, high-tension wires had been strung from huge towers. They were high enough to allow big ships to pass underneath. As we approached the wires, we saw blue-white sparks flying around the insulators and suspensions on the steel towers. Dark clouds in the background promised a thunderstorm. The atmosphere was close and oppressive. If lightning were to strike, it would mean the end of the *Trillium II* and of us.

Harry connected heavy chains to the stainless steel rigging and dropped the ends into the water. That created a cone of protection around the ship. Everything went well and we sailed stately beneath the overhanging cables. Ahead of us, over starboard, we saw Messina on Sicily.

Below threatening clouds, the harbour and the city did not look very attractive. It was a dirty place, so we sailed on. Over the port side on the mainland, another place came into view. It was Reggio di Calabria, and seemed much more inviting than Messina. We located an empty yacht harbour, and met a friendly harbour-master. He did not charge us a fee to stay and did not expect any gifts. That made us feel welcome.

During our visit, he dropped by frequently to chat and to improve his English. He offered us rides into town to do our shopping. His little old Fiat was always at our disposal and he directed us to the best mercados. After a few days of rest, we said goodbye to our new friend and thanked him warmly for everything he had done for us. As we made the final preparations for departure, a French yacht sailed into the basin and docked on the opposite side of the basin. The harbour-master took off in his Fiat to greet the newcomers.

I started the diesel, and Harry jumped ashore to free the lines from the bollards. Diana stood at the railing to take them in. All of a sudden, the harbour-master came racing down the quay frantically waving his arm and sounding the horn. Did he want money after all? With squealing brakes, he jolted to a stop and bounded out of the car. In his best English-Italian, he explained his problem. The skipper of the French yacht had dropped off two girls, with all their belongings, on the quay. He did not want them on board his ship any longer. Why, the harbour-master did not know, but he did know that the two signorinas were *molto triste*, very sad. Could the Signor Capitano not take the girls on board. Por favore?

Oh, those Italians, always gallant and helpful, especially when it concerns the fairer sex. Harry and I looked at each other. We could use some extra crew, and replenishing our ship's kitty was welcome, too. I asked him to introduce us to the prima donnas and away he raced. Harry, still on the quay holding the mooring lines, threw the loops back over the bollards. This could take some time. I turned off the diesel. Harry might be right.

Five minutes later, the knight in shining armour returned. Two girls, dressed in clean jeans and colourful blouses, stepped out of his war horse, carrying heavy backpacks. I signalled to Harry to begin the preliminaries and negotiations. The harbour-master listened with interest. Harry then pointed to me. I had the final say-so. He invited them aboard and the girls told us their names and where they were from. Silently, I examined them. The first thing I looked at was the inside curve of their elbows. There were no needle marks. Their appearance was neat and tidy and they seemed strong and healthy. Their bright eyes looked me straight in the face—I liked that.

I recovered my politeness and welcomed them aboard. Catherine spoke English very well, and Dominique knew a bit of German. I thought to myself that we would get along just fine with each other. Harry remembered to be practical and advised the girls to go shopping first. They were given an hour and then we would depart.

Our Italian friend was overjoyed. He ran to me, gave me a big hug and kissed me on both cheeks. "Si, si Signor Capitano." He would drive the girls into town and be back within the hour. "Mille grazies, Capitano." With gears grinding, he dashed away.

The harbour-master of Reggio di Calabria should buy a new car sometime.

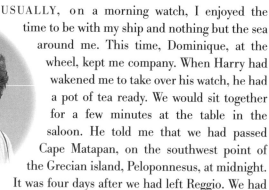

USUALLY, on a morning watch, I enjoyed the time to be with my ship and nothing but the sea around me. This time, Dominique, at the wheel, kept me company. When Harry had wakened me to take over his watch, he had a pot of tea ready. We would sit together for a few minutes at the table in the saloon. He told me that we had passed Cape Matapan, on the southwest point of the Grecian island, Peloponnesus, at midnight. It was four days after we had left Reggio. We had made good time and the new crew had had the oppor-

Catherine and Dominique

tunity to adjust to the ship's routine. They performed their duties with pleasure. They shared a cabin, but each had a double bunk and privacy. Compared to the cramped quarters on board the French yacht, they had a super-deluxe residence.

During my watch on the bridge, we crossed the Gulf of Lakonikos. When rounding Akra (Cape) Malla, I advised Dominique on a new course to the island of Spetsai, almost due north. We sailed close to the coast of the peninsula, the mountains mere silhouettes against the dark sky. Stars twinkled above, but night would soon pass. The eastern sky already revealed a shimmer of light, with dawn soon to follow.

In the distance, a fully-lighted ship passed. It was probably a ferry on its way to Athens. At the foot of the mountains were strings of light in the sleepy villages. Higher up, lights winked in the windows of small houses where I pictured an early-rising farmer eating his goat's milk porridge with his family. We heard the rumbling of the ferry's diesel in the quiet hours of the morning, both of us steering in the same direction.

Then, daylight announced itself and the mountains lost their deep, black shadows and became more clear. One by one, the village lights disappeared after illuminating the foot of the craggy Alps all night, like candles on a Christmas tree. A haze formed on the eastern skyline and presently the sun rose behind it, spreading a golden glow, its rays casting a fan-like pattern across the sky. My mind's eye snapped a picture of the orange, mauve, pink, and gold against a pale blue background. Suddenly, a wonder unfolded right before us. On either side of the sun's orb, bright green spots came into view. Very few people were privileged to behold the rare, stunning phenomenon of the Mysterious Green Lights. Dominique and I gazed at the marvel, momentarily transported into a dream world of kaleidoscopic colours. We would never again see anything like it.

Gradually, the green faded. The rising sun became stronger and brighter. The villages and houses at the foot of the mountain came into perspective, exposing the barrenness of the slopes. This was not the land we had been searching for—the land of ouzo and retsina, the land of temples and wild, gyrating music in village inns, or terrazzos beneath oleander and olive trees. No, the land we dreamed of was farther north, and *Trillium II* would take us there.

THE SUN had dropped toward the western sky when we reached Spetsai. Only one hour of daylight was left. We did not possess a chart of that part of Greece, but we did have a sketch of the harbour. By motoring around the island, we soon found Balza Creek, and let our anchors drop between many other yachts. The weather was pleasant and calm, although in the morning we noticed that the wind had turned *Trillium II* completely around and the two anchor lines were twisted, lines tangled together.

Before long, a friendly customs officer paid us a visit. He was immaculately dressed in a starched, white uniform. A white cap, decorated with gold embroidery, balanced on his jet-black hair. He allowed us to go ashore to purchase our necessary stores and provisions, but advised us to sail to Nauplia for clearance and a 'permit of stay' in Greece.

Nauplia was a four-hour sail into the Kolpos (Bay) Argolikos. The wind in the bay was treacherous. Strong gusts blew from one direction and then changed to winds from another side. After that, we were becalmed for about five minutes. Our crew loved the resulting action and the sail changes. One moment there was boiling, foaming water under the wind decks at an exhilarating speed, and the next we were becalmed, the sails hanging as limp as a dish rag.

The quay in Nauplia was similar to a boulevard, with potted plants all along the water's edge and palm trees lining the median. We had the whole place to ourselves, and because of the conveniences that Nauplia offered, we stayed for three days. Customs had given us clearance and permission to sail in Greek waters for as long as we wished. It had cost only a few dragmas, which was not much if figured in dollars.

SPETSAI—a gathering place for yachts from all over the world. Skippers with unshaven faces held curved pipes between hairy lips to make sure they would not be mistaken for landlubbers. Their jolly crews were dressed in tattered jeans. Sidewalk cafés were filled to capacity with people drinking ouzo or retsina, a drink that tastes like turpentine. When we arrived from Nauplia, we had anchored at the same place, but now I was suspicious on account of changing winds. I specified that only half of the crew could go ashore to sample the ouzo; the rest were to remain on board...just in case.

The evening was calm, the sky clear. There was nothing to worry about. The two German boys we had picked up somewhere along the route lowered the sloop and seated themselves on the middle bench. They would be the oarsmen. With Catherine in the bow and me in the stern, the sloop had little freeboard left, but we reached the landing with no problem.

Coloured lanterns lit the sidewalk cafés. Sounds of Nana Mouskouri, a hit of the seventies, drifted to our ear, and we were eager to get to where the fun was. We found a table close to the seawall that had sheltered the village from the sea since time immemorial. The waiter suggested we try the ouzo of Spetsai. Catherine and the German boys agreed to his recommendation, but I stayed on the safe side and ordered a Heineken beer, even though it was more expensive. Suddenly, the village square that had been so crowded became empty. People quickly vacated their seats at the café. Tour boats, moored below the seawall, clanged and clattered against each other, their chains jangling. The sea had turned inky black. Small whitecaps smashed the wall. Still, Nana droned on and on.

What was happening? Gusts of wind whirled papers over the

village square. One of the tour boats, with passengers on board, left the mooring, setting my mind at ease. They would not go out in deteriorating weather, would they? The puffs of wind became stronger, blowing dust high over the square. It was then I realized we had to return to *Trillium II* anchored in the bay. Harry and the two girls were alone, and I was unsure of the conditions in Balza Creek.

In a sudden panic, we hurried along the seawall. It seemed as though we were miles from the sloop at the landing place. Finally we found her bobbing amidst some rubber dinghies. The condition of the bay was worse than I had anticipated. Dark waves with mean-looking whitecaps were rolling in. Wild, swinging masthead lights showed us where the yachts were anchored, but where were the lights of *Trillium II?*

The captain and his two Parisiennes.

The boys rowed vigorously, but we took in a great deal of water. The sloop was unable to rise against the oncoming waves. Catherine, sitting for'ard, received the brunt of the onslaught of water. She was drenched. The sloop sank deeper into the sea with every boarding wave, and we had no bailer. Where was *Trillium II?* Had she gone adrift?

Then a fierce, bright beam of light swung back and forth over the wild water until it caught sight of our small, white sloop. Harry had found us. Harder and harder, the boys pulled on the oars. The sloop had only a few inches of freeboard left. She would go down any minute, that was for sure. We heard the humming of the diesel and Harry manoeuvred the ship so we were in its lee. Diana and Dominique were in the cockpit ready to catch our painter. Would we make it? At the first throw, they grabbed the line. The sloop sunk, and we clung to the railing. A moment later, we stood on the solid deck of *Trillium II*.

No true sailor would leave his sloop behind, so with all hands we dredged her from the deep. Harry then set course to the north against wind and waves, away from Spetsai and the deadly trap in Balza Creek.

Thanks to Harry's capable seamanship, the four of us had survived a perilous situation where we had little chance of escaping our foe, the sea.

Cruising the Greek Islands

Mykonos

In Piraeus, the Port of Athens, we were booked full. We had heard about Mykonos, where the jet set loved to romp, and decided to make it our next destination. The island was located on our route to Rhodes, and we were interested in how the rich and famous amused themselves. Of course we were not of their calibre, but surely we could find a spot to park *Trillium II.*

The sea chart showed us that we would pass many other islands and also an area of magnetic anomalies that would affect our compass. We were not unduly alarmed. Navigating in the Greek

Archipelagos was simple—shortly after leaving one part, another island would show up on the horizon.

In Mykonos, the pier was packed solid with plastic yachts, mostly rentals from chartering companies. We found a spot close to some sharp boulders. With a few extra mooring lines, we would be fine. To get to the village on Mykonos, we had to walk along a narrow beach which was dirty and smelly and crowded with young

Mykonos in her summit days. This is the playground of the European jet set.

people. Some of the boys and girls lay on the sand, arms and legs entangled. Others leaned against their backpacks on the retaining wall, glassy-eyed, staring into nowhere. Beer cans and plastic waste was strewn everywhere. We had to step over inert bodies to reach the end of the beach. There, by the far wall, was their toilet. Millions of green, golden flies buzzed over piles of excrement. Were these poor, drug-poisoned young people the jet set of Europe? How on earth had they arrived on this island? The explanation was simple. Once a day a ferry dumped them off and returned for them the day after or even a week later.

At the sidewalk cafés in the village there were also young people, but they were clearly of a different breed. Quietly and peacefully, the young men and their girlfriends sat over a cup of café espresso or a bottle of wine. In the distance, we heard music coming from a bar. However, even here, we did not find the rich we had so eagerly anticipated.

The village sprung to life in the evening. The narrow streets were overcrowded with strolling people, the music more lively. Soon Harry with his Diana, and I with my two Parisiennes, were caught up in the stream of the festive bustle. There were no empty seats at the cafés, but we finally found a bar where we could stand like sardines in a can. We were hemmed in by pseudo sailors in woollen jerseys and dito caps, and pseudo chic women wearing colourful, shapeless dresses similar to Hawaiian mumus. It was plain to see that they did not belong to the jet set either.

The real jet set had escaped from Mykonos long, long ago. We too had seen enough of this place and left the island with no regrets.

IN AGREEMENT with our guests, we called at the islands of Naxos and Paros in the Cyclades Archipelago. Here we hoped to

Naxos and Paros

rid ourselves of the bitter aftertaste of Mykonos. Both the little port and village of Paros had the same name as the island. It was refreshing to rest here where there were no activities and nightlife was non-existent. On the beach, we watched as some Greek fisherman tarred their small boats.

We bought some fresh, crusty bread at the bakery on the waterfront. It would taste good with the French onion soup Catherine and Dominique

had prepared for our lunch. Delicious aromas wafted from the tiny galley. They did most of the cooking together.

Skipper Jerry and Catherine in Athens.

At lunch time, people hungrily found their places at the table. Because there were so many guests, Dominique, wearing only a bikini, was crowded in the middle at the back of the table. Harry placed the huge pan of steaming hot soup on the table and Dominique took the ladle to fill the bowls for the guests. She had a full bowl in her hands when it tipped and spilled the hot contents all over her breasts, belly, and thighs. Screaming, she ran outside and I followed her with a kettle of cold water. How she had jumped from behind the table with so many people was a mystery that no one could solve when we later discussed the mishap. She continued to scream while I poured cold water over the fast-rising purple blisters on her body.

Harry kept his cool. He ordered the boys to drop the sloop into the water and we lowered Dominique backwards into it. We put soaking wet towels on the burned areas, and the boys rowed her ashore as fast as they could. On the quay, Harry flagged down a passing car but the man refused to take them to the hospital. They would not take no for an answer. After much yelling and gesturing, the man finally gave in.

Late that afternoon, they returned with Dominique all wrapped up. In the hospital they had given her a can of spray to ease the pain of her burns. It was a wonder spray, so one of us went to the drug store to stock up on it just in case. I hope never to hear anyone scream again as Dominique did on that fateful day. Harry agreed with me wholeheartedly.

In Rhodes, Dominique left the ship to go back to Paris. She tried to persuade Catherine to come along but to no avail. Catherine wished to continue travelling—to sail down the Suez Canal, see the Pyramids near Cairo, visit the Valley of the Kings. She was adamant. Adieu, Dominique, adieu. Dominique looked so pitiful stumbling away from the quay in Rhodes, toting her backpack. Her legs had not completely healed. She did not look back to the ship, not once.

Cyprus

PAPHOS ON CYPRUS was a dangerous harbour, wide open to the unpredictable Mediterranean Sea. As we entered, people moved some rowboats from the pier and gestured as to where we could moor. They were friendly people with welcoming smiles on their faces. When we had tied up, they looked amazed. *Trillium II* had taken up the whole length of the pier. In no time we had aroused the curiosity of tourists, and they pointed to our Canadian flag.

The Harbour of Paphos—wide open to the dangers of the Mediterranean weather lies Trillium II moored with her stern to the quay. She can leave immediately in case of sudden storms. Mooring this way is a safety measure.

That evening, fishing boats arrived with their day's catch and noticed how much space we had taken. They waved and moored on the other side of the mole. One fisherman brought us a huge slab of swordfish caught that afternoon. Five minutes later, the same man marched down the pier again. This time he had a gift for Harry. It was the three-foot sword of the fish he had given us, with razor-sharp edges. No wonder a swordfish has no enemies...except man. Harry had the honour of frying the steak, and it was indeed delicious.

The pier and a restaurant annex pub were the centre of activity for locals and tourists alike. We answered the usual questions about where we had come from and where our next destination would be.

Some of our crew disembarked to explore Cyprus, but Diana and Catherine stayed with us. We could afford a few days rest, but we were expected in Port Said, Egypt, by a certain date. The agent from Holland would be waiting for us with a new crew.

The evenings in Paphos were quite peaceful. The sea did not pipe up once, and all four of us enjoyed ourselves immensely. Harry sat in one of the cockpits with his Diana, and I in the other, with Catherine.

About the time the fishermen returned from the sea, a pelican flew down from the restaurant's roof to the pier, where he was treated generously with a portion of fish by the fishermen. It was not necessary for the bird to go out to sea for his dinner; this was a lot easier. Tourists gathered to watch the spectacle. Stuffed and satisfied, the bird swooped back to his perch on the roof, and after some snapping of his beak, he placed it under his wing and had an after-dinner snooze.

Catherine in the Harbour of Rhodes. The ancient mills are built on the mole.

One morning, a motor scooter came racing down the pier. Our peace and quiet was over. Gloria had arrived. A tall, good-looking woman with healthy, tanned skin steered her vehicle alongside. On the pillion of the scooter sat a full-figured woman. It did not take us long to realize that they were mother and daughter. Mother and daughter had seen our Canadian flag and were curious as to what we were up to. In no time, they had invited themselves aboard.

Their bold invasion caught us off-guard. We learned that the daughter's name was Judy, and the mother's, Gloria. They had been on Cyprus for three months, had seen everything, and were ready to try something new. Judy planned to leave for western Europe in a few days. They asked where we would be sailing to. We told them our route was to Port Said, through the Red Sea and to Ceylon. Mother wished to come along and be dropped off at Djeddah in Saudi Arabia. We had never heard of that place so, of course, had no plans to make a landfall there. Harry pulled a chart of the Red Sea out of the drawer and yes, there was Djeddah, also known as Jiddah.

Gloria arrives, in all her glory

It turned out that Gloria's husband worked for the Arabs. They had a house and a valid visa for the country. There were no problems. We also found out that Gloria was rich. That helped us to make up our minds. After telling them of the vacant bunk in Catherine's cabin, we offered the ladies a cold Dutch beer to celebrate the happy occasion. First they wanted to go back to their hotel. "I'll pack my belongings and also pick up my cheque book. I might as well come aboard right away," said Gloria. We informed her politely that we could not accept cheques, only cash in American dollars. Gloria understood. They buzzed away from the pier and were back in no time, a taxi following with their luggage.

Gloria reading a book, facing a tanker in ballast and bound for the Persian Gulf.

AS IT TURNED OUT, Gloria was a very dear woman and lots of fun to have on board. She became good friends with our quiet Catherine, and Harry's sweetheart, Diana, did not seem as talkative. That was a blessing. Gloria, with her loud mouth and her tender heart, was also a blessing. She rose early in the morning and baked scones so we could eat them warm and crusty for breakfast. She handled the wheelwatches like a pro. The compass never wavered off course. She cooked, scrubbed the decks with the other girls, and kept the captain's cabin clean and neat. And she paid for many things.

Gloria had arrived on a scooter, but how she left our ship in Djeddah is another story.

Port Said

The weather had become warmer by the hour, by the day. We had sailed away from Paphos in the evening, and if conditions were favourable, we could be in Port Said within two days. Things did not go as we had planned.

There was no wind at all, so we were forced to use the diesel. Fifty miles out of Paphos, the propeller axle shot out of the clutch-housing. Harry climbed into his coveralls and descended to the engine room. Several hours later, we were under way again.

On the second day out, we noticed a vague coastline in the distance. It was already late afternoon and the sun stood in the west. We could not see anything on the radar that resembled a harbour, only that straight line. The sea was deserted, not even a fisherman in sight. We motored closer to the coast, where there were sand dunes as far as the eye could see. I tried getting a channel on the marine radio, hoping to hear busy conversations from shipping to the Suez Canal, but all we got was static.

Where were we? Were we east or west of Port Said, and how in the world had we ended up here? After much thinking and scratching our heads, consulting the charts and double-checking the radar screen, Harry and I came to a sort of conclusion. An unknown current must have set us off course to the east of Port Said. The lonely, empty coast we saw was the north side of the Sinai Desert. Gloria, holding the wheel, was given a new course, a simple one: "Sail into the sunset Gloria, until you see Port Said...."

Before dark, the coastline broke and a broad waterway could be seen. We had found the Suez Canal after all. In the background were huge buildings, definitely the city of Port Said. Although we seemed to be in the right place, Harry and I had a feeling of uneasiness. Here, we were the only ship. The waterway should have been teeming with ships, tankers, and freighters, but there was nothing in sight. We were sure Port Said was a big harbour, but where were the docks?

On we sailed until we noticed that we were in a huge basin with no exit. The buildings were dark warehouses. Night fell quickly, and somewhere in the middle of the basin we threw our anchor out. We decided to stay put for the night and do some searching in the morning. The real harbour must be right around the corner.

Early the next day, we turned into the port of Port Said. A motor launch sped toward us, crashed into our starboard side and some dark-coloured people jumped onto the deck of *Trillium II*. An obese fellow approached me. "You captain of ship? We health inspection. Welcome to Port Said." With tongue in cheek, I welcomed him aboard.

He explained that it was his duty to check our safety equipment and to make sure there was no sickness among the crew, and also to see if there were rats aboard. I assured him everything was in order, that there was no sickness, and not even a tiny mouse was hidden on the ship. He didn't seem the least bit interested with my report. Then came the surprise attack. "Do you want to go through the Suez Canal? No problem, Captain. Did you remember to bring present from Canada?" There it was loud and clear— *baksheesh*.

On Cyprus, the people had warned us to bring cartons of cigarettes and chocolate bars as well as soap, tea, and American dollar bills. We had done so, but something inside me resisted this practice of bribery. Luckily, Harry was wiser than I. He produced

***Baksheesh* in Egypt**

a carton of cigarettes and the eyes of the "health inspector" glittered with greed. The rascal broke open the carton and spirited the packages away. He hid two under his uniform cap, some in his socks, and the rest in his grimy white shirt. Obviously he did not want to share the loot with his buddies on deck.

Without further ado, he stamped some forms and showed us to the marina where we could stay. The marina, in a small inlet, was opposite the city with its harbour works. Two small yachts

The youth of Greece.

bobbed in a corner, and once *Trillium II* was secured at the rickety dock, there was no room left. Under a canopy sat a soldier holding a sten gun across his knees. We wondered why he was on guard. We had not been moored for more than half an hour when two girls, screaming excitedly, came running into the marina. Behind them, somewhat calmer, was our agent from Harlingen. Following closely was the soldier, his gun poised menacingly.

It turned out that no one was allowed into the harbour without a permit, and certainly not aboard a foreign ship that had just arrived. The guard rambled on in his broken English while we greeted our guests. They had arrived the night before and were anxious to get sailing. The two girls, both named Tina, had booked as far as the Maldives. The agent would disembark in Djiboutie and a fourth passenger, yet to arrive, would travel as far as Colombo on Ceylon. The guard with his pop-gun was uncertain about how to handle the situation. Maybe he would shoot us in cold blood. To pacify him, the girls and our agent returned to their hotel on the other side of the Suez Canal in hopes of obtaining a permit soon.

Harry and I were beginning to understand the ways of the East. They used military power where it was unnecessary, and were very suspicious of westerners. The matter of *baksheesh* (bribery) was something we had to cope with, as well as the excessive formalities.

First the police came on board demanding a list of the crew members in "triplo." My old German typewriter came in handy. I clickety-clacked the forms in triplicate. Then we had visitors from the customs office who wanted forms, forms, and more forms. They searched the ship for contraband. We were ordered to move our bottles of liquor into the shower stall, which they sealed. After that, the mighty men from immigration, dressed in sparkling white uniforms and gold trimmed caps, arrived in a launch with a small cabin aft. We welcomed the gentlemen aboard *Trillium II*. They also wanted a list of the crew, and for some unknown reason, they wanted it six-fold. Our passports were confiscated and replaced with a proof of surrender with which we could enter the city of Port Said. Upon departure, the passports would be returned.

This was done in a courteous manner, but with an undertone of unflinching power. Reluctantly, I surrendered. There was no use in arguing with them. I was left with a stack of forms to fill out and told to drop them off at their office. They clambered back on board the launch, saluted, and roared away. Slowly and half-heartedly, we brought a finger to our sailor's caps.

THAT AFTERNOON, we smugly showed our permits to the soldier. He retaliated by inspecting every piece of paper slowly and carefully. We took a five-minute walk to the ferry that would transport us across the canal. It left every 10 minutes and there was no fee to pay. The whole crew had come along; Harry, with his Diana, I with Catherine, and Gloria tagging behind. *Trillium II* stayed at the marina, guarded by a soldier with a machine gun.

The immigration office was located at the quay where the ferry had dropped us off. The officers recognized us immediately. We handed them the forms I had filled out. Indifferently, they tossed them on a shelf without even glancing at them. They showed us to a room and invited us to join them for tea. An attendant brought in a large, oriental teapot, and with a deep bow for each of us, he poured a black, sweet tea for "L'illustre compagnie du Canada." Their French was every bit as impeccable as the English they spoke.

After numerous cups of tea and some small talk with the immigration officers, the papers and forms were tabled and provided with large stamps with Arabic lettering. Then each of us was asked to fill out another form requesting personal information, and these were also stamped. Forms and stamps seemed to be an obsession with Egyptian officials.

While we were busy, a man peeked his head in the door and introduced himself as the missing passenger for Colombo. He was

The elderly of Greece.

a retired administrator from the KLM, the Royal Dutch Airlines. He told us his sob story about being sent from one office to another, from one side of town to the other, still accomplishing nothing. Finally he thought he must be in the right place. He began explaining how he had come to Cairo by plane from Amsterdam, by taxi from Cairo to Port Said to board a ship from Canada bound for Colombo. No one so far had understood his mind-boggling itinerary, and refused to grant him the necessary permits.

Unfortunately, he still was not in the right place. One of the officers gave him another address and told me to go with him to help explain his situation. Then he could come back, exchange his passport for the permit, and everything would be fine. I inquired of the officer why this could not be done here and now. The immigration officers threw up their arms, "Non, non, Monsieur le capitaine. C'est impossible."

The little road sweepers of Port Said.

Hank, the KLM man, had a taxi waiting outside which he had hired for the day. It was the cheapest way to travel around Port Said. We seated ourselves in the back of the rusty old jalopy and Hank gave the driver a new address. He had to stop often to ask for directions, but assured us we would arrive soon. We drove through a part of the city that had been heavily bombarded by the Israelis in the Six Day War in 1968. Entire housing complexes had been reduced to rubble. We passed a mosque in a dismal street and at that moment the Muezzin began summoning to Allah through tinny-sounding speakers from the tower. The driver stopped his taxi in the middle of the street, jumped out, and entered the mosque. Hank and I looked at each other and shrugged. There was nothing we could do. We hoped the session would not take long.

After 20 minutes, the driver returned, pushed the starter button and nothing happened. With typical eastern fatalism, he shook his head. "Inshallah...it is God's will." He tinkered under the hood, and with a bang the engine started. Triumphantly, and with a big grin on his brown face, he drove us on to our destination.

Four hours and several American dollars later, the immigration authorities clapped a stamp on a piece of paper and Hank was given a permit to board our ship. Our ship's company was now complete. The two Tina's were busy installing themselves in a cabin and Hank would share one with the agent. And then, once again, came the inevitable question, "When do we sail, skipper?"

"Sail?" I asked like a simpleton, "Sail? What about provisions? What about diesel fuel, and a pilot? Without a pilot we will not be allowed to enter the Suez Canal. All those things must be looked after first before we start talking sailing."

Faces fell, and I could see I was no longer their friend. But Harry and I got things moving. The agent organized a shopping spree with the girls from Amsterdam. Harry took Diana into the city to buy a flight ticket back to Holland, and Catherine and I roamed the streets of Port Said in unbearable heat to find diesel fuel, a pilot, and clearance for the canal. And Gloria? Well, she stayed on board holding the fort and prepared a meal in a galley as hot as an oven. Our guard sat in his armchair keeping an eye on *Trillium II*. Did that man never go home? Hank, the man from KLM, did not want to do anything but drink cold Heineken beer.

Catherine and I were taken for a ride by the Egyptian bureaucracy. We were sent from here to there without getting anywhere, stupid, stumbling fellow that I was. If I had left a handful of American dollars at the right place, we would have had the fuel delivered in no time, the permit for the canal, plus arranged for a pilot with no problem. Now, after a whole day of running around in a stinking, hot city, we were not sure of anything. Harry and Diana had returned in the evening after beating their heads against walls of incomprehension, unwillingness, and stupidity. There was no ticket to Holland; Diana cried.

How to get along with people in Arab countries had to be learned. South and east of Port Said existed another world with completely different values and views on life. As the saying goes, east is east, and west is west, and never the twain shall meet. We had not realized that Port Said was such a closed city. One could not go anywhere without permits for this and permits for that. Every paper had to have half a dozen stamps in blue ink and Arab letters. The more stamps, the better, it seemed. But each stamp cost us a small fortune in Egyptian pounds.

I could not help Harry and Diana. My own problems were rising sky-high and the mood of our guests deteriorated by the hour. After a four-day wait, Diana could leave for Holland, the fuel was delivered, and we held our permits to sail through the Suez Canal. At 9:00 A.M. on Monday, a pilot would be on board.

We had to help Diana after all. Her flight ticket back to Holland cost so much that she did not have sufficient funds to pay for it. We had to raid the ship's kitty.

On Saturday night, we had a mutiny on our hands. I had announced that on Sunday, Harry would take Diana to the airport and I would go to Cairo with Gloria and Catherine. Monday morning at 0900 hours, we would sail, and not a minute sooner. A storm of protest arose. Our four guests reminded me that they had not paid to lie in this harbour for five days, and why were we not sailing until Monday? Coldly and authoritatively I answered, "None of you has offered to take a turn cooking meals. It is always Gloria who has breakfast, lunch, and dinner ready on time. None of you ever offered to keep us company on our dreadful days in the city running from one building to another. None of you was pleasant to us when we returned at night, hot, sweaty, tired, and disappointed. All this time you have been asking for beer, beer, beer. Our stores are not everlasting!"

Cairo—so near...and yet so far

TAKE THE BUS and go to Cairo. It seemed simple enough, but we were in for a rude awakening. We had contacted the immigration office, which we were very familiar with by now. We told them we would like to see Cairo, with its pyramids, the museum with all the treasures of Tutankhamen, and anything else of interest. The officers were enthusiastic about our plans and assured us there would be no problem. "If you come early tomorrow morning, Captain, we will have your passports and a day permit for you to leave the city all ready for you."

At 7:30 the next morning, we ferried across where the officers waited for us with beaming smiles on their faces. As promised, our passports and day-passes were ready, but there was a hitch. The passes cost 150 Egyptian pounds each. They had pulled a fast one on us. In unison we gasped. What was the reason for charging us that amount? The officers laughed and tried to explain that it wasn't as serious as we thought. All we would have to do was go to a bank, deposit 450 pounds in cash or traveller's cheques, return to their office, show them the deposit slip, and they would stamp the day-passes. Then we would go back to the bank and our cheques or cash deposits would be returned. It made me dizzy just thinking about it. How long would all that running back and forth take? We had hoped to take the 9:00 A.M. bus. The officers were positive that we would not have any problems, and added that the last bus left at 11:00.

We thanked them and quickly set out. The day was still young. Maybe we could make it in time. Heat engulfed us. The girls' dresses already showed wet spots on their backs and under their arms. We sat down at a sidewalk café, ordered colas, and asked the waiter if he knew where there was a bank open on Sunday. He said there was one, but it was only open from 10:00 A.M. until noon. No nine o'clock bus for us.

Promptly at 10:00, we stood on the steps of a stately building. Gloria had enough traveller's cheques to exchange for the three of us. The deposit slip worked wonders. Not only were we given our passports back, but also day-passes that allowed us to leave the city. We looked forward to a long, carefree day. On to the 11:00 bus, and then to Cairo.

When we arrived at the bus stop, it had just left. Gloria began to cry and Catherine, too, was ready to give up. An old beggar wearing filthy rags straggled by, muttering, "Baksheesh, Madame? Baksheesh, M'sieu?" We were definitely not in the mood for *baksheesh*. We had trudged and tramped in unbearable heat, and now there was no bus to Cairo. At that moment, an unshakable, stubborn will arose in my whole body. I exclaimed defiantly, "Do not give up, girls. We shall go to Cairo, no matter what. To the devil with all the bureaucracy in the world, especially in Port Said. Look, there's a taxi on the corner."

Four taxis were parked at the curb, each with a driver asleep at the wheel. We aroused the first one and asked him to take us to Cairo. He shook his head. One after another told us they had no permit to drive outside the city. Then the first driver motioned us aside. "Step into my taxi. I will drive you to a taxi who will go to Cairo," he informed us. When we reached it, I asked the driver how much the ride would cost. He declared, "One hundred American dollars, M'sieu." I offered him $50 and he agreed to it immediately. I should have offered him $25. Maybe he would have accepted that, but we were in no mood to resist any longer. Sweat oozed from every pore in the intolerable heat. We could not wait one moment longer.

Gloria sat beside the driver, a man with a kind, round face and a straight nose, contrary to the hooked noses of pure-bred Arabs. Catherine and I climbed into the back seat. The cab had no windows, allowing the air to blow in freely. It felt so good.

Located at the city limits was a military barricade. We were ordered to leave the taxi and show our day-passes. The floor mats were thrown outside, and the trunk searched. Our chauffeur glanced at us in an apologetic manner. He was accustomed to this sort of treatment. No contraband was found. The soldiers retreated to their place under a verandah and our driver was expected to replace the mats himself. To top off the idiocy, one kilometre farther the same nonsense was repeated at another barricade. Then, the road was clear. We were finally on our way. Cairo, here we come.

The noon heat shimmered above a long, narrow strip of asphalt. On both sides were the rolling sand hills of the Sahara. "Four hours," said our driver as he wriggled himself into the corner between the door and the seat.

Halfway to Cairo, we stopped at a brown wooden shed on the side of the road. The driver hand-pumped gasoline into the tank. He went inside, and a moment later he stood at the window and offered us three large portions of ice cream in plastic cups. We enjoyed the present immensely and were surprised at the situation. How was it possible to be parked on the side of a straight, black-topped road (why did the asphalt not melt in this heat?) halfway between Port Said and Cairo, to be handed a delicious helping of ice cream by a friendly, non-Arab driver in 50°C heat, seated in a windowless cab?

At 3:00 P.M. we entered the suburbs of Cairo, and not long after, we were at the museum. I was as thrilled as a high school boy who had taken his girl to a prom. I had studied Egyptian history, and now, for the first time, I would see things I had only seen pictured in books: Tutankhamen, the boy Pharoah, and his treasures, or Ank-Hesn-Aton, who changed the pantheistic religion into monotheism, making the priests hate him and his wife, Queen Nefer-ti-ti. Even if there were only a bust of her, I would be satisfied.

Inside the museum, it was dark and dusty. The old, plank floors creaked, showcases and cabinets were not illuminated, but so dark that labels could not be read. It was a great disappointment. There was no justice done to the valuables. The gold of Tut's treasures had only a faint glow, and the lapis lazuli on his breastplate was the colour of watery milk. Those historic riches should have been displayed on dark blue or black velvet with hidden lamps or infra-red lights to make it a play of colour and glorious sparkle. "Poor young Pharoah," I thought. "They should never have found your grave, your body and your riches. They should have let you sleep for ever and ever without disturbing you."

Gloria lost interest quickly and moved to the inevitable souvenir shop. Catherine and I followed her. The museum and shop would be closed at 4:00 P.M. We didn't have much time. I was not in the habit of buying trinkets at every place we made a landfall. If

I had done so from the beginning of our travels, *Trillium* would have sunk under the weight of all that useless stuff.

Yet I was interested in one thing—something to do with Nefer-ti-ti. The original bust of her had been stolen from Egypt long ago, and rested in the palace of Charlottenburg, in Berlin. I hoped there would be a worthy replica of her in this shop. There were many copies, but they were all ugly duplicates made of Mexican onyx. They were so poorly done, I turned my back on them. It was an insult to that lovely queen who had lived in the land of Egypt so long ago. Catherine must have noticed my disappointment. She asked, "Don't you want them, Skipper?" I shook my head in disgust. "Oh, look here then," she said, "Is this what you are looking for?"

There was Nefer-ti-ti, alone in a glass showcase. On black velvet, stood a little bust in low-lustre black on a heavy, rose onyx pedestal. Proudly she wore the royal headdress, her breast plate inlaid with gold. There was no price tag on it. I had learned to be careful with lovely things without a price tag. Under no circumstances would I allow myself to raid the ship's kitty. I was right. The price was far too high for me. I shook my head and went outside to look for our taxi.

THE PYRAMIDS OF GIZEH were impressive and awe-inspiring. My special interest concentrated on the Pyramid of Cheops, or Khufu, which had passages inside. Regretfully, we had arrived too late to inspect the interior. I had read and studied this Tomb of Cheops, and now I actually stood at the very foot of it, a pyramid that had been built more than 4,000 years before, in the fourth dynasty of the Egyptian pharaohs. King Cheops had had to get a "mortgage" on it by selling the honour of his daughter to the highest bidder. That was quite common in those days.

From the plateau on which the three large pyramids were situated, we had a marvelous view of Cairo. It was breathtaking when the sun sank low toward the western sky and the city's buildings turned in a hue of pink with mauve shadows. I snapped a few pictures of Gloria sitting on a camel with the pyramids in the background. She did not want to miss the chance to ride such a beast. It was a cantankerous animal, and she hung on for dear life.

Nefer-ti-ti was queen consort of Pharao Ech-N-Aton from the 18th Dynasty. The limestone bust of this lovely queen was secretly smuggled out of Egypt and is now in the Museum of Charlottenburg in Berlin. Understandably the Egyptian government wants it back.

TIME SPED BY and we had to return to the city for dinner. At the foot of the pyramids, we had met an American couple who had recommended the Rose Garden as a very good restaurant. I asked our chauffeur if he knew where it was. He said, "No sir, but I will find it." The Rose Garden did not disappoint us. It was exactly what its name implied—a gigantic rose arbor. There were roses overhead, boxes of roses between the tables, roses everywhere. The scent was strong and sweet.

Since it was still early, there were not many guests. We chose a table at the back with a view of an irrigation canal. Behind it were women busying themselves turning hay cocks. Far in the distance the pyramids glowed in the late sunlight.

Catherine and I at the great pyramids of Pharaoh Cheops, sometimes called Khufu.

Napoleon Bonaparte had once stated, "Soldiers..., forty centuries look down on you." Here we were, Gloria, Catherine, and I looking down on those forty centuries over the head of direct descendants of builders of pyramids—the Fellaheen.

There was no canned music in the Garden. Noiselessly, waiters served us. We selected an authentic Egyptian meal of lamb stew with rice along with many dishes of unrecognizable contents. Nevertheless, it all tasted superb. Inaudibly, a young waiter stood beside my chair and offered me a wine list. I must have looked surprised, because he explained that non-Moslem guests were allowed to order wine in this restaurant. We decided on a light, sweet Hock wine which turned out to be a good choice.

An evening in paradise with my lovely queens

The three of us didn't talk very much. We enjoyed the evening and each other's company. Just sitting there was a reward for all the misery of the morning. Our table was cleared without so much as a tinkle of the cutlery. For dessert we ordered an ice-cream sundae, but it was not served right away. The young waiter told us that the table was ours for the rest of the evening. "No hurry, Madame," with a bow toward Gloria, "Mademoiselle," a bow toward Catherine. We were certainly in no rush to leave the Rose Garden and its tranquillity, with the waiters silently moving about in their formal wear. Beyond our reach, the mighty pyramids stood proudly in the glorious twilight.

Catherine reached into her shoulder bag and pulled out a package wrapped in tissue paper, which she carefully set on the table next to my wine glass. I eyed it suspiciously and Gloria silently looked at Catherine. "For you, Skipper," she said, a hint of excitement in her voice. I unwrapped the present slowly and cautiously. There she was, the black Nefer-ti-ti, Queen of the Land of Egypt, on the pedestal of rose onyx. I stared at Catherine and then at the bust with startled surprise, I noticed that their faces were identical. I took Catherine in my arms and kissed her tenderly. Gloria, with tears in her eyes asked, "Are you two in love?"

What could I say? The afternoon and evening had been so unreal it was as though all three of us had been in a dream world. We had seen the pyramids, smelled the sweet roses in the Garden of Eden, tasted the sparkling wine in tall goblets that tinkled musically when we toasted each other, wondered at the Egyptian chauffeur who knew where to find the Rose Garden, and sensed the Presence of One who had made it all possible.

Catherine in the "Rose Garden."

"Dear God, let it last forever." There was such a peace and unbelievable atmosphere that seemed to cast a spell on us. Here was no snake, no cunning devil amidst the roses of Paradise. Here was love, tender love. I loved our loyal Gloria and the golden, blonde Catherine.

I gazed once more at the little statue on the table decked in white damask that showed drops of wine from when I had refilled our glasses. Suddenly, I remembered something Catherine had shared with me while we were sitting in the cockpit one evening in Paphos. Catherine was an Egyptian. Her father had come from this country. This was the land of her ancestors. Catherine had come home, and I had brought her here. It was I who had sailed her to the Land of Egypt.

Gloria and I must have been aware of something strange. It had hung elusively in the air and had followed us during the afternoon and evening. But Catherine had known all along. Catherine—Nefer-ti-ti—had the wife of Akhenaton returned in the blonde Catherine? Was she the re-incarnation of this Queen? Who could tell? They looked identical to us that evening, Catherine and Nefer-ti-ti.

Alas, a snake slithered through Paradise after all. It was called Time. Time had ticked away the hours and cast us now out of the

Garden of Eden. The taxi driver was waiting, *Trillium II* was waiting, and we had a long way to go.

I went to the restroom and when I came out, a cherub dressed in miniature coat-and-tails with a white starched collar and a bow-tie stood waiting. Little black eyes looked up at me innocently from an olive-skinned face. Then the little angel held out his arms and presented me with a freshly-laundered white towel.

With my arms around the shoulders of Gloria and Catherine, we reluctantly left Paradise. At the gate I said to them, "There are no angels with flaming swords here to prevent us from returning. But here is a little angel sent by Allah. Let's greet him." Bowing politely, he accepted his *baksheesh*, gracefully.

Back to Port Said, and bureaucracy

TAXI AND DRIVER waited at the curbside. The heat of the day had tempered. Coolness rushed in through the glassless windows. Again the chauffeur found his corner between the door and seat back. An esoteric calm accompanied us through the desert. We did not speak.

Halfway to Port Said, a shadow of the shed loomed up beside the road. Its doorway stood out in yellow light. The driver parked the vehicle and vanished inside, soon returning with the tasty ice cream. Again he went inside, but stayed away for quite a while. We became curious, so I stepped out of the car to investigate. The man was seated on a wooden chair, smoking a pipe with a long, straight stem and a bowl like a hollow chestnut. On top of the bowl glowed a little ball of opium. The room smelled like strong incense. I knew what was going on, but I wondered how long such a sitting would last.

Once behind the wheel, he drove straight on. We had expected drunken behaviour, but that was not the case. He must have been an experienced opium smoker.

At the barricades of the city limits, we were waved on by a lone soldier. It was well past midnight and we were dead tired, especially Gloria, although she had been fast asleep beside the driver. When we arrived at the ferry, I paid the man his fee plus something extra for the ice cream and the opium.

The ferry was still running and the guard at the marina was sound asleep in his rattan chair, his gun across his knees. We tip-toed past him, and on board Harry was waiting for us. That afternoon the whole crew had gone to the immigration office and paid four Egyptian pounds each to have some papers and their passports stamped. The officers also wanted to see us on our return from Cairo. We were not up to it. We just wanted to crawl into our bunks and sleep.

"Allah commands it," so let's go. We were requested to leave our passports until tomorrow. Angrily I shouted, "Tomorrow? It is already tomorrow! At nine o'clock our pilot comes aboard and we want to sail immediately. Here is 12 pounds for the three of us. Stamp the passports so we can go."

We should have known better. They said the stamp was in another office and the man who collected the money was not there either. It was impossible to stamp them tonight. Catherine and Gloria slumped on a bench in the hall and wept from exhaustion. While I argued with the officers, a servant treated us to a cup of tea. Finally, one of the younger officers took pity on Madam and Mademoiselle and motioned to me. "Come, Captain. Come with me in my car. We shall try to find the man with the stamp and the man who will collect your money."

At 1:00 A.M., we raced through the dark streets of Port Said. We stopped at bars and opium shacks in dead-end alleys. No men could be found. We drove to a building also belonging to Immigration, but there were no lights on and the double front doors were solidly closed. The young officer rattled the doors, but to no avail. Soon a police car came by to see what was going on. After some explanation, they picked up a screwdriver from their car and tried to force the door open. I could not believe my eyes. Police officers trying to break into an Immigration building just to get at one of those damned stamps.

Finally the young immigration officer said, "Let's go back, Captain. I have done my best. Give me the passports and the money. I will be personally responsible for it. I am on duty until eight. Send one of your people over at seven to pick up the stamped passports and clearances to leave Port Said." For a moment, I was speechless. Here stood a life-sized angel in front of me, not one with wings but with gold bars on his epaulettes. At the office, Gloria and Catherine had already left. Since the ferry had discontinued service for the night, my rescuer took me across in their launch. Inshallah, everything is in Allah's hands....

GLORIA AND CATHERINE stood in the open cockpit, as naked as the day they were born. With the marina's water hose, they rinsed dust and sweat from their bodies, and hopefully also the emotions of the day. In no time, they aimed the hose at their skipper, likewise clad only in his skin. It was heaven to be scrubbed and massaged by two beautiful nymphs. I thought it was an appropriate end to a very eventful day. The soldier in his chair, awakened by the splashing of water, looked on with interest. But it did not matter. It was 3:00 A.M. and still dark.

The friendly Egyptian immigration officer was true to his word. One of the Tina's had taken the first ferry across and was back before 9:00 A.M., waving passports and clearances. We could sail! But where was the pilot? When would he arrive? Tomorrow? When he got there at 10:00 A.M., we were pleasantly surprised. The two Tina's had the great honour of casting off the lines. With the diesel in reverse, I backed out of the marina, and *Trillium II* entered the Suez Canal. We were finally on our way.

Then, with horn blaring, the immigration launch approached from the other side, loaded with men in white uniforms, the gold embroidery on their caps glistening in the morning sun. What did they want now? Another round of stamps? *Baksheesh?* Harry, busy on the after deck, motioned me to swing *Trillium II* around. The launch bumped our starboard float. He secured their line with a half turn around a cleat. All the men jumped aboard our ship. They only wanted to wish us bon voyage and seal it with smacking kisses for everyone.

"Au revoir, Catherine. Goodbye, Gloria. Bon voyage, Harry. A safe arrival in India, Captain. Happy cruising to all of you." We had argued with them about passports and stamps. They had given us the run-around, but I believe we left some friends behind in that stinking, hot city called Port Said.

Djeddah–
A Harbour in Saudi Arabia

Djeddah (Jiddah), in Saudi Arabia, is a port on the Red Sea, 600 miles south of the Suez Canal, or halfway between Suez and the Strait of Babel-Mandeb. Thirty-five miles east of Djeddah, lies Mecca (Makkah), the holy city of all Moslems. Five times a day, followers of Mohammed the Prophet kneel on their prayer rugs, facing east. Since time past, white western men have been called Nazarani's, men from Nazareth, by them. It means as much as "Christian dogs," somebody to despise.

We made a landfall in Djeddah, but we were not left with good memories of that port. My advice is to stay away from Djeddah. Although we had business to do in Djeddah, we have regretted going there ever since. It is not a place for westerners.

THE EGYPTIAN PILOT who had accompanied us from Port Said seemed to be a very friendly man. He had asked to be allowed to steer *Trillium II*, and we had granted his request. Normally a pilot does not steer the ship he travels on, but a pleasure yacht was an exception to the rule. We thought we could sail the canal in one trek, but he informed us that it was not permitted to small ships and yachts. At Ishmalia, halfway through the canal, we stayed over one night.

Usually the pilot is given some *baksheesh* when leaving the ship, so after our ship had been secured in a harbour near Ishmalia, we handed him an envelope of American dollars and also a bag of goodies for his wife and children. With a beaming face, he said his goodbyes and stepped over into the launch that had come alongside to pick him up.

At 4:00 the next morning, the pilot-launch slammed against *Trillium II*, and a very noisy man stomped on deck before we had a chance to open our eyes. We woke up quickly when the new pilot announced an ultimatum: Sail now, or wait over two days. We had no choice. Within ten minutes, we were under way.

He had brought along some warm rolls, and after Gloria had made tea, we had breakfast at 5:00 A.M. The buttered rolls tasted good, and our new pilot seemed to be a jolly fellow.

Control posts were set up at regular intervals all along the Suez Canal. The pilot reported our passing by marine-radio telephone. Our previous pilot had not bothered to do this. Behind the posts were little man-made bays large enough to accommodate medium-sized ships. Suddenly, the man cornered me and demanded fifty American dollars. If he was not paid, he would steer *Trillium II* into one of the bays and chain her up. Harry and I both looked at him in astonishment. Fifty American dollars? It was pure blackmail. The man was a scoundrel.

After discussing the situation, Harry and I decided to pay the man what he asked. We did not want to inconvenience our passengers. It was naive on our part, but we were not used to such criminal behaviour. As if that weren't enough, he also wanted Harry's leather jacket that hung in the wheelhouse, Harry's diver's watch, and bags full of goods to take home. Harry refused to give him his jacket and watch. In the galley, he had demanded that Gloria prepare a special meal for him because he was a Moslem and could not eat our western food. A bottle of whiskey would go well with the "presents," he said.

Aha! We had him. Liquor was strictly forbidden for every Mohammedan. I found my captain's voice and angrily shouted at him, "I will report you to the authorities of the Suez Canal for blackmail and misbehaviour on board of my ship! I'll tell them you demanded whiskey. It will cost you your job!"

The rest of the way he was very tame and submissive. He took the wheel like his friendly predecessor had done. In Suez we had to clear customs because we were leaving Egypt. He followed me around like a dog that had been whipped, afraid I would make true my threat to report him.

A wrong turn in the Gulf of Suez

THE NEXT DAY, we sailed from the canal into the Gulf of Suez. In that gulf, we were introduced to suffocating heat that hung over the ship like a dome, making breathing difficult. One could not walk in bare feet over the decks without getting blisters. For the next two days, the wind was in our favour, but it did not bring any relief from the heat.

Djeddah, where Gloria planned to disembark, lay halfway up the Red Sea. According to information we had received in Paphos, coral reefs blocked a direct approach to the harbour. We did not own a large-scale chart to navigate the channels between the reefs. There was a small yacht harbour a few miles to the north of Djeddah that we could try. We sailed for seven days from the Gulf of Suez to Djeddah. Seven days in a savage, burning sun, seven days of cranky Tina's and a sulking KLM man. We had put the beer on ration. Thank God we had Gloria and Catherine to boost our spirits.

We missed the small yacht harbour and had the port of Djeddah in the bearing. Harbour control was called, but we received no reply. Between us and the port lay the Ten Mile Reef. We didn't dare get any closer. The ship was turned north in search of a better place to land. We scanned the coastline, and soon we saw buildings and also a small inlet with one concrete pier. Hesitatingly, we cruised up and down the mouth of the inlet. It did not seem too inviting.

Little brown men appeared on the mole and pointed to their feet, a universal signal that we could come in and land. For some reason, Harry and I did not feel right and Gloria was very uneasy. The men at the mole did not look trustworthy, and after our experience at Port Said, we had become suspicious of anything to do with Arabs.

Our premonitions were correct. We had hardly thrown our line around some cleats on the mole when at least fifteen buffoons jumped on deck yelling, "We plice, we plice!" (police). In their dirty bare feet, they stomped over the decks and snooped in the cabins. One of the bandits discovered our stock of liquor and ordered us to set all the bottles on the table. He started counting them, but in all probability he could not count beyond ten. It was quite a while before he finished.

We were commanded to go ashore and stand on the mole where an armed soldier guarded us. There were no houses in sight except some barrack-type buildings. From one of them emerged a military man in khaki battle dress with knife-sharp creases in his trouser legs. He introduced himself as the captain of the garrison, and asked why we were there. This was not a yacht harbour and foreign yachts never landed here. Gloria explained that her husband worked for the American aircraft company, Northrop, and was stationed in Saudi Arabia. She asked permission to phone him so he would know where she was and could pick her up.

I was then questioned as to the reason we had not gone directly to Djeddah. We told him we had called Djeddah but had not received a reply. We had not dared to cross the Ten Mile Reef because we had no chart. The captain was a friendly and understanding man. He asked us to wait on the mole while he took Gloria with him. Most of the "plice" had dispersed except for the bandit in the saloon still counting bottles. The soldier with his rifle stayed to guard us.

Four men came from a barrack. Two of them carried a rolled-up carpet and the others had large baskets with them. They said we were the captain's guests and rolled out the carpet on the concrete and invited us to sit down, without shoes, please. Out of the baskets came all the wonder of an occidental kitchen, worthy of a rich oil sheik. The mood of our crew had improved greatly during the meal of unknown delicacies. The servants continually filled our cups with the customary sweet, black tea.

I was annoyed about the fellow in the saloon, so Catherine and I went below to check on him. There he was, with all the bottles uncorked, stone drunk, still counting. I took him by the arm and guided him back ashore, where he swayed and retched on the edge of the mole. I secretly hoped he would fall into the deep six.

I made my way back to the carpet with its intrinsic, oriental pattern. Exotic and dried fruits were invitingly arrayed. This was a strange situation we had ended up in. Even the tasty treats could not expel my misgivings as to what had happened to Gloria. She had been gone for quite a while.

Harry and Catherine were taking pictures of the unbelievable happening on that mole, but the sentry quickly tore the cameras out of their hands. Presently, Gloria returned with the captain. She had not been able to get through, but had left a message for her husband telling him that she was in Saudi Arabia.

Lunch was over, the carpet rolled up, and the captain ordered his servants to carry the leftovers to our ship. He accompanied us and when he saw the uncorked bottles, he understood what had occurred. He told us to put our supplies away and under no circumstances were we to allow any of those bandits on board again.

The Arabic captain was a gentleman. He had arranged a pilot for us so we could sail to Djeddah. We were to stay for the night, and the next day we would be able to leave. Only then would our cameras be returned. Since it was a military harbour, photographs were off limits. Our tomorrow had a surprise in store for us.

Early the following morning, the two servants arrived with baskets. That gift from the captain contained fresh fruit, canned rations, cream, milk, cheese, figs, freshly baked rolls, and butter. There was enough to feed the entire crew for at least two days. The servants, with a few American dollars in their pockets, left happily with the empty baskets.

At eight o'clock, the captain arrived with our pilot. Behind him stood two grim-faced soldiers, heavily armed with machine guns and semi-automatic pistols in their holsters. They posted themselves in the cockpits, one at each side.

Our faces fell. Was it necessary to have such an armed consort? The captain nodded to the soldiers, "Orders from Djeddah." He gripped my hand and wished us all a safe voyage. "Allah be with you, Captain," were his parting words.

The soldiers were surly, hostile fellows, but the Arab pilot was worth his weight in gold. He chatted with Harry incessantly and guided us safely through the coral reefs. We called the harbour control and this time we got a reply. Our estimated time of arrival was reported, and a voice with a clipped English accent acknowledged.

Outside the Ten Mile Reef, ten or more freighters were anchored in the roadstead. The harbour itself was a huge complex of piers, cranes, docks and dry-docks, and numerous buildings.

That same voice directed us to a more distant section of the port. A welcoming committee was present at the quay. People in burnous, others in more western dress, and of course, the inevitable armed and unfriendly military were there to greet us. While we were busy securing the ship to the quay, shouts were heard coming from the mob. We felt the hatred in their voices, and heard the word "Nazarani" for the first time in our lives.

Gloria, pale and frightened, explained that women were not to be seen in the open. They had to go below even though the saloon was like an oven and there was no breeze. The Tina's did not heed Gloria's warning, and I paid the consequences for that later.

The Arab world is a man's world. They keep their womenfolk hidden behind veils and concrete walls. They are always clad in the *hyab*, a tent-like robe which conceals every trace of the female outline. Women must produce sons and are forbidden any sexual pleasures, hence the mutilation of their reproductive organs. Our ship was a Canadian ship from a free world where women had the same rights as men. Why, then, should we hide our women?

Men in blue coveralls approached us. They were English, hired to organize the shipping in the harbour, and loading and unloading of ships that bring in the products of the western world. Saudi Arabia buys unprecedented quantities of farm equipment, bulldozers, tractors, trucks, tanks, and other war machines. They pay with the petrol-dollar. Arabs had the money, but lacked the expertise to handle the flow of import. The English Nazaranis had taken on that task.

Arab interrogators and an English guardian angel

One of those Englishmen would later become our guardian angel and the liberator of *Trillium II* and her crew. It was obvious we were being detained, but for what?

The soldiers who had been on board were replaced by two others who sat on deck with rifles across their knees. The crowd on the quay grew steadily, and became louder by the minute. Would they attack us in a Islamic frenzy of "Death to the Christian dogs!" if abused? In such a case, I hoped the soldiers on our ship would defend us.

Our English friend returned and explained that we had been suspected of being spies for Israel. We had been condemned before any hearing had taken place. By setting Gloria ashore, we had been accused of infiltrating the land of Arabia. "Death to all Israelis and their western spies. Death to the Americans!" notwithstanding, we prominently flew our Canadian flag high in the mast.

Harry was not at all intimidated by all the commotion. When the guards began to walk over our decks with their hob-nailed shoes, he shouted at them and pointed to the gashes they had made in the paint. He told them to guard us from the quay-side, which, to our amazement, they did. They seated themselves on the heavy iron bollards with their rifles on their knees. The whole thing seemed so ridiculous.

A jeep drove down the quay, carrying two armed soldiers. They wanted the captain of the ship to come along to speak to the port captain. When I boarded the jeep, the Englishman jumped in beside me. "I will go with you. You need me," he said. The captain of the port was a huge Arab with hands like shovels and a behind like a beer barrel.

In spite of the animosity, tea was brought in and it tasted so good in the brutal, desert heat. After the first cup, the Arab flung wild accusations at me, half in poor English and half in Arabic. I looked over at my friend, and he translated for me. "They have not seen your ship on their radar. You had not called harbour control. You wanted to put someone ashore. Your ship has come straight from Israel. You are a spy for Israel. Now you better confess."

I looked the port captain straight in the eye and said, "I will not confess to anything. None of your accusations are true." For a moment it seemed as though he would explode, but then he ranted on about throwing me into jail, The Englishman warned me to watch my words. The man would do what he said. Then my friend spoke to the Arab in a pacifying manner and the bully calmed down.

It was time to call upon Allah. The table around which we were sitting was pushed aside with my English friend's and my help. A prayer mat was taken from a wall closet and spread on the floor. The Arab fell to his knees and began praising Allah, the Compassionate, Allah, the Omniscient, and His Holy Prophet, Mohammed. The session with Allah lasted about fifteen minutes. We, the two Nazaranis, waited timidly against the wall, It gave us an opportunity to collect our thoughts.

When the prayer mat had been stowed away and the table put back in place, there was another round of drinking tea. Then the port captain started a new kind of interrogation. He wrote down a question in Arabic and passed it to the Englishman, who scribbled the translation underneath. I was expected to write my answer and sign it. It was a time-consuming process, but it allowed me a moment to discuss it with my friend and come to a decision. Each time we returned the paper to him, his beady, black eyes would stare right through me, but I would stare back at him just as hard.

Categorically, I denied the charges and explained why.

They had not seen my ship on radar: I replied that my ship was built from wood. Radar beams penetrate wood but it does not throw back an echo. That was the reason we were not seen.

We had not contacted harbour control by radio: to that, I explained that we had called several times on the proper frequency, but had not received a reply. We had wanted to get bearings or radar guidance to sail through the Ten Mile Reef, but without radio contact, we did not dare to cross the coral banks.

To the accusation of spying on their military installations, I told him we had mistaken the small military harbour for a yacht marina and had landed of our own free will in broad daylight.

When questioned about setting an American spy ashore, I informed him that there were no spies on board of *Trillium II*. We had simply taken Gloria to her home which was here in Saudi Arabia, in a place called Khamis Muskayt. Her husband was employed in their country. Gloria had a legal visa, passport, and other papers to prove her residence.

To the charges of being American spies, I answered in our defense that we were not spying for anyone. We were Canadians with Canadian passports and our ship was registered in Canada. We also had four Dutch people on board, one of whom wished to return to the Netherlands.

He seemed to accept each of my written replies. Then I asked if our agent would be permitted to take a plane back to the Netherlands. I thought he would jump out of his skin, and again my friend advised me not to pursue the matter. He had taken it the wrong way.

At that moment, a scooter stopped at the door and a young, rat-faced fellow entered the room and reported something to the captain. His brown face became purple and he shouted at me, "Those whores you have on your ship are flirting with my guards. Get into the jeep and go back to the harbour. If you cannot control them, I'll sling you into prison. I'll manacle you, you Nazarani!"

My English friend and I jumped into the jeep and raced back to the quay, where there was still a throng of belligerent Arabs watching my ship. Sure enough, the two Tinas were on deck and I told them in no uncertain terms to go below. Harry's face lit up. I had been away for five hours and he had not known where I had been taken. I assured him that everything would be fine. I hoped to be finished with the port captain soon.

We returned to the office and my friend looked very pale and concerned. "Something is wrong," he said as we sat down. The interrogation started all over and the port captain told us that he had turned our report over to his superiors. We would be informed in the morning as to what our fate would be. I politely thanked him, but at the door I turned and asked, "We are low in provisions, captain. May we get some tomorrow?" He acted as though he were having a heart attack. My friend pulled me outside and back to the jeep. "He will cut off your head! Let's get out of here before he calls us back."

We were in luck. We heard him move the table. It was time to kneel, head toward Mecca. In-sha-allah.

Trillium II ... OUT!

WHAT TERRIBLE CRIME had we committed to be interrogated for an entire day? What was the meaning of all the threats and abuse? What was the cause of the display of power and hatred against a small ship and a few men and women from western countries? Could it be fear of Israel? I think that was one reason and the other reason...Islaam. Allah is the Compassionate, but not for Nazaranis. Every action of the last two days would not have stirred the least bit of interest in the western world, but here it had been intolerable and treated like an unforgivable crime.

My crew heaved a sigh of relief when they saw me stepping out of the jeep. Even the two Tina's had been worried. My friend came aboard with me and advised me to write a letter of apology to the port captain. He assured me the worst was probably over and that everything would turn out fine. He was familiar with the behaviour of that bully and he expected that we would be given permission to leave. With that, he was gone, but within half an hour he was back with a friend carrying baskets loaded with fruit. They had passed the hat around and this was the yield. He also had a photocopy of the approach chart of the harbour. With the aid of that chart, we would be able to cross the reef with a minimum of risk to the ship.

The next morning there were still two soldiers posted at the ship, but they were no longer armed. It was a good sign. Soon a harbour official gave us permission to move the ship to where we could fill our water tanks. A desert Arab may be one's worst enemy, but he will never refuse to give one water. That is the unwritten law of the desert.

Gloria invited the soldiers into the cockpit and presented them with glasses of apple juice that looked suspiciously like whiskey. Along came young Ratface, the harbour spy, who stopped his scooter, jumped aboard, and snatched a glass out of the hand of one of the soldiers. He sniffed at it and took a sip. He was out of luck. I kicked him off the deck, literally, and the soldiers smiled, raising their glasses in a toast of recognition.

Later in the day, Gloria's husband arrived to pick her up. Because I had tried to "smuggle" her into the country, there were many formalities to go through. Finally, all the problems were solved and Gloria's husband was given permission to take her home with him. Down below, in the hot saloon, we said our good-byes to her. We didn't dare kiss her on deck. That would have been an unpardonable sin.

Our agent from Harlingen did not get permission to leave for Holland. He had to remain with us until our next landfall, which would be Djibouti, in the French part of Somalia. The Tina's and Hank, the KLM man, tarred with the same brush of impatience and chagrin about the delay, became antagonistic and discontented. There were complaints about not enough cold beer and why, for heaven's sake, had we landed in this out of the way place? I could not stand another minute of their whining. Angrily I shouted, "Shut up! Shut up! I have already told you that the trek through the Red Sea would be difficult." As an after-thought I added, "Shut up from now on or get off my ship!"

The last part was nonsense on my part. No one could leave the ship. I had fallen out of my role as the unperturbed captain— understandably. I had had my full share of misery. Without my three pillars of support, Harry, Gloria and Catherine, I don't think I would have made it.

We were not in the clear yet. There was no official permission to leave and passports had still not been returned. After lunch, an obese sergeant delivered all the necessary documents— unstamped. We had to go to a specific office to have that done. He said he would send a jeep with driver to finish the last proceedings. The jeep arrived, Harry and I hopped in, but the driver did not know where to find that particular office. For two hours, we drove around an immense complex of government buildings around the harbour works.

The driver took us back to the sergeant who was half asleep behind his desk. He offered to phone to find out what was going on. In one hand he held the phone, and in the other, a hose connected to a water pipe from which he inhaled puffs of smoke. It was a long one-way conversation, and then Harry noticed that he was fast asleep. What else could we do but wait? In walked our Guardian Angel and asked us how we were making out. We pointed toward the sleeping sergeant. He motioned for us to follow him. Outside, he pulled the (also sleeping) driver from his seat in the jeep, took his place without much ado, and off we went. Within half an hour, we had all the stamps we needed. Finally we could leave. There was still half an hour of daylight left when our friend dropped us off at the quay. "Goodbye," he said, "I will go to the radar station and guide you to open water. Leave directly. Leave now."

Before jumping aboard, Harry and I had already whipped the lines from the bollards. Harry started the engine, and I turned on the radio. News travels fast. The quay was full of English people in blue coveralls, waving us out. Not one hostile man was in sight. The Arabs had lost all interest in us.

In the dusk of the evening, with the help of the chart and guided by the radar information, we were outside the Ten Mile Reef in less than two hours, and in the open waters of the Red Sea. Thankfully, we reported to the radar operator and closed radio contact with the usual phrase—"*Trillium II*...Out!"

POSTA SCRIPTA: My dear English friend in blue coveralls. Man from Albion, I do not know your name, but I would like to write it in gold. Your unselfish assistance was a sublime example of human greatness. You did not ask the why or the wherefore. You were always there when we needed you most. Your deeds are written down in our ship's log book and in this Book of the Sea. But most important of all, may the God of all people have your name written in His Book— the Book of Compassion.

From Djiboutie to the Maldives

Island of dreams...silver white beaches...whispering palm trees...moonlight and shadows...wavelets murmuring over the coral reefs....

In Djibouti, a port on the northwest point of French Somalia, our agent from Harlingen took a plane back to Holland. He could not stand the heat any longer and he had business to tend to. We had left Gloria in Djeddah, in the care of her husband.

Worst of all, we lost our sweet Catherine, too. It was so hard to say goodbye to her. We took her to the airport to catch her flight to Paris. The parting was heartbreaking. Together, Harry and I, Gloria and Catherine, had been through many predicaments that had bonded us strongly. Every farewell means a bit of dying, losing someone dear to your heart. But we had to sail on. Our destinations were still far below the horizon to the Maldives, Sri Lanka, India, and the Far East.

With sadness in our hearts, Harry and I set sail from Djibouti, pointing the bows of *Trillium II* eastward. For six days we tackled the tremendous heat in the Gulf of Aden. For six days there was no wind, and the sun burned like hot, melting copper from a white sky. For six days we lived with an impossible crew who refused to do any work. They had paid for a cruise, not for wheelwatches. Why should they do any work?

Hank, from the KLM, demanded cold beer, and the two Tina's expected the ship to stop a few times a day so they could have a swim. Harry sneered, "Listen, girls. If we stop the ship five or six times a day, we will never make the Maldives. But you are welcome to jump overboard and swim to those islands." He also had a solution to their unwillingness to help with the watches and the galley chores. He cooked a pot of rice big enough to last for at least three days. Good for you, Harry. Three days of rice, curry, and pepper will keep the malaria at bay.

SIXTEEN MILES to the north of the island of Sokotra lay a very important point. The sea chart indicated it has a rendezvous point for all the shipping to and from the Red Sea. Sixteen miles was just the range of our radar. Once that point was reached, we would be out of the Gulf of Aden and entering the Arabian Sea. We had heard tell that Sokotra was an island of pirates. A ship sailing too closely was taking the chance of being boarded by the bandits. As the story goes, they even attacked tankers and freighters. They probably had radar on the island to scan for unsuspecting passing vessels. They would come in super-fast speedboats, throw a grapple over the railing, and climb aboard like monkeys. Whatever was on deck would be taken. The crew of the ship stayed in their quarters, doors locked. To go on deck and try to chase the pirates away was suicide. They were well-armed and known cutthroats. Sharks always like a piece of fresh seaman's meat.

We kept our distance, and at the expected time the radar showed the coast of Sokotra at the 16-mile range. As the island is 100 miles long, it would take a full night's sail to pass it. Harry revved up the diesel from its usual 2400 rpm to 2800. The sooner we were away from the island, the better. The crew agreed wholeheartedly. Even Hank volunteered to take a wheelwatch. A steady

Keeping a distance from bandits

radar watch was kept, but the night passed peacefully with no pirates in sight.

It was a bit late in the season to traverse the Arabian Sea and part of the Indian Ocean. The southwest monsoon was due any time. Once we were from under the lee of Africa, it might hit us in full force. In the Gulf of Aden we had had no wind whatsoever, not even for one hour. Harry and I were pleased to have a new diesel installed. That machine ran smoothly for seven days without missing a beat.

Late in the afternoon of the day we had passed Sokotra, small ripples appeared on the sea's surface. The "cat's paws," forerunners of the wind to come, had arrived. The sun's glare on the water disappeared and a grey tone matted the surface. First we felt a zephyr on our cheeks. Then a light breeze from the southwest brought cooler air. The cat's paws changed to little waves that nibbled and lapped at *Trillium*'s sides. The ripples became slapping waves. Monsoon weather had reached us. Far out on that immense Indian Ocean, something lay in wait for us: a large low-pressure area—*la Niña*—that would determine the weather for the next six months. Something else also lay in wait for us, but it was not the monsoons. It was far more deadly...coral reefs.

Gusts of wind followed. Harry and the two girls hoisted the sails—jib, mains'l, and mizzen. *Trillium II* picked up speed, heeled over to port, and the water under the wing decks began to gurgle. It was music to our ears. Nine knots! This was sailing! For ten days we had the passat in our canvas. Every day ticked off 180 to 200 sea miles. Sometimes we had a downpour in the afternoon, and in the evening, thunder and lightning on the horizon. The sun sank in a welter of colours, bright and unusual, mostly yellow.

It lasted for ten days, then it was over. The wind died down to a steady, light breeze. The heavy mains'l was taken down and replaced with a light genoa.

The Maldives could not be far off anymore....

The attitude of the passengers changed. They became more pleasant and manageable. What had they expected, a cruise ship with waiters in frocks to serve cold beer at their beck and call? Hank attended breakfast in a floral housecoat and a sash with tassels. Harry and I smiled about this absurdity at sea. Breakfast was no more than hot porridge with sugar and a bit of butter that melted into a yellow puddle. Since Djibouti we hadn't had bread. Long ago, our cook Gloria had risen at 6:00 each morning to bake fresh rolls and scones. We ate them hot from the oven. Now, Hank gagged on the oatmeal porridge. Our stores were depleting; that was all there was.

Because Hank and the girls refused to perform their wheel-watches at night, Harry and I divided that duty. But early in the morning we were given a reward. The decks were covered with fly-ing fish that had jumped on board during the night. We cleaned them, flopped them into the frying pan, and five minutes later, we enjoyed the finest sea breakfast we could think of. No night watches, no treats, dear passengers....

Many times we had noticed the girls going through our stores. If they found tins of fruit, they would take them to their cabin. At last, Harry hid all the fruit that was left. We liked it too. Hardly a word passed between us except to give orders pertaining to the ship's navigation or sail changes. Harry and I felt like lost souls on board of our own ship, but deliverance was in sight. The passen-gers had all planned to leave in the Maldives, and that was the best news we had heard in a long time.

Only 100 miles to go. Only 100 miles to Malé, the capital of the Maldives. With some navigational calculations, we concluded that we would arrive at the atoll at night. That was unfortunate for us. The *Pilot*, the seaman's bible, had explained all about the dan-gers of the coral reefs, especially the heavy risk of approaching at night. The solution was to remain at sea during the night and lose time by reducing sail and therefore speed. There was still a hun-dred miles to go, lots of sea room.

A storm of protest arose from Hank and the two girls. They asked for the diesel to be turned on so we could arrive just before dark. I did not answer. Harry turned his back to them and said, "Tonight, we stay at sea." Grumbling and sulking, they retreated to their cabins, only to show up for meal time. Clearly and simply, it was mutiny, and as such it was entered into the ship's log.

HARRY WENT ON DECK and dropped the genoa. Under jib and reefed mizzen, we had just enough speed to handle the ship. Four or five knots was just fine. We stayed on an easterly course, but what we were doing was completely, awfully wrong. We did not have 100 miles to go, we were nearing the deadly reefs...and we did not know it.

At 4:00 A.M. I took over the watch from Harry. The ship, so very well balanced, sailed herself and we drank our usual cup of tea together, sitting in the cockpit. The night was dark, but with the light of the stars we could see clouds high in the sky. The

Danger from the coral reefs

wheelhouse doors were open on both sides. The atmosphere was clammy. We were right at the edge of monsoon territory. In the wake of the ship, plankton sparkled in rainbow colours, illuminating the sea.

Tea finished, I seated myself behind the wheel and checked the compass. Harry had trimmed the sails perfectly. The ship had not wavered off her intended course. The spokes rested lightly in my hands. The radar was on standby, and before Harry turned in, he switched the range from 16 miles to eight, to four, and then to two miles. Everything in that particular range would show up clearly.

The radar beam searched the surface of the sea and caught something. Harry's back blocked my view of the radar screen, but he noticed something on a quarter mile dead ahead—a jagged line, a coral reef with the surf breaking over it. Thinking quickly, he pushed me aside and grabbed for the wheel, turning it hard over to starboard. We were lucky the ship had enough momentum to bring her bow through the eye of the wind. The booms smacked to the other side and *Trillium II* sailed away on a westward course, away from the fatal coral reefs.

Within five minutes, we would have been driven over the razor-sharp edges. The hulls would have been split wide open from stem to stern. It would have meant the death of our ship and in all probability, the death of us, too. Harry handed the wheel back to me, stuttering, "That was a close call, Skipper, a very close call." His face was ashen. I wondered what had prompted him to turn the range to two miles so we could see the danger clearly. All I knew was that he was at the right place at the right time. His sea-sense had saved our ship and all of its crew.

Harry did not return to his bunk. Sleep was far from him. First the fear and shock had to wear off. He posted himself at the radar. If our passengers had wakened by the sudden manoeuvres, we never knew, but none of them had come on deck to see what was happening. In the morning, we did not bother to let them know that their lives had balanced on the edge of Eternity. Gradually the image of the coral reef disappeared from the screen. After about five miles we dropped all sails and waited for daylight. A greyness showed on the eastern horizon. It could not be far off.

At 6:00 A.M. the sun broke from the horizon and silhouettes of islands rested on the skyline. Palm trees, like black filigrees, stood out against a bright sky. Harry had rolled the sails around the booms and also put the blue covers over them. The genoa, still lying on the foredeck, was replaced in its bag and dropped into the forward hold.

Everything was ship-shaped in Bristol fashion. I started up the diesel and cautiously moved closer to the atolls. On the chart, I had set out a course from the rendezvous point north of Sokotra to Rasdu. There the transit of the Arabian Sea would be completed. Every day I had made corrections on the compass course with the aid of running fixes. We must be close.

What we saw before us could not be Rasdu. We laid the chart of the Maldives on the deck and tried to compare the profiles of the islands and atolls with the drawings on the chart. We were aware we needed to be careful in doing that. One was inclined to make things fit to the detriment of being wrong.

Were we too far north or too far south? The two girls had woken early to help us look. It turned out we were too far south, so at a slow pace, depth sounder whirring, we coursed north at two cables' distance from the dreadful reefs. After a couple of hours, Rasdu came into sight. We were in the four-and-a-half degree channel. We could head for Malé without any further trouble. After navigating the Arabian Sea for more than 1,200 sea miles, to be off by only ten miles was not much. But where reefs are concerned, it was too much, way, way too much. Had it been bad navigation on my part or had an unknown current set us off that far?

That afternoon we turned into the harbour of Malé. Suddenly, the depth sounder indicated a zero. We were aground. The harbour was very shallow with a bottom of mud. We backed out to deeper water, and at a safe distance, threw our anchor out. There the water was so deep we could not reach the bottom with the length of anchor rope we had available. After drifting around for awhile, we saw four soldiers waving at us from the mole. They jumped into a runabout and headed straight for us at full speed. Would this be Port Said or Djeddah all over again?

No. The soldiers were friendly. Though armed with small pistols, they remained in their holsters. The lieutenant of the group kindly informed us in perfect English that the harbour was only suitable for the proas of fishermen, not for yachts. We explained to him that the water was too deep where we had dropped our anchor. Help sprung from an unexpected corner.

HANK REMEMBERED about an island he had visited the year previously. It had a hotel, and more importantly, a pier for mooring. Everyone's face lit up, including those of the soldiers. The lieutenant offered to take us there. He expertly navigated his craft through the atoll of North Malé and within an hour we were at our

Kurumba, the coral island

destination—the coral island of Kurumba.

A rickety pier jutted out just beyond the coral. The soldiers and some people from the hotel helped us with our mooring lines. The lieutenant hopped aboard and asked for our signal pistols, telling us he would return them when we were leaving. The hotel manager also came aboard and he said he would phone Customs and Immigration to give us clearance. Once the formalities were out of the way, we were welcome at his hotel, the first drink on the house.

The Customs and Immigration officers had to come from Malé Island, a half-hour trip by motorboat. On that island was also Hulule International Airport. We had to wait for them before we could disembark at Kurumba.

The two Tinas became bothersome again. They wanted to go ashore immediately. I had to raise my captain's voice: "Not until the officers from Immigration and Customs have been here." The manager of the hotel was right. In thirty minutes they came alongside. They were dressed neatly in marine blue pants and white shirts. The two women wore blue skirts and white blouses. Not one speck of gold could be seen. There were no shoulder pads or white caps with gold embroidery. Their uniforms were clean and simple.

Gratefully, they accepted a cola from our refrigerator. They stamped our passports, allowing us three months' stay in the Maldives. It was only for designated islands that were open for western tourists. The rest of the 1,200 islands (not all are inhabited) were forbidden to vacationers. With many thanks, they left and wished us a pleasant stay which, by the way, we did have. It must have been a compensation for the weeks of annoyance and wretchedness by having those mutineers aboard *Trillium II*.

During all of the activity, Harry had managed to cook up a pot of hash. Our guests devoured it greedily, and then trooped ashore, leaving the dishes for Harry and me to clean. At 10:00 P.M., we were finished and we made our way to the hotel to have our free drink. The hotel was no more than a verandah with a roof of palm leaves, and the bar in the back was only a straw hut. With our free drinks in hand, we looked for a place to sit under the palm trees or on the beach of silvery-white sand. Twenty-five or thirty guests had already found deck chairs and were parked in a large circle around the bar. Speakers hidden high in the palm trees produced soft, melodious music. In the week we stayed on the island, we never heard pop music, pounding rock, or the nasal whining of eastern instruments. The hotel manager must have been a very sensitive man.

The Tinas chatted with other young people, and Hank told us

they had eaten a nice dinner at the restaurant. Harry and I did not react. The three of them had rented cabins, and told us they would come aboard later to pick up their belongings. That was good news, and Harry clapped his hands sarcastically.

Trillium II was not moored properly at the ramshackle pier, so the next morning we took her out to deeper waters and dropped a hook. It held securely in the sandy bottom, which was about 40 fathoms. The ship was safe and we were at ease.

Harry was enjoying himself and had already made friends. We did not eat aboard. We found out it was cheaper to eat at the restaurant and we did not have to bother in the ship's galley. Hank and the Tinas approached us once more. They wanted a refund for the unused portion of the cruise. We told them that they were staying behind on the island of their own free will. There would be no reimbursement. I said to Harry, "Come, mate. Let's celebrate our new freedom at the bar."

THAT WEEK we sat always at the same table to eat our meals. Next to us was a friendly, attractive lady who usually dined alone, but sometimes she was in the company of a younger man. I mentioned to Harry that it wasn't nice to let her sit alone, and once, after a meal, I went to her table and invited her to share a bottle of wine with us. She rose so quickly that her chair fell over. Politely, I picked it up and shoved it back under the table. The bartender had looked on with a smile, and without being asked, brought a clean wine glass to our table.

Another friendly German lady

We engaged in a delightful, animated conversation with her and learned that Ingrid was from Germany, from the city of Mainz on the Rhine. Her husband owned a TV repair shop and she also worked in his business. It had kept them so busy that there had never been time to take holidays. Her son had generously treated her to this vacation. She could still not believe that she was on a beautiful, tropical island. To top it all off, she was sitting at a table of world-renowned sailors.

We did not consider ourselves world renowned, we told her modestly. Frieda from Hamburg had used those same words when we met her in Helgoland in the North Sea. When the wine bottle was empty, we invited her to keep us further company in the chairs under the palm trees. Harry would order a banana split from the slender man at the bar. We found empty seats at the beach and gazed out over the ocean where a crescent moon drew a path of yellow light from the horizon to the ripples over the coral bars.

Trillium II lay to at a cable's distance from the island, impassive and indifferent to the romance of the evening. Moonlight peeked through the palm trees while the leaves rustled in the soft breeze.

Harry had gone to sit somewhere else and the conversation between me and Ingrid had stilled to a dreamy murmur as we looked out over the sea. Soft dance music floated from the speakers. The only dance floor was the warm sand of the beach. Her hands hung loosely over the arm rests of the lawn chair. I reached out and took her by the hand. It was warm and dry and soft. Without saying a word, we both stood outside the circle of the other guests, and shuffled to the tune of the music, barefoot in the warm sand. She squeezed her body softly against me and I placed my cheek against her head. Her hair smelled fresh, like the sea, the salt, and the scent of heather. The evening was like a fantasy. We felt like we were dancing in a dream world where we never had to wake up.

THE NEXT MORNING, Harry picked up Ingrid and her son at the beach and rowed them to the ship. Ingrid could hardly believe her eyes at all the luxury and comfort of an ocean-going vessel. Harry gave them the grand tour. Ingrid was speechless and sat down on the settee with a bewildered expression in her nice eyes. We offered them a Dutch beer, and later the son asked Harry to row him back to the beach. He had met a girl on the island and wanted to spend time with her before a rival got the chance. Ingrid remained on board and begged me to tell her about our adventures on the Seven Seas and roaming around the world so carefree. The sailor's live, with its liberty, was beyond her comprehension.

The pretty, slim woman was also a revelation to me. She had longed for a world she had never known, and run into it, head first. The city of Mainz, in remote Germany, no longer existed for her. The here and now, this little Paradise, this was her reality, her truth. Germany and her TV business had become completely forgotten. Her forget-me-not blue eyes were misty. Only last night had we become acquainted. This morning she leaned against me on the settee hanging on my every word. She seemed to be hungry for a life she had never known existed.

Fair, blonde, of Nordic descent, I imagined her blue eyes could be cool and collected. Had she shown passion before she landed on the island of Kurumba? Had she been asleep all her life, hidden away in the dark recesses of her very being? Did she realize that she had awakened like a beautiful Sleeping Beauty? I was the lucky one to see the real Ingrid, the Ingrid who had matured overnight into a very desirable woman. She herself was desirous and longing, longing to escape the monotony of her daily life in Germany. Ingrid took my face in her soft hands and gazed straight into my eyes. "I don't want to leave," she whispered. "I want to stay with you, sail with you, always." The bumping of the sloop against *Trillium II* interrupted the moment. The three of us returned to the island for lunch.

In the heat of the afternoon, Ingrid went to her cabin for a sièsta. Harry and I walked around the shore just within the shade of the palm trees where the sand was cool. I was very quiet, and finally Harry asked, "Is something wrong, Skipper? Is there a problem?" "No, my boy. What could be wrong?" My voice was unsure, and Harry sensed it. We had travelled together too long to hide our feelings from each other. Then I added, "Day after tomorrow, we go under sail again, Harry. You are the best first mate there is, son. I am so happy to have you aboard our good ship, *Trillium II*."

Harry looked at me with astonishment and disappointment. He could not help asking, "Sailing already? But Skipper, we like it here. Why can't we stay a few days longer?"

That evening, the three of us found it difficult to make conversation. Each of us struggled with our own thoughts. Harry did not want to leave. Ingrid wanted to come with us...but what did I want? Should we leave the day after tomorrow? We truly enjoyed this island. Could we remain just a few more days? Ingrid was unaware of my plan for departure, but I could not bring myself to tell her at this time. I would wait until the next evening.

After dinner, Ingrid and I walked to our seats and sat under the palms. The crescent moon loomed over the far horizon, silently climbing the heavens. Music played from somewhere in the trees and the murmur of voices could be heard in the background of this romantic island. That night, we did not dance. Ingrid stroked my hand that rested on the arm of her chair. Had I actually just met her last night? It seemed as though I had known her since time began. We clasped hands and beheld the wide expanse of ocean, the moon high in the faded blue sky, and the surf lapping at our feet.

Not far from us, our ship rocked slowly, contentedly on the calm ocean. She had experienced other oceans, wild and furious. Ingrid wished she could sail away on her, not return to Germany, to Mainz on the Rhine. Poor, beautiful Ingrid.

THE HEAT OF THE DAY had long since passed as we walked through the warm coral sand of the beach. Our little sloop was pulled high out of reach of the surf where Harry had left it. Slowly, Ingrid and I strolled around the island, arms around each other. The sea surrounded us on all sides. When we returned to the place where the sloop had been, it was not there. Harry had gone back to the ship. The evening had lapsed into midnight. All the guests had retired to their cabins, the bar closed, the music silent.

Harry, my friend, my best first mate, had understood. Ingrid looked up at me with eyes that sparkled like stars. Ingrid, the lovely blonde girl from a land in the far, cold north. I couldn't resist reciting a poem that originated in the mysterious east. My voice quavered as Ingrid listened with the glistening eyes to the words that had been written so long ago on the banks of the sacred river Ganges, in India.

> Da hupfen herbei, und lauschen
> Die frommen, klugen Gazellen;
> Und in der Ferne rauschen
> Des Heiligen Stromes Wellen...
> Da wollen wir niedersinken
> Unter den Palmenbaum,
> Und Ruhe und Liebe trinken
> Und traument seligen Traum.

> *Swift jumping by, listening sharp,*
> *The quiet, shy gazelles;*
> *And far away murmurs*
> *The sacred river Ganges.*
> *There we will lie down*
> *Under the palm tree, repose,*
> *Taste the tenderness of love*
> *And dream sweet dreams.*
> *Come, my love, come.*

Ingrid pressed herself against me and I could feel the warmth of her body, the softness of her full breasts. She was shaking, and so was I. "Komm, Lieber Jerry," she breathed softly, "Kommst du?" Together we faded into the night beneath the silhouettes of palm trees that sighed in the gentle, ocean breeze.

THE SUN AROSE in a blaze of gold, as Harry and I lifted the anchor of *Trillium II*. We were thankful that our troublesome passengers had decided to stay behind on Kurumba. Only Harry, my very best mate, and I would be on board. That suited us just fine. The ocean was blue and calm. The four day's sailing to Sri Lanka would be a pleasure to undertake. We turned the ship's bows to the rising sun.

Farewell to Kurumba... farewell to a lovely dream

On the beach stood a small, forlorn figure in a light, cotton dress. The sea breeze blew the skirt against her bare legs. Ingrid had promised to wave us off at our early departure. There she was on that deserted beach, waving both arms above her blonde head in a last farewell. Through the binoculars, I could see that she was shouting something, but we could not hear her. The distance between us was already too great. Her lonely form became smaller and smaller. I watched as she sunk to the sand and held her head in her hands. She was crying so helplessly, her shoulders shook. Was she weeping for the loss of something that could never be? She wanted to stay with me forever and sail together, from one horizon to another.

For ever and ever, I left her on that secluded shore of a small coral island in an immeasurably large ocean... KURUMBA.

A soft seabreeze blowing the cotton dress against her legs.

Chartering in Tropical Waters

To many, it is a dream to buy or build a boat and sail to warm climes, charter, and become rich. What's more, you can see the world for a bargain. Dear readers, to come straight to the point, I must destroy your dream of getting rich. To charter with a fair-sized yacht on the North Sea, in the Mediterranean, the West Indies or the Far East, and the Pacific Ocean is easier said than done. Chartering, no matter where, is very competitive, hard work. If the wrong people are on board, it can be a bitter disappointment.

There are times when you may be idle in a harbour for months at a time. There is no income, but the expenses continue. A ship is an extremely expensive undertaking. The upkeep costs a fortune, especially if a diesel engine needs to be replaced or new sails need to be purchased. Even theft of equipment might occur.

As soon as the bow hits the deep, blue water, insurance premiums rise to unaffordable heights.

No one becomes rich, but if you are lucky you might break even. We have sailed the Seven Seas from east to west, from north to south and back again. In twelve years of extensive sailing, we covered 100,000 sea miles. We saw so much of the world, met many people of different races. Harry and I would not have missed one moment of it for the world.

The Maldives—a rickety dock, pure white beaches, blue sea and sky. Dhonies sailing by.

Our ship carried us safely over the oceans, always reaching our destination. Hundreds of people were picked up at one location and dropped off at another. There were young people out for adventures or older ones living out their dreams of taking a sea voyage. The odd time we carried passengers who refused to adapt to life on board of a sailing ship resulted in many problems and troubles.

As the saying goes, "Men stay at home, fools go to sea." We, the fools, had heard of golden opportunities in the last paradise on earth—Sri Lanka (Beautiful Island) in the Indian Ocean. There, the charter business was up for grabs. No one had thought of it before. We wanted to take a chance and try our luck. But Sri Lanka was not next door. Ten thousand sea miles separated us. Our agent from Harlingen saw potential in the venture and promised to help us finance it. After all, Sri Lanka was a tourist attraction.

Trillium II was given a complete overhaul. Cabins were redone, new carpet was laid in the saloon, new upholstery put in, and even a new diesel engine and an electrical aggregate were purchased. In the merry month of May we departed from our beloved Tulip Land. After four and a half months, we secured our lines around bollards in Colombo harbour. It was October and the southwest monsoon had just begun. We now had to accustom ourselves to a totally different climate, and completely different people.

Evidently we were the first charter yacht with official permission from the government of Sri Lanka. We were given a formal welcome by a TV station, a radio station, and an assortment of newspaper reporters. Cameras clicked as we answered questions of curious reporters. When the media had dispersed, it was the turn of our agent in Sri Lanka, who had been waiting at the quayside with his secretary and righthand man, Krish.

Krish, a pleasant and helpful young man, and his boss had thought of a good plan. The agent showed us a long list of dignitaries of Colombo to whom we must offer a free cruise and dinner and drinks as a token of goodwill and acquaintance. Their spouses, too, would be invited, and as an afterthought he added, "At your own expense, of course, Captain." Harry was doubtful of the generous proposal. Hadn't the ship's kitty shown the bottom long ago? He asked the agent if he already had some paying guests for us, with the emphasis on "paying." The agent patiently explained that such a thing needed time, much, much time.

We understood and made him a contra-offer: only one free day-cruise at our expense and he would pay for all the extras such as dinner and drinks. This time he seemed uncertain, but before he could protest, Krish piped up and said, "That sounds reasonable to me, boss. Let's do it the Captain's way."

Krish, a man after my own heart.

Stuck in Colombo

FOR MONTHS we were stuck at that dirty concrete pier in Colombo. No charters, no income, no nothing. Each day we made trips to the office of the agent and were always greeted with a happy smile that showed white, perfect teeth in a brown face. "Give it time, give it time" was his never-ending song. It was a lovely tune, but in the meantime our kitty was empty and we lived on rice and fish as the poor men did. If Krish saw us coming, he hid in his own office.

We learned that time meant nothing to the men of the east, and to make an appointment was a fruitless undertaking. They were broken without notice or guilty feelings afterward. We westerners could not get used to this conduct.

IN THOSE EARLY DAYS, Harry had met a man from Germany who lived and worked on Sri Lanka. He owned a bungalow in a small village outside Colombo. From his home in Moratuwa, he operated an import-export business. He had many contacts from the hotels near the village of Beruwala, and he began to act as our unofficial agent. Through him, we were able to obtain charters. They were mostly German tourists who spent several weeks in the hotels and were anxious to break the monotony of hotel life with a spell at sea.

The agent noticed that we left the harbour frequently, and became quite concerned that we would not return. "When are you coming back?" he questioned with a furrowed brow. Invariably, our reply to him was, "You have no customers for us, so you will see us whenever we get back." It was not to his liking, but he could not stop us.

We established a sailing route from Colombo down the west coast to Galle, on the south point of the island. In between, we had discov-

ered and explored several bays and lagoons which we used as stopovers. It was always a seven-day cruise, and it worked out well for us and also for Harry's German friend. The stay-over in a lagoon would be for a day and a night. The guests could swim, dive, and explore to their heart's content. If they didn't want to take a wheelwatch, it was fine

Galle—our port of call on the south point of Sri Lanka. Krish, secretary of our agent on the island, in white shirt and hand on the seawall, part of the 15th-century Dutch fortifications of Galle. To the left is his chauffeur.

with us. The weather was always pleasant, and the distance between stop-overs was short.

Galle was an interesting harbour town which had preserved many of the old colonial ways of the Dutch. The port itself had been walled in and had an impressive, arched gateway as its main entrance. Above it, clearly chiselled, was the name "Fort Frederick Hendrick," after a Dutch prince, Frederick Henry (1583–1647), the youngest son of William the Silent.

The Dutch East India Company had retained the place for 175 years. After the conquest of Ceylon by the English, some of the Dutch settlers chose to remain, and formed a group which to this day is called "The Burghers" (The Citizens). They own a club building and are guardians of a museum which contains ships' journals, utensils, books, paintings of East Indian governors and famous sea captains, and further memorabilia from past years of glory and riches for the Dutch.

Caught in a scam

ONE DAY we acquired clients from an unexpected source—Wagon Lits from Holland. They wanted to rent our ship for a week for two people who were on a world tour. One condition was stipulated: no oher people on board except the permanent crew. It seemed to be a favourable proposition and Harry and I were pleased with the wind-fall. As usual, between gentlemen, fees and prices were not mentioned.

When we were notified of the arrival of the VIPs at the hotel in Colombo, we hired a taxi to pick them up. They were welcomed aboard with high regard. The young lady was the daughter of a former Dutch athlete who had won four gold medals at the first Olympic games held after World War II. Of course we were honoured to have her as our guest. She was accompanied by her boyfriend. Since they were the only passengers, they were given the choice of any of the free cabins.

Very discreetly and politely, inquiries of payment were made. The lady assured us they had paid Wagon Lits the full amount and that company would settle up with us later. It seemed a rather strange arrangement. The young man offered his two cents worth that everything was fine, and then suggested that we start sailing right away. The way he spoke, it was more an order than a request.

Harry angrily flung the lines on deck. It was obvious he was not pleased with the situation. Misgivings gnawed at the back of our minds. Our business instinct was alert and this couple's credibility was slipping away quickly.

The next day, we dropped the hook into a beautiful lagoon south of the fisherman's harbour of Beruwala. The white beach was enticing, the water crystal clear and warm. Dugouts rested above the waterline and hidden under the palm trees was a small settlement of huts. Soon the male population rowed out toward *Trillium II*. Escorted by her companion, our female passenger came to me riding her high horse. "For goodness sake, Captain, why did you come in here?" she asked, tossing her head in the direction of the approaching canoes. "I have seen enough monkeys lately. We want to sail, Captain."

She had offended me completely. With my voice in control, I sternly replied, "It is February. You came from Holland where the snow and rain make life unpleasant and miserable. Here, you can enjoy warm sunshine and water so clear it is a delight to swim in. You have the freedom to sunbathe on a beach where no one will disturb you. What more could you possibly wish for? If you want to sail, fine, but not today. We will not leave until tomorrow morning. By the way," I added, "those monkeys in the canoes happen to be our friends." It was a long speech during which Harry shot me looks of approval.

We continued the cruise, remaining on the ocean, wind or no wind. Late in the day, before the end of the charter, we arrived in Galle. The couple went ashore to explore the old town we had described to them. Before they left, Harry told them their farewell dinner would be ready at 7:00 P.M. We went into town, too, to buy provisions for the "Captain's Table" that evening.

By seven, the table was beautifully set, the dinner prepared, and we waited for our guests to return. At 8:00 P.M. they had not yet arrived. By 9:00 P.M. the dinner was ruined. Finally, at 10:00 P.M., her highness and her mate came in to inform us they had eaten dinner in town. They picked up their suitcases, and without saying thank you or goodbye, they were gone. Good riddance!

Harbour of Colombo—Harry, brown as a native, works on something hidden from our eyes. In this place we waited for customers from our agent. It didn't work the way we expected but we found paying guests in some other manner.

Harry dumped the remains of the dinner overboard. The fish had a feast. We never saw a penny for that week of chartering with those impossible people. A seaman's job is to sail. He leaves deceit and corruption to a select few on shore. And as for Wagon Lits, your guess is as good as mine.

Faith in humanity restored by pleasant passengers

WITH AN EMPTY BOAT, we sailed back to the lagoon near Beruwala. Our German import-export friend had contacted us in Galle. He had a load of German tourists waiting who would meet us at the lagoon to embark. True to his word, when we dropped anchor, seven people were waving at us. Our friends, the "monkeys," ferried them over. Laughing noisily, they climbed aboard, carrying suitcases and boxes of wine.

We made our acquaintance with a father, two of his daughters, their husbands, and two other young ladies. As usual, we left it up to them to decide which cabins they wanted. Not only did they man the cabins, they took possession of the entire ship. Every nook and cranny was explored by the curious women. Harry immediately explained the ship's protocol and what was expected of them once we got under way.

The girls had already changed, and clad in colourful bikinis, they jumped from the railing to keep the fish company. The men had uncorked the wine, and before we could count to ten, a party was in full swing. "*Prosit, Herr Kapitan,*" they shouted. "*Auf eine gute fahrt. Prosit.*" ("Let's have a nice cruise...cheers!") We wished them welcome on board, but just to be on the safe side, we took Father down to the saloon to settle financial matters.

The party remained lively and Harry made snacks to go with the drinks. Dusk fell after the last sun rays had disappeared behind the palm trees. Twilight passed quickly, so we turned on the deck lights. With the free spirit of youth, wine, and song, the swimming continued in the nude. Father kept his trunks on, however, and Harry and I did not swim at all, but kept an eye on the festivities. It was a happy-go-lucky group and was very refreshing after the bitter disappointment we had had with the two stuck-ups who had wanted the whole ship to themselves.

Harry set some portable loudspeakers on deck and shoved a tape of dance music into the player. Our new guests kicked up their bare heels, with the Skipper and his first mate joining in. At an hour when most people would have been asleep, the deck party was still going strong. More wine bottles were popped open. Then someone suggested we leave the lagoon and go sailing on the ocean. Whoopee! Everybody thought it was a great idea.

Radna, our volunteer deck-hand, in front of the Toko Annex post office in Beruwala (toko means shop.)

Behind my back, Harry allowed one of the girls to push the button that started the diesel. I pretended not to notice. I was too busy practising my rusty German with Marlies, Father's youngest daughter. All the ladies were dressed very scantily, but the night was balmy with no chance of catching cold. The men hauled the anchor aboard and Harry pointed the bows toward the break in the reef. There was no risk, since we knew our way. As long as we kept close to the lighthouse on the coral rocks, we would be safe. Its four flashes were our guide.

Communal bath house in Beruwala. Young and old splash water pulled up from the well freely.

Once in open water, Harry turned the wheel over to me. With the help of the new crew, he raised the genoa and a slight breeze filled the sail. I gazed through the wheelhouse doors and saw a yellow path of the moonbeams rippling toward the ship. Strangely, I could see not one moon, but two. Then there were four. Two moons in the heavens and two moons in the sea. I blinked a few times and sure enough they were still there. I called Harry into the wheelhouse to tell him about the phenomenon. He patted my back and calmly said, "Why don't you go on deck, Skipper, and keep our guests company? I can manage the wheel and those four moons of yours quite well." What else could a skipper do but take the advice of his best first mate?

A nightly sail on the Indian Ocean with a jolly group of German people. The wine flowed freely, Harry played the mouth organ, and the lovely girl in the middle of the picture, Marlies, didn't want to leave the ship when the cruise had ended.

In the wee hours of the morning, the party began to lose its fire. One by one, our guests disappeared into their cabins. Harry stayed at the wheel and I tidied up. Tomorrow we would teach the new crew to pick up after themselves. There was only one moon now, sinking low in the western horizon. The four flashes of the lighthouse were a mere twinkle in the distance.

With a chuckle, Harry told me that some of the merrymakers had wanted to take a turn at the wheel. He had shown them a compass course and solemnly, aware of the responsibility, they had held the spokes. He hadn't bothered to let them know that the ship was hardly moving at all. The soft breeze had merely filled the sail, but there was no real pressure in it.

Daylight brought with it an unexpected storm. Under storm jib and reefed

These beautiful girls in colourful saris were delightful.

mizzen, we skated back and forth so as not to lose the dim outline of the island from sight. We were still unaware of the plans our revellers had for the next five days. Now and then a head would pop up through one of the deck hatches to find out that all was not amusement on a windy day with a rough sea and rain whipping across the deck. They had a double hangover—one from the wine, and one from the waves pounding against the hulls.

Harry and I had to change wheel-watches every hour. We were exhausted and took catnaps on the settee in between. Our crew could not be counted on. Later we would catch up on our sleep.

OUR GUESTS had been good sports. The little storm had not deterred them from remaining the full week of cruising on the Indian Ocean, visiting little ports, and diving and swimming in the enchanting lagoons. On the last day of the cruise, we stopped at the small harbour of Dehiwala, just south of Colombo. This time we held the "Captain's Dinner" in a hotel and it turned out to be a great success. From there they would go by taxi to Beruwala for the last few weeks of their holiday in Sri Lanka.

The girls with their colorful parasols, watching Trillium II *from the mole.*

Once more we were forced to say goodbye to people we had come to love. Harry and I received many hugs and kisses from the girls. Father had hidden a substantial farewell present under the tablecloth in the saloon. We found it the next day.

Our faith in humanity had been restored.

The Forbidden Island

On one of our many voyages, we met a group of young men and women of diverse nationalities. Harry and I had been sitting at a sidewalk café, each enjoying a litre-sized glass of refreshing cold beer. As we were between charters, we had ample time to sit and relax. Patiently we awaited our second drink. Over the past few months, we had earned a fair dollar. The ship's kitty could afford a splurge. After the beer, we intended to have dinner at a first-class hotel in Colombo, the capital of Sri Lanka.

Good times with a party of young travellers

We struck up a conversation with some members of the group, and listened to their stories with much interest. They had been roaming around Nepal for some time, had visited its capital, Kathmandu, and from there, flown to Delhi, India. Disillusioned by India, they had arrived just that morning by plane to Colombo and were seeking suitable accommodations.

Harry and I pricked up our ears. "You are just in time," we said. "Our ship is tied up at a wharf in the harbour. There is plenty of room for all of you. Why not stay aboard tonight?" Our proposal was accepted with enthusiasm. We had snared them. Tonight we would try to sell them a cruise. Harry was a convincing salesman, and the money would fatten the kitty some more. Of course, our dinner plans were abandoned but we didn't mind.

This was more important.

Eight eager young people were invited to use the two float cabins. They were given the freedom to divide them any way they chose. Later in the evening, Harry brewed a pot of coffee and explained to his audience what we were doing with our ship. He painted a beautiful picture of the islands of the Maldives, snorkelling amid coral reefs, white, sun-drenched beaches, and the blue, blue ocean.

Not much more needed to be said. Harry sold them a four-week cruise with a promise that we would go fishing for sharks. I set out a course on the sea chart while our new guests looked over my shoulder. First we would sail to the Maldives and stay on Kurumba for a week. Then, onto the Indian Ocean for fishing. From there to the interesting place of Cochin, on the Malabar Coast of India. On the way back to Colombo, we would visit the old town and port of Trivandrum.

The group paid cash in American dollars. We noticed they had a lot of ready money in their pockets, and warned them that it was a dangerous thing to do. Our crew was sent ashore the next morning to buy food for those four weeks, while Harry and I took care of the loading of diesel fuel and water. Customs and Immigra-tion officers were notified of our plans. By slipping a couple of dollars into each passport, we sped up the process. Stamps were smacked onto our passports in no time. Big smiles assured us that we had done the right thing.

Fish pedlar in the streets of Colombo.

Back to Kurumba, our beautiful dream island ...and a mirage

WE HAD FOUR beautiful days sailing to the Maldives, a calm, blue ocean, no seasickness, and eight pleasant passengers on board. *Trillium II* danced like a young ballerina across the swells. A breeze gave us four knots, and that was good enough for us. When we arrived in Malé, the friendly, well-dressed officials came on board. While they enjoyed a non-alcoholic drink, they clapped the usual stamps in each passport, good for a stay of three months.

Harry steered the ship on to Kurumba village. With steady hands, he manoeuvred us through the reefs. We were now in famil-iar waters. The boys stood on the foredeck, ready to drop the anchors, and the girls trooped to the top of the wheelhouse in antic-ipation of seeing the tropical island we had told them so much about.

In the cockpit, I stood alone, staring ahead over the turquoise water. My mind wandered, flashing back to a white beach and a hazy form of a delicate little figure. Would I see her again? Would she be waiting at the strand to wave at us in welcome as she had waved farewell in sorrow on that early morning so long ago? It seemed like only yesterday.

Beautiful Kurumba.

Excitedly, the girls pointed toward the distant horizon, where the outline of an island appeared. Kurumba, our dream island. Harry called to the boys on the foredeck to be ready to let the anchor go as soon as the depth-sounder indicated 25 fathoms. Slowly, we approached, coasted, and there was Ingrid, standing barefoot in the warm sand, her hair blowing around her lovely face. She waved, her arms high above her head. The sea breeze pressed her light dress against her legs.

Nothing had changed. The girl from that far Nordic land waited for us. I stood stiffly, lifting my arm to greet the slender figure. Harry shouted for the boys to drop anchor, and the rattling chains sunk to the sandy bottom. Quietly, *Trillium II* came to rest a cable's length from the island. Harry came out of the wheelhouse, stood next to me, and informed me that the anchor was holding good. As though in a trance, I mumbled, "Ingrid...?" I felt my son look at me in wonder. Then softly he answered, "That is almost two years ago, Skip." I sighed in disappointment.

Inside the lagoon.

THE BOYS set the sloop into the water and ferried the girls to the island. They landed at the old rickety pier where some Maldavians from the hotel welcomed them. Harry and I stayed aboard for awhile to steady our emotions. This reunion had awakened many memories of happiness and carefree days, which had ended in such a sorrowful farewell.

We stayed for a week, frequenting the bar under the palm trees. The music from the hidden speakers still added a note of sensual enjoyment to the romantic atmosphere. In no time, our guests had formed couples. Long after the bar had closed and the music stopped, they walked around the island under a starlit sky with the breeze rustling through the palm trees. They sat on deck for hours, arms around each other, silently listening to the sounds of the sea washing over the coral reefs, and to the beat of their own hearts. Luckily, the ship had such large decks that every couple found a spot away from the others.

What was a week on a beautiful island? Time raced on ceaselessly, the island a mere dot in a boundless ocean. So we weighed anchor to explore other horizons. Our young guests were in favour of roaming the seas. I set out a sailing pattern for about a week, west of the Maldives. We would return to the Malabar coast by way of the Lakkadives, a group of islands north of the Maldives.

Deeper into the Indian Ocean, Harry taught the crew how to bait a line for shark fishing. A piece of red meat, bought in Colombo for the occasion and saved in the freezer compartment, was slung on a good-sized hook. The line was so strong, I was sure we could tow a ship with it. We had not seen any sign of sharks, but we were confident that these waters would be teeming with the monsters. They would surely smell the meat from miles away and reach it in no time.

Harry had fastened the line to a heavy cleat on the aft deck, from there to a winch to pull the catch in (if we were that lucky), and an indicator line attached with a clothespin to a backstay. At the first pull on the fishing line, it would let go, signalling our catch. For half that day we trailed the line behind the ship. Finally, in the afternoon we got a hold of one. It was an enormous fish and it put up quite a fight. The boys worked on the winch and the girls shrieked in excitement, pointing with outstretched arms as the great fish beat the surface of the water to foam in its effort to get free.

Suddenly the line went slack. When it was brought in, we saw that the hook had been either bitten or broken in half. The business end, with the barbed hook, was probably in the shark's jaws. Unless that monster has seen a dentist, it is still swimming around with that piece of steel in its mouth. We all had a good laugh, and the shark had its freedom instead of being fried in the pan.

Slowly I changed course toward the north, into the Arabian Sea, the northern part of the Indian Ocean. Days dreamed by. The young people had carried their mattresses on deck and slept under the bright stars. There was no swimming during the hottest part of the day. Our friend with the hook in its mouth might have followed us to take revenge.

The sun rose on the eastern horizon and spread her golden light over the ocean. It sunk in the west and coloured late-afternoon monsoon clouds day after day. I took my sights on that sun in the morning, at noon, and again in the evening while the crew curiously looked on. I explained how my calculations gave us a position at sea from where we would set a course to a new destination.

Day after day, the ocean remained calm, with a lazy swell from the southwest and a breeze just enough to fill the light genoa. The girls fried the flying fish that landed on deck during the night, and also the tunnies we hooked in the day. Not one day were we without a sea banquet. We did not see any sharks after the first encounter.

Then, one day, I announced a course change toward the east for a visit to Cochin, in India. The Dutch had used that port when they sailed for the Dutch East India Company in the 16th and 17th centuries. It was a place full of mementoes of colonial times. The governor's home had been turned into a distinguished restaurant without having lost any of its charm. Harry and I had treated ourselves to a delicious Java rice table there many times on our visits to Cochin.

The course I had drawn on the chart ran between two groups of islands, but one afternoon I noticed something strange looming over the skyline. Had an uncharted current set us back to the south? I was sure it was not the Lakkadives. By checking the chart, I suspected the islands to be in the Ihavandiffulu atoll, which were covered with dense groves of palm trees. Instead of sailing through the Nine Degree Channel and straight east to Chochin, we had somehow made our way down to the Eight Degree Channel, just north of the northernmost atolls of the Maldives.

Harry instructed the boys to lower the sails, and carefully we approached the atoll under diesel power, the depth-sounder sweeping the bottom. Within the atoll were several islands, the closest one thick with palm trees.

The sun sinking toward the western edge of the world cast her golden rays over the surf, the lagoon behind the reefs and the sandy beach where fishermen's proas had been pulled up above the waterline. The sea bottom had risen quickly, so we decided to drop the hook and stay for the night. The weather was steady, and we expected the wind to die down completely by dusk. The island

**Ihavandu—
the forbidden
island**

had been identified as Ihavandu.

Some of the natives had appeared out of the trees and pushed their proas, or as they are called there, *dhonies*, into the water. They rowed across the lagoon toward an opening in the reef, recognizable by smooth water. A moment later, they hung, as usual, on our railings, speaking a language we didn't understand. An elderly gentleman was accompanied by a young boy who could speak a bit of English. He informed us that the man was his father and the chief of the island. He bid us welcome and warned us it was not safe to anchor outside the lagoon. We were encouraged to come inside and they would guide us through a breach in the reef.

An approaching dhonie. Is it friend or foe?

It seemed like a fine invitation, but for some reason I didn't trust it. Every time we landed in the Maldives and cleared Customs and Immigration, we were given a list of the nine islands we were allowed to visit. We definitely had no permission to make a landfall on Ihavandiffulu, and Ihavandu was a forbidden island. To call on any of these islands might lead to the confiscation of our ship.

Patiently we explained the rules to the chief through his son, the translator. But the big brown man would not take no for an answer. The men in the *dhonies* amused themselves with our guests in a confusion of tongues. When some tokens of friendship were offered, the brown faces split wide open in thankful grins of white, flashing teeth. They were extremely polite and disciplined. Not one of them attempted to climb aboard the ship. Our guests thought it was a great experience, a new adventure to be enjoyed to the fullest. Cameras clicked and laughter rose when they used both hands and feet to gesture to the natives.

Meanwhile, the chief insisted we anchor our ship in the lagoon instead of outside the atoll. "I chief of village," he exclaimed. "I chief and you come to village with me. You my guest. You may come inside lagoon. You may come to village." He was a stubborn, persistent man. Harry and I let him know that if we did go inside and visit his village we would be breaking the law. His reply was, "I am chief. I am chief. You my guests. You come with me."

We were in a serious dilemma. We were well aware of the rules, but on the other side of the reef lay that beautiful lagoon and a village of friendly natives who had invited us to tarry awhile. Eight pair of eyes looked at Harry and me imploringly. Should we take the chance? There was still some daylight left, and the sun, low in the western sky, had painted everything a soft red. It was so attractive and tempting, we were unable to resist any longer. Harry told the boys to weigh anchor. The island and the chief had won the battle of wills.

The natives cheered as I started the diesel and aimed for the entrance of the lagoon. They clung to the railing and let themselves be pulled along. The lagoon was very shallow and with the calm weather the weight of the anchor chain alone held *Trillium II* in place.

We invited the chief and his son aboard and treated them to a cup of tea and some Dutch cookies. The man was very impatient. He was the chief and wished to be obeyed at once. "Now we go to village." Harry and I, still unsure, discussed the situation and decided that half the company could go ashore and the others would hold the fort.

A friendly chief comes aboard Trillium II.

The men in the *dhonies* paddled us to the beach where the chief ordered me to walk on his right side, the others on his left. Islanders had formed two rows leading to a path under the palm trees. Men greeted us hands together, heads down. The women curtsied as we passed them. Although we were strangers, we were given a welcome fit for a king. I couldn't help but notice the finely chiselled features of the young women whose skin varied in colour from light brown to black. Most of them were clad in sarongs, but some of them wore colourful western dress. Even though they were Moslems, none of the females wore veils or shapeless Arab attire. On the contrary, they appeared to enjoy showing off their beauty.

The road beneath the trees led to the centre of the village. The chief first took us to the mosque, his pride and glory. The people who had welcomed us at the shore followed in a long file. The streets of the village were made of raked coral sand. It was immaculately clean with no visible sign of waste. Chickens ran freely, but their droppings were removed constantly.

The chief's house was the largest in the village. Halfway up, the walls were constructed of coral blocks. The roof was thatched with palm leaves, the usual means of protection against the sun and monsoon rains. Children pushed open the heavy gate. The procession which had followed us remained outside the fence. With harsh words the chief spoke, and reluctantly they dispersed.

At the front of his house were two rocking benches which he dusted off before we sat down, I on his right, the others wherever they could find a spot. He barked an order to one of the older children. When the boy returned, the family paraded behind him.

Cochin, India. An old Dodge flanked by rickshaws and a hole in the ground. Two of our young guests walked into such a pit, but one much deeper than this. At night they are invisible, with no street lights, no barricades, no warning signs.

Mother came first, holding a baby. We soon discovered she was his favourite wife. Next in line were his four young by-wives and children of all ages, then the grown daughters and last of all, grand-father. He wore the old-style loincloth which revealed loose brown skin hanging from his thin frame. The poor fellow was blind in one eye and coughed incessantly.

With that ritual over, the chief gave us the grand tour of his palace. It must have had at least ten bedrooms, each with a large bed and scoured concrete floors. There were no ornaments to be seen. In the meantime, darkness had fallen and the older boys placed coal oil lamps in the trees. Tea was served by the daughters, along with platters of sweets. A large bag of fudge was presented to us to take along for our crew on board.

After the ceremonial tea was finished, a new procession began with grandfather first in line. I was asked if we had medicine on the ship that could cure him of his dreadful cough. Indeed, we carried cough syrup in our medicine chest. I promised the chief I would give him a bottle when he escorted us back.

Next, one of the chief's by-wives came to us with a baby in her arms. The helpless child had a huge lump on his forehead. It was believed he had been stung by an insect, which seemed odd to us since those islands were virtually insect-free. Whatever the cause, the small, brown heap of humanity was also suffering from a fever. Mentally, I ticked off our medical supplies and all I could come up with was aspirin. I resolved to consult the paper doctor.

As the evening wore on, I urged the chief to take us back to the ship. He insisted we join him for a drink. Again, his beautiful daughters waited on us. This time they brought a fruity lemonade. With Allah's blessing, the chief was allowed to have four or five wives. We could see that he had made full use of that privilege.

FOR SOME REASON we no longer felt at ease. With more prompting, the chief rose and walked us to the beach where the *dhonies* were parked. In the prow of one of them sat a man with a portable two-way radio. It seemed so incongruous on this island without electricity or modern conveniences. The chief overheard the conversation and we noticed the expression on his face change. He snatched the radio from the man's hand and began shouting into it. We understood. The islands were linked by radio in a kind of relay system. We had been reported. We had landed on a forbidden island.

A primitive smithy in Cochin.

The chief continued his conversation, but I nudged him, gesturing for him to return us to our ship. Some of the men pushed a *dhonie* into the water, jumped into it, and we followed. As soon as we stepped aboard *Trillium II*, we felt greatly relieved. The chief, still holding the radio, clung to the railing, jabbering and arguing into the microphone.

Harry quickly got some of the promised medicines and gave it to the boy-translator. I heard the irritable prattle in a strange language spew forth from the speaker. We pried the fingers of the chief from the railing, and Harry gave his *dhonie* a good shove with the boat hook. The chief had one last message for us: we were not to leave the lagoon. He ordered us to stay until morning.

Harry and the crew members who had remained on board had dinner ready. While we ate, we discussed the situation. If we waited until morning, the MTBs from Malé would surely arrest us and confiscate our good ship, *Trillium II*. We would never give her up! By the time the girls had served dessert, we had the solution. We would simply go. We would leave the lagoon and head for open water.

The chief was a very shrewd man. Upon our last inspection around the decks, we saw that we were surrounded by a cordon of *dhonies*. We were prisoners. By the light of the stars, we could see three or four shadowy figures in each boat. Our plan of escape

**Escape from
the forbidden
island**

would have to be changed. We huddled in the saloon and turned off all the lights with the exception of one small lamp in a corner. At 11:00 P.M., when those brown devils thought we were fast asleep, we would break out.

Our guests were excited at the prospect of this thrilling adventure. Even Harry and I were ready for action. The diesel was started and left to run in neutral at the lowest possible rpms. She ticked over, hardly making any sound. Some of the boys peered over the freeboard of the cockpit but were unable to tell if the guards heard the slight rumble. At ten minutes to 11:00, three men volunteered to crawl forward over the deck to lift the anchor. Hand over hand they palmed in the chain and got the hook on deck without so much as a tinkle of chain. In case the guards heard anything, they would soon be lulled to sleep again because everything was so still. *Trillium II* floated freely in the still night air.

The tension among our guests rose by the minute. The boys lay at the bottom of the cockpits, peeking over the freeboard every now and then. We waited another fifteen minutes. The position of the cordon had not changed. Harry, ready at the wheel, shoved the gas handle slowly forward until the diesel clicked into gear. To our ears, it sounded like a hammer blow on an anvil. Outside, nothing stirred. Very, very slowly, Harry turned the ship on the few ticks the propeller made. It looked as though *Trillium II*, of her own volition, moved in slow motion.

She turned in the right direction, her bows toward the opening in the reef. It was a visibly dark spot between the luminescence where the ripples played over the coral. The strain was almost unbearable, but Harry kept his cool. It was all up to him now. "Now, Harry, now!" the boys said, trembling and stomping their feet against the boards.

Harry thrust the handle forward all the way, and with a roar the Volvo-Penta diesel instantly gave all the power she had. The bows shot skyward then bounced back onto the water. With increasing speed, the ship headed for the break in the coral. Six knots, then seven, eight, and before we reached the reef barrier, *Trillium II* ran nine knots, her maximum speed under power.

Screaming and yelling, the brown bandits rose up in their *dhonies*, fetched their paddles, and frantically rowed after our ship. There were three *dhonies* directly in our path, the men standing and waving wildly in a vain attempt to stop us. I gave Harry the only order I could: "Run them over, Harry, if they don't get out of the way." Glancing at me, he knew I was serious—and the islanders knew it too. Furiously, they paddled their dugouts away from the path of the onrushing *Trillium II*.

Our young people cheered and danced and clapped Harry on the shoulder. "Well done, Harry! Well done," they praised him. Once outside the reef, Harry pulled the handle back a bit and with eight knots we set a course due west. After an hour we were in international waters, where patrol boats from the Maldivian government had no say. Still we continued, and carried no navigation lights that could be spotted from a distance, just in case.

At sunrise, we changed course to the north, and during the day I took some sun sights to find our exact position. By sunset, the helmswoman was given a new course, and by the next morning we passed Mincoy Island and were safe and sound in the Nine Degree Channel. Our paying guests looked forward to a new adventure once we reached Cochin on the Malabar coast of India.

Spooky

One night, we had the distinct pleasure of having a beautiful guest on board *Trillium II*. We had invited Spooky, a young English girl, to join us for dinner. Of course, Spooky was not her real name, but that is what everyone called her. Perhaps it was because she was so capricious and loved to wander. She seemed like a Jack-in-the-box popping up here and there unexpectedly. Her hair was golden-blonde and her eyes a very light greyish blue. One's eyes become that way when at sea for a long time scanning the horizon. Freckles were sprinkled across her cute little turned-up nose. She loved to talk and was extremely bright. Her golden locks framed a lovely face. Was it any wonder that I fell in love with her? Harry, my first mate, was also enamoured by her. Like two young fools, both of us were infatuated with her beauty. But Spooky was very sensible and shared her attentions evenly.

We gave her the grand tour of our ship, explaining anything she did not understand. Having her aboard was like being in seventh heaven.

We had met her in Galle Harbour on Sri Lanka upon returning from a difficult charter cruise. The Indian Ocean had been tempestuous because of the monsoon storms. Also, the approach to the harbour had caused problems. The red and green buoys that marked a channel between coral reefs were frequently hidden

A beautiful English girl

by spray from incoming waves. When we had made it into the harbour and made fast at the mooring buoy designated for us, a sloop belonging to an English yacht rowed toward us. In it were three girls and one young man. After greeting us politely and inquiring about our cruise, they extended to us an invitation for tea aboard their yacht. How could we refuse an offer by such charming company?

That afternoon, I rowed to their ship alone. When I arrived, tea was ready. On that ship there was no exception to the rule. Along with the tea, crisp biscuits, cold meats, cheese, and a sweet, homemade raisin cake were served. Spooky saw to it that I, as guest of honour, was treated royally.

I am not too fond of sweets, but I took big bites of the cake and rinsed it down with tea. A fellow will do almost anything to impress the girl he has fallen for.

This beautiful tropical bay led to the entrance of the Harbour of Galle. We made many landfalls in such bays with our paying crew members when we circumnavigated the island of Ceylon.

After tea, Spooky announced that she would like to row back with me to have a better look at our ship. Gallantly, I helped her into the sloop. Once on board of *Trillium II*, I awakened Harry to let him know we had a guest. Spooky was taken aback by the size of our saloon, the galley, and the cabins. Their yacht of eight tons was not capable of giving them the roominess we had on the thirty-ton *Trillium II*.

Harry did his utmost to please Spooky, and he seemed to succeed miraculously. I watched with suspicious eyes. We invited Spooky to stay for dinner and informed her people by radio that she would stay for a while and was dining with us. The rest of the afternoon passed too quickly for my liking. Spooky was an interesting conversationalist. She told us all about her adventures at sea and we, in turn, told her about ours.

In the tropics, dusk falls at 6:00 P.M. so when the dishes were done I rowed Spooky back to her ship. There was no moon and the water in the harbour was pitch black. Here and there the reflection of the lanterns on the quay glimmered in rippled bands of yellow light. It was quite a task to locate the English yacht among the other boats in the dark.

As we rowed, we spontaneously made up a little song and loudly sang it together:

This is my ship/And there is your ship/And we are rowing/From my ship/To your ship/Row along, row along.

Then we laughed at our own silliness. I gazed at Spooky's profile and wished that the rowing could go on forever, but it ended abruptly when the bow of the sloop bumped into the side of her yacht.

At her departure from *Trillium II*, she had thanked Harry for the nice dinner and given him a big kiss. As she climbed back aboard her own ship, I was expecting the same reward, but with a mere "Thank you," she disappeared below. Can you imagine, how disappointed I was? Disillusioned, and deeply saddened, I rowed back to my own ship somewhere in that dark harbour.

Spooky...would we ever see her again?

Spooky...a dear little English girl with golden hair.

Spooky...all of five years old.

Galle Yacht Harbour just before sunset. Spooky lived on one of these yachts.

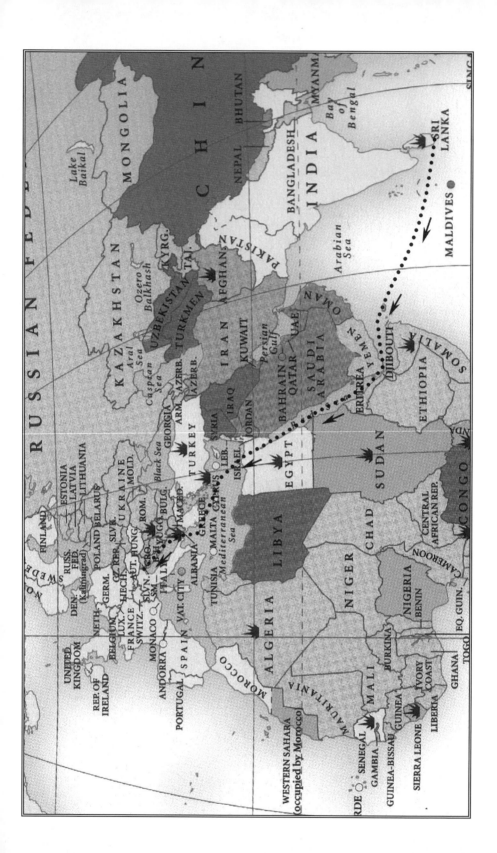

From India to the Mediterranean

Trillium's *Fight with the Red Sea*

W e were returning to civilization: Cyprus. I considered the idea of civilization and what we had experienced on our travels. For more than three years we had tolerated *baksheesh*, blackmail, military despotism, and official bureaucracy. I couldn't shake the thought that revenge was taken on western man for hundreds of years of colonialism and exploitation by white oppressors.

By sailing to the "East," we had hoped to find Paradise, but we were extremely disappointed when we encountered nothing but ignorance, laziness, and lust for power by small-minded bureaucrats. Fortunately, we discovered a little peep-hole through which we could glimpse into the history of the lands of the east. Books and excursions taught us of a high civilization with un-equalled architecture, knowledge and wisdom, gods and idols. We felt humble when we learned of the rich past of these lands.

MANY TIMES I was afraid of losing our dear *Trillium II* to the blackmail of corrupt customs and immigration officials. Rebels in some countries were in need of weapons, and we were suspected of smuggling them into the land. *Trillium II* was a large ship. She could easily hide contra-

Trillium II ashore in Galle Harbour, Ceylon, for her yearly inspection and maintenance of the hulls and keel. Algae and gooseneck barnacles grow fast in tropical waters, and also the dreaded marine-borers are a constant worry for owners of wooden ships. On this occasion we prepared the ship for the long haul back to the Mediterranean.

band. Often she was searched from top to bottom for drugs.

Harry and I decided it was high time to leave this part of the world. There were many options open to us. I dreamed of sailing to Cape Town in South Africa and fitting *Trillium* out for the Roaring Forties, or going via Cape Leeuwin, Australia, into the Pacific. I imagined her skimming the Horn of South America, the Screaming Sixties, and exploring the exotic, poetic islands in the largest ocean of the world–the South Pacific. Harry's desires were to return to the Mediterranean. It was closer to home and we had seen so little of it.

As Sudan

Along the coral reefs of the Red Sea, we sailed. At our port side stood the mountains of Africa, the mountains of As Sudan. Arrogantly, they rose from the desert, their peaks red in the early morning light. As the sun rose higher, their colour changed to mauve, then to violet, and finally settled on pale blue for the remainder of the day. Far above their tops stretched a filmy veil of translucent cirrus, an omen of wind to come.

Four days before, we had left Port Sudan with favourable weather and calm winds. An Arabian beachcomber at the waterfront had predicted a south wind (for a fee, of course). However, our weather chart indicated something very different: strong winds from the north. The chart was correct, as usual.

After leaving the harbour of Bur Sudan, we stayed on an easterly course to clear the Wingate Reefs. Once free of the sharp corals we could turn north, heading for the Suez Canal, 500 miles away. We were also heading into a norther with Beaufort 5. Waves two to three metres high slapped into our bows. The torture lasted four weeks. Four weeks of fighting against an unrelenting foe.

Days of rest in Khor el Mar'Ob lagoon

NOW WE WERE ANCHORED in the beautiful, calm lagoon of Khor el Mar'Ob. We needed the rest badly. We had struggled for five days against wind and waves. Every wave that slammed into the bows of the ship had brought her to a near standstill. Our Volvo-Penta was not strong enough to withstand such adverse force.

Huge areas of low pressure develop over the deserts of Africa (Sahara) and over Saudi Arabia (An Nafud) during the first part of the year. Cyclonic winds reinforce each other over the Red Sea causing the dreaded north winds. The latitude of Bur Sudan, the midway point of the Red Sea, is a region of calms between two weather systems. From the south of Port Sudan to the Strait of Bab-el-Mandeb reign the south winds of anti-cyclones.

Between Bab-el-Mandeb and Port Sudan, with the winds over the stern, *Trillium II* had sometimes reached speeds of 20 knots or even more. She had fearlessly planed down the waves. When that happened, the crew shouted with joy. It was an exhilarating experience.

This time we were all exhausted, feeling powerless against the forces of nature. Inshallah. It is Allah's will.

THE WATER SURFACE in the lagoon was calm, but high at the top of the masts we heard the howling wind. We were lucky to have found such a protected bay. We looked for a break in the reefs and then moved cautiously through the coral barrier with all eyes searching the water for any obstacles. Once through, the bay spread open in all its splendour and beauty.

Somewhere in the centre, we dropped anchor. As soon as it had set, Harry jumped overboard. We could see his lean, tanned body working the danforth deeper into the coral. Colourful fish swam in the clear water around him. They had probably never seen a human so close. Our first mate popped up to the surface, giving us the thumbs-up signal. We were riding safe behind the anchor. Eagerly, some of the crew joined Harry in the clear, blue water of the bay.

Judith and Bob, an English couple we had on board, packed some goodies and water and rowed the sloop to shore. They wanted to explore the interior of the Nubian Desert. We watched as their two tiny figures became smaller and smaller in the immense, golden sea of sand. In the distance between some dunes the sand twirled and rose higher. Suddenly the top of the dunes disappeared as though a giant hand had swept over it. Farther off rose the Jabal Oda mountain range, over 7,000 feet high. Its shades of dark grey and hazy blue made the mountains seem severe, even forbidding. Had human feet ever trod this part of the world? Was it possible that we were the first to step foot on these shores of the Dark Continent? Could we be the first to feel the wretched loneliness of this forsaken place, the first to taste the mystic atmosphere since it had been created so very long ago?

AS THE SUN moved toward the western sky, the palette of the mountains changed to darker hues. They were quite different from the *Alpen-gluhen* (Alpen glow) in Switzerland. Here it was cheerless. We were far from human habitat which concentrated in a few harbours along the Red Sea. In between was nothing but barren land as it had been formed in the beginning.

We began to worry about our two desert trotters. They had been gone for the best part of the day. Had they lost their way in this constantly changing land? Dunes blew down in minutes only to be built up somewhere else. We did not belong here, I realized. We were not Bedouins, the roving, nomadic desert dwellers. The mountains in the distance were our enemies, the vast, sandy plains an antagonist of monstrous proportions.

Judith and Bob, come back, please! They had only a mouthful of water and a few snacks with them. Long before dark, we turned on the masthead lights, a guiding light to safety and comfort. Everyone was on constant lookout.

They appeared at dusk on bare feet, their shoes hanging around the necks. Tired, but content, they flopped down and we plied them with many cups of tea, relieved at their return.

The sun had sunk below the mountains, and our crew began preparations for dinner. Some of them grumbled that we had no fish for our meal. Were there not thousands swimming around the ship? The cook invited them to catch their own. Harry spoke up. "Those fish have never met an enemy and we shall not be the first. Did you not see how they swam around me in such a friendly manner? Tonight we will have dinner without fish."

THE DARKNESS of night was black and solid around the ship. We went out to gaze at the stars. There was no smog or disturbing city lights. The stars sparkled like diamonds. The wind blew harder, and we needed to wear sweaters or jackets to keep the chill off. Our eyes grew accustomed to the dark and we could see the mountain ridges cutting a sharp silhouette out of the sky.

A flash of bluish light shot heavenward from behind the ridge, renting the celestial dome in two. Then it started to sway back and forth. It looked like a searchlight, but what would one be doing here? It was a great mystery to us. After a short while it disappeared as suddenly as it had come. We were certain of one thing. This part of Africa was not as deserted as we had thought.

All of us retired to our bunks. Tomorrow was sailing day again.

The next morning we learned differently. Outside the lagoon, huge waves in endless procession passed by on their way south. Compared to the hell of raging water mountains, it was heaven in the lagoon.

"No sailing," I informed them at the breakfast table. "No sailing," echoed the crew. Plans were made to spend the day at anchor. Two daredevils went ashore to explore the desert, but soon returned. Sharp, blowing sand made it impossible to go far. There was plenty of other entertainment: snorkelling, exploring the coral reefs, feeding the fish. And Harry had his work cut out for him— maintenance of the Volvo-Penta, our faithful, hard-working diesel. I sat constantly at the radio trying to catch a weather report. My tuning was in vain—no stations, just static.

Before darkness fell, I cast my eyes over the sea. The waves were not as high as they had been that morning and there were no whitecaps in sight. At daybreak, the sea was calm and the wind had died down to a pleasant breeze. This time it was a sailing day. The anchor was quickly freed from the coral and we carefully found our way back to open water.

Wind and waves were handsome and we made five knots at the usual rpm's for cruising speed. Later in the morning we met up with an Arabian *dhow* carrying four men, who pulled nets aboard. I called out to Harry, "Hold your course to that *dhow*, Harry. Maybe they'll sell us some fish for dinner."

As we closed in on the fishermen, they reached for their paddles, turned their lateen sail around, and took off like the devil was on their tail.

"Well, what do you know," chuckled Harry. "They're afraid of us." Smiling, he steered us back on our own course. All we had wanted was a batch of fresh fish for our midday meal.

Purposefully, we continued our voyage. Suez was a long way to go.

Al Ghurdaqah

After our departure from Port Bernice, towns with reasonable harbours appeared more frequently along the Egyptian coast. Wind and waves remained abominable, and the weather reports we were now able to receive spoke of winds reaching 50 miles an hour. We could not believe our ears. Winds of 50 miles per hour could sweep the seas up to nine or ten metres. It meant Storm with a capital S. We couldn't help but feel despondent, yet we struggled

Rendezvous with old friends, and blackmail anew

on until approximately 130 miles north of Port Bernice. There we found an anchorage in the partly protected harbour of Al-Quasayr. Although there was a small pier, we dropped the hook in the open bay. The shoreline was completely surrounded by basalt blocks. Fortunately, the sand had a grip on our anchor like a vise. It saved *Trillium II* and her crew.

Early the next morning, the direction of the waves changed. Enormous swells rolled into the bay to break on the basalt-reinforced shore. *Trillium II* was in the path of the rolling monsters and swayed in a frightening arc on her long anchor line. Normally a stable ship, she heaved so violently that our crew could not stay in their bunks, and even walking on deck was impossible. We could see clearly what was approaching from the sea and how quickly the swells rose sky-high on the upcoming bottom of the bay. *Trillium II* definitely took a beating. She was picked up as though she were a matchbox and smacked back down with a resounding clap. It was terrifying!

Our sloop was secured on the aft deck, but a boarding water mountain snatched her up, broke the ties, and swept her over the railing and into the sea. She would probably have smashed to pieces somewhere on the shore but Harry refused to give up on the sloop. With a line around his waist, he jumped overboard. Rising and descending with the gigantic swells, he swam toward our little boat, managed to grab hold of her, and both were pulled in. Strangely, the whole event had taken only a few minutes.

Trillium II still clung to the feeble nylon line. The wonderful danforth anchor had bitten so deeply into the sand that it would not let go. It was our life-line, but we wondered how long it would hold under the conditions. Something had to be done. We decided to creep deeper into the bay to find shelter behind that little concrete pier.

I turned the diesel on, and Harry, with four women, moved to the bow. Slowly, I manoeuvred us forward, and the men took up the slack in the line. When we were positioned straight over the anchor, Harry cleated it and the next incoming wave heaved the ship up, up, up. The anchor broke loose. We were free! Relieved, I motored to a spot behind the pier where the water was more calm. It was a safer place, so the boys let down the hook again. Soaked to the skin, they made their way to the cockpit where the girls were waiting with a large pot of hot tea. They had accomplished a herculean task and it had not been without danger, even though they had been clipped and harnessed to forestay and pulpit. The risk had been great, but everything had gone well. *Trillium II* was safe.

THE STORM that had been forecasted had blown itself out at Al Quasayr. We had only received the tail end of it. The weather had calmed enough for us to proceed. Presently we were sailing in a vast lagoon. The sun shimmered brilliantly over smooth, tranquil waters. On the horizon rose the city of Al Ghurdaqah or, to make it easier for the tongue, Hurgada. The white cubicles of houses and buildings seemed to hang suspended above the borderline of sky and water. In about an hour, we could be in port.

Hurgada, situated at the mouth of the Gulf of Suez, was the beginning of the end of the long trek from India. We certainly deserved a good rest after the tortuous weeks we had experienced on the northern half of the Red Sea. It was hot, dry, and the port swarmed with soldiers carrying rifles. Worst of all, it was hemmed in by barbed wire. There was no way we could get out and into the city. We endured the usual procedures of relinquishing our passports and were ordered to stay within the compound.

The *Hornet* with Dale and Maureen had arrived two days earlier. They were sure the others would follow soon. We cleaned up, dried out the ship and the cabins. At meal times, plans to visit Luxor and the land of the Pharoahs were discussed. But how were we to get out of this prison-like harbour, especially without passports?

The gate was heavily guarded, but fortunately Customs and Immigration were located next to it. Together, we paraded to the office and a friendly official listened to our plight. His smile broadened as he informed us that a bus travelled daily from Hurgada to Luxor. We inquired about our passports and he told us there would be no problem in having them returned. For the price of 150 Egyptian pounds, we could *buy* them back. All the passports? No, it would be 150 pounds (cash) for each passport. His eyes glistened viciously. Our faces fell. It was a fortune. Seven of our paying crew fell for the extortion. Harry and I declined the "generous offer." Somebody had to stay aboard anyway. Jens Jorgensen also chose not to go. It would be over a 1,000 pounds, more than the man's yearly salary. That explained the gleam in the official's eye and the snicker as he pocketed the money.

The next morning our crew boarded the bus, planning to be away for at least four days. We assured them we would not leave without them. Harry and I settled into a calm, daily routine. Our bookkeeping showed that we had not made as much profit on this cruise as we had expected. We had had many expenses and because of the strong headwinds since Port Sudan, we had burned a lot of fuel. We had to be careful with our ship's kitty from now on.

**A passenger
becomes
unhinged**

JENS JORGENSEN had booked in Sri Lanka for the full voyage to Cyprus in the Mediterranean. He was a young Danish fellow, a quiet type who kept to himself most of the time. Harry hoped that he could make a good deckhand out of Jens, but it did not work out that way. When Jens had no wheelwatch, he stayed in his cabin. We had this type of people aboard quite often and the behaviour pattern was always the same: first at the table at mealtime and last one to come on deck when there was some work to do. During inclement weather, with rough seas and howling winds, this type does not respond to "All hands on deck," they cower in their bunks. It didn't bother Harry or me. *Trillium II* was easy to handle.

Jens started to behave oddly for the time we were cooped up in the harbour of Hurgada. The dry desert wind played on our nerves. It became hotter by the day. A full moon rose in the east and stood overhead by midnight.

With his white, curly hair, white eyebrows, white eyelashes, and light eyes, Jens was the centre of attraction among the dark-skinned, black-eyed Egyptians. All the staring caused Jens to become unbalanced, and adding wind, sand, heat, and a full moon finally drove him over the edge of sanity. One day we noticed he had disappeared and had not slept aboard that night. Harry assumed he had stayed on a Dutch tugboat from Smit & Co., which was permanently stationed in Hurgada. Jens perhaps had discovered country men on board that tug.

At 10:00 A.M., as Harry and I sat at a late breakfast table, Jens showed up. I asked him where he had been all night, but an unintelligible mutter was the answer. He refused to eat, and all day he sat as in a trance, looking straight ahead with empty eyes. When the moon came up, Jens took a Bhudda-like position on deck, facing east. Suddenly he jumped up and started pacing in circles on the shore. Patrolling soldiers looked at him but said nothing. Then, as if by magic, Jens vanished. By midnight he had not yet returned and we were becoming very worried. If he were caught outside the barricade we would be held responsible. We were also concerned about the soldiers. They might be trigger-happy, shooting first and asking questions later.

Next morning at 8:00, he appeared once more. Harry and I had no idea how he slipped away or passed the military guards. Jens was becoming a liability to us. We were going to run into trouble with his escapades. To my questions, Jens did not offer a reply.

Harry made breakfast and boiled some eggs. When we were sitting around the table, I asked Jens again where he had been during the night. He began to shout, "I am free. I am free. I am a child of the sun. I am free. I am free." Then he gobbled up his egg. After he had finished it, he hollered, "I killed a chicken. I killed a chicken." Harry and I looked at each other and Harry said, "You're talking nonsense, Jens. Come to your senses, man." But over and over Jens repeated his cry that he was "free," whatever that meant in his befuddled mind. He went ashore and started his walking in circles again as we observed him from the deck. Suddenly he dashed to a corner of the compound and crawled through a hole where the barbed wire was fastened to a stone wall. So that was how he escaped. No one had noticed, not even the guards.

From our high position on deck, we could see him dash to a street, then disappear around a corner. We did not know what to do, whether to alert the guards or keep quiet. But it was too late. Soldiers had noticed it, too, and yelled at us, pointing to the hole. Jens came back into view, stark naked, and ran toward the sea until he stood up to his neck in water, arms outstretched to the sun and chanting, "I am a child of the sun," over and over.

I jumped off the ship and ran toward the hole, shouting to the guard, "Don't shoot. I'll pick him up." At the water's edge, I called out to Jens to come back, but he swam into deeper water. In the meantime, quite a crowd of Arabs and Egyptians had gathered around me. One told me he had seen Jens undressing himself in the middle of the street. He tried to grab him but Jens had run to the beach and jumped into the water.

The locals became agitated, cackled hysterically, and pointed to the sea. Jens was not swimming anymore. His head was down. Only his white back floated on the surface. What was he doing? Swimming under water? Suddenly I realized that he was drowning. In a flash I reached him in chest-deep water and pulled his lifeless body on shore. By pressing his chest and stomach, water gushed out of his mouth. He must have swallowed the entire Red Sea. I did not feel a heartbeat. The locals circled around us and looked on curiously, but no one offered a helping hand. Then Harry arrived and together we worked on Jens by applying mouth-to-mouth resuscitation and pounding on his heart.

Jens was fortunate. His heart started beating again and his eyelids fluttered, but he was still unconscious. That stupid sun-worshipper. What trouble he had caused in the past few days. One of the Arabs brought Jens' clothes and we tried to put his pants on him, but it was not so easy on a limp body. Finally we had covered his shrivelled manhood. Four Arabs lifted him up to carry him back to the ship, this time not through the hole of the fence, but in pomp and style through the main gate. The guards stood aside and a procession followed us to the ship, where the Arabs laid the body on the floor of the wheelhouse.

Now what? The answer came in the form of a screaming siren. An ambulance stopped right in front of *Trillium II*. A doctor came aboard and had a look at the pathetic white body on the floor. He lifted one of his eyelids and asked us if Jens was a user of drugs. We told him that we had suspected it, but had never seen him using anything in public. We also mentioned his behaviour of the last few days, his antics and his nonsensical talk. The good doctor gave Jens an injection and summoned the ambulance attendants. On a stretcher, Jens was shoved into the ambulance like a loaf of bread into a baker's oven. The doctor needed to keep Jens under observation, and Harry was allowed to accompany him to the hospital.

I HAD EXPECTED Harry back in the afternoon, but when he had still not shown up at midnight, I became worried. I stood on deck looking at the gates but they were closed for the night. Early the next morning I went to the gatehouse to inquire where Harry could have been taken, but the guards could not make me any wiser. Would Immigration know? With a shrug of his shoulders, the official told me not to worry; Harry would be back soon.

During recent days, we had made friends with the first mate of the tugboat of Smit & Co. International Tug Service. On this trying day, he kept me company, and even though he was a Muslim, we both sat on deck drinking beer and keeping an eye on the gate. Allah, in his eternal kindness and wisdom, closed his eye for this poor sailor as long as he did not get drunk.

Who but Harry and Jens did we see marching through the gate as cool as cucumbers? How was it possible? I welcomed them as if they were the prodigal sons of an old biblical patriarch. Jens was not a child of the sun anymore. He had absolutely no recollection of what had happened to him.

The hospital had been out of town at the edge of the desert. Twenty-five doctors had manned the place, and Jens had been the only patient. They had examined him from top to toe and an injection had sent him into dreamland. Harry had played soccer with the doctors in the empty halls, and had slept in one of the many vacant beds. The next morning, Jens was tested again, and with a slap on the back, discharged from the doctors' care. He and Harry were given a free ride into town and dropped off at the harbour gate. I expected a peppered bill from the hospital for all the service, doctors, ambulance, and injections, but it never materialized.

We heard later that the locals had been astonished to see how two white people had brought a man back to life. It had been a miracle to them. Allah is great. There's no denying that.

ALL OUR FRIENDS from the fleet had arrived in Hurgada. Even George and Liz had made it through that unexpected storm. The damaged hull of their yacht had not sprung any leaks. But all were glad to be here for a good, long repose. Everyone needed a breather. Also, our passengers returned from their excursion to Luxor and were very enthusiastic about all they had seen...the Valley of the Kings, Karnak, the huge statues of Ramses I and Ramses II, the burial sites of the pharoahs like Tutankhamen, the boy king, and so much more. As I had studied Egyptian history, I listened with much interest to the stories of our guests and I felt a slight pang of jealousy. Well, perhaps one day I would return and see it all for myself.

On through the Suez Canal

The skippers of the fleet agreed to stay close to each other during the last part of our cruise, the Gulf of Suez, a mere 150 nautical sea miles. Our passports were returned with no problem, clearance was issued by the Customs officers, and the latest weather reports and forecast were good. Close to Suez, the shipping was heavy. As we approached the port, we saw a barque steaming toward us and someone shouting through the Tannoy, "Do you want to go through the Canal immediately? Three hundred dollars!"

My thoughts drifted back more than three years. At that time, I had been a stupid mule because I was not willing to pay *bakshees*. That had caused so much misery, not only for Harry and myself, but also for Gloria and Catherine. I had learned an expensive lesson, so I resolved to give in this time. The barque had come alongside, and a man, introducing himself as a shipping agent, jumped over. I could not resist to dicker and said, "Three hundred dollars? Way too much." The agent looked aft where the five ships sailed in keel-line, and he asked, "Do those belong to your fleet? A hundred and fifty dollars for you, a hundred dollars for each of them."

Harry radioed the other ships and we accepted the man's offer. I ordered fuel, provisions, and water. The agent promised with a firm handshake that it would all be waiting for us at the marina. Then he took off with a roaring engine and a huge wash behind his boat. His day had begun very profitably.

The agent was true to his word. As we made fast in a place assigned to private yachts in the harbour of Suez, an oil truck waited for us, ready to pump our tanks full. A ship chandler's annex provision store was across the quay, and a canal pilot hopped aboard our ship. We were the largest and therefore the leader of the pack. One pilot for all six yachts, that was economy. On top of all good things, this man was honest, polite, and had no blackmail tricks up his sleeve.

The trek through the Suez Canal was a piece of cake and at long last, the Mediterranean spread out before our longing eyes, blue and beautiful. We had accomplished what we had set out to do. Civilization and the Horn of Plenty were just below the horizon waiting for us...the Isle of Cyprus.

Larnaca, Cyprus

IN LARNACA on Cyprus, Liz and George put their damaged ship on shore for repairs. We organized barbeques and parties with the crews of all the ships. And as for Jens? One morning his cabin was empty. He had simply vanished.

Oh, well...

The fleet in Larnaca, Cyprus. Trillium II enters the marina of Larnaca.

Let's have a cookout.

Louise

We couldn't decide whether she was an experienced actress or a born deceiver. But one thing was for sure; she could lie with glee, even believing herself. Did she merit our sympathy, or should we bid her good riddance at the next harbour? We just couldn't decide what to do with Louise.

Kidnapped in Yugoslavia

IN RAB, a beautiful place in Yugoslavia, Louise was one of the many Sunday strollers along the boulevard that bordered the long quay. Many yachts had found a place of rest there. Harry sat in the cockpit reading a book and I had settled myself in the saloon doing absolutely nothing. As was customary among the passersby, a woman stopped and chatted with Harry. He invited her aboard for a cup of tea.

She was a captivating story-teller and described to us her travels and the people she had met. She had just arrived from Austria and had not yet reserved an hotel room. Before we realized, she had wheedled herself aboard our ship for the next cruise, and the skipper was accompanying her to pick up her car—an enormous American monster—so she could bring her belongings on board.

Instead of returning to the ship, she headed down a remote country road. She had kidnapped me! After driving for about an hour on a macadam road through the interior of Otor-Rab, an island connected to the mainland by a bridge, she stopped by a stump of an old, uprooted tree.

"Now we will eat something," she said, and from the ample trunk of her car, she produced forks, knives, plates, a two-litre Thermos, and a large melon. The trunk was crammed full of utensils, towels, glasses, cups and saucers, with monograms from restaurants and hotels printed on them. Was she a kleptomaniac?

As we sat, Louise told me the story of her life. She was raised on the American east coast, owned an electronics firm, and was very rich. She showed me a photograph of her home and her daughter, a very pretty girl. Louise was taking a trip around the world and had spent the last six months touring Europe.

Later, parked beside the ship, she withdrew a couple of weekend bags from the back seat, and we installed her in one of the aft cabins.

No amount of payment for cruising on *Trillium II* was mentioned. As the days passed, it became more difficult to bring up that important subject. Each time we landed in a harbour, Louise bought food and then prepared lovely meals. She bestowed gifts on us daily. We were in a dilemma—had her cunning beaten our business instinct?

CRUISING ALONG the coast of Yugoslavia had been a profitable venture. We were never without passengers. There were Germans, Dutch, English, and even Yugoslavians on board. We sailed up and down that scenic coast and every evening we stayed in another harbour, another town with a history reaching back to the middle ages.

Sailing in Yugoslavian waters.

Brent, a New Zealander of Harry's age, had booked in Cyprus for the long cruise to Venice. He and Harry became such good friends and Brent was so handy that we kept him on as a non-paying deckhand.

THE CLOSER we came to Venice, the more Louise could tell us about the places we passed along the coast. She was interesting company but it was hard to know when to believe her.

In Louise's narrative, the skipper was the best sailor in the world, and as a navigator had no equal. Harry and Brent were darlings—the three of us could do no wrong. The tables were turned when Louise tried to play boss on board of our ship and arrange things to *her* liking. Since she would disembark in Venice we did not make a big issue of it. Financial arrangements had still not been made, and we knew for certain that she was a kleptomaniac.

Harry and I discovered this when we went for a walk in a small tourist village along the Yugoslavian coast. We found a cosy terrace under some trees, and Louise ordered coffee. She was going to pay. When the waiter came to collect his money, she complained that the coffee had been bad and too expensive. As we rose to leave, she snatched her cup, saucer, and spoon and took off like a greyhound.

We followed her shouting, "Louise, bring that cup back!" But she didn't stop until we had reached the ship. Once aboard, she stowed her newest acquisitions in her locker with a satisfied smirk. From then on, we kept a sharp eye on Louise.

More sly than intelligent, she seemed to be a good business person, one who was usually the winner in transactions. Her face was pleasant, and she did not look her age of 65. Her short, silver-grey hair was becoming. She must have been a beautiful girl.

Louise was not a careful housekeeper. It did not bother her in the least to mop the teak floor of the wheelhouse with our nice, embroidered tablecloth, or dry the dishes with a bath towel from the shower stall. Everything on board the ship had a permanent place, but after Louise had done some housekeeping, we found the bread knife in the box with the shoe polish.

She was the biggest human puzzle we had ever encountered in all our years of chartering and travelling. "Skipper, shall we go for an evening walk?" she asked in a sweet, seductive voice. Of course, the skipper cheerfully agreed. Hand in hand we strolled down cobblestone streets of one or another romantic town. Shortly, she suggested we have a drink in a dreamy sidewalk cafés and promised with a sugary whisper, "I'll pay, Skipper." But when it was time to pay, my goodness, she had forgotten her purse. I reached for my wallet time and time again.

ONE LATE, SUNNY AFTERNOON, Venice and the San Marco loomed up in the distance. The lagoon was enormous and we sailed back and forth trying to locate the famous Lido, the playground of the rich. We were not able to find it, so we moored at a part of the lagoon called La Salute, which was directly behind the Giorgio Maggiore, a gigantic old church. The water in that harbour was turbulent. Ferries, commercial vessels, and boats of all kinds, shapes, and sizes churned the waters day and night. To park at the rough, concrete quay was impossible. Harry and Brent fastened lines to different pilings so we could ride free and easy, the stern of the ship about two metres from the sea wall. With a painter, we pulled the stern closer and could hop ashore.

A much needed rest in Venice

Louise was at her best behaviour. She knew Venice and had many friends there. We believed her instantly. Everyone was eager to see Venice under Louise's guidance.

Every day, Louise took us in tow. Because of her, we saw more of Venice than the average tourist. She also introduced us to some of her friends. One was the owner of the largest and most expensive hotel in the city, close to the San Marco. Harry and I, with Louise, were promptly invited to an oyster lunch. The owner, a lady, took time to sit at our table with us. Later we were given the grand tour of the hotel and were shown the bridal suite where the grandeur and riches of ages past seemed to drip from the walls.

Louise invited us for a drink at the bar of the hotel. It looked very expensive with its mirrors in gilded frames and numerous bottles on the shelves. Even the bartenders had an expensive demeanour, and the drinks were certainly expensive. Louise performed her usual disappearing act. Fortunately Harry had enough money on him to pay.

Another disappearing act by Louise

THE NIGHTS WERE BALMY and across La Salute the old city lay spread out in all its glory and dignity. They were such romantic, dreamy evenings long to be remembered by all of us. On one such an eve, Louise played her trick on us again. The four of us were seated at our regular table. Louise went inside the café and presently returned with three bottles of wine, enough for the whole evening. She announced triumphantly that she had already paid the padrone. With wine, women, and song, the evening flew by and toward midnight the padrone wished to close his café. Louise had already left long ago. The proprietor came to our table and presented a bill for three bottles of wine. We looked up at him in surprise. Hadn't the signora paid when she bought the wine? "No, no Signores. La Signora non pagare," the padrone insisted. The bill was too high for the cheap, sour vinho we had been drinking all night. Harry once again emptied his wallet and Brent chipped in.

On our way back to the ship, there was Louise sitting on the iron railing of a bridge. With the heels of her shoes she beat against the pipes, her victory march. How could we have let her sucker us again? Angrily, Harry reprimanded her. Brent and I were fed up, but Louise showed us her sunniest smile. She had lied so convincingly I think she believed that she *had* paid for the wine.

On another occasion, Harry and Brent had gone to our usual haunt. They had made plans with some young people to go to a disco. Louise and I would join them later. I dressed up in white trousers, a Hawaiian shirt with an exuberant flowered pattern, and on top of my sparse hairs, the white sailor's cap with gold ornaments, which I wore at a rakish angle. Louise had donned a flowery gown which left her arms and shoulders bare, and with a modest decolleté, she looked very attractive, the little cheat. I was proud to be her escort.

One evening ...two baths

MOST OF THE NARROW alleyways in Venice run alongside small canals which look so picturesque on postcards, especially when a gondola passes through. In reality, those canals are nothing but stinking sewers. The houses drain their waste products straight into them and tidal action flushes it toward the Adriatic Sea. Quaint little bridges connect both sides. One of the largest bridges is the Rialto, spanning the Grand Canal, which divides Venice in two parts.

Concrete steps lead down to the water's edge of the narrow

canals. There, the gondolier takes on or sets off his passengers. At low ebb-tide there is no water covering the bottom steps, but the green slime makes them very slippery. They turned out to be my downfall that evening.

Dressed for an enjoyable night on the town, Louise and I set out in great anticipation. We strode along the canals bathed in stripes of late, warm sunlight, until we came to a little stone bridge. The entire setting reminded me of a beautiful painting done by an old master. Curiously, I wondered how the scene would look through the arch of that bridge. Nearby were steps I could descend for a better view. Yes, every step down improved the vista. The bow of the bridge was like a frame around a tableau. I bent over and stepped down once more to get a look from a different angle. It just happened to be low tide, and as my foot touched that mucky bottom step, splash! I landed right in the filthy sewer, up to my neck in the ooze. My sailor's cap was still perched jauntily on my head.

Louise laughed uncontrollably, dancing with glee. It must have been quite a sight, just my head in that sailor's cap sticking out of the water.

Once back on board *Trillium II*, Louise was kind enough to douse me with pails of water from the lagoon. At least it rinsed the muck from my pants. Not paying attention to the Venetian laws of virtue and morality, I stripped out of my soiled clothing under the curious eyes of onlookers and let Louise scrub me clean with fresh water from our tanks until I smelled human and emerged as pink and rosy as a baby. And tomorrow I would assign to Louise the task of laundering my white sailor's pants and Hawaiian shirt to get my revenge for her laugher at my expense.

A WEEK LATER, Louise was still on board. By this time we were really fed up with her and I told her she had to leave the ship. She was very upset. She accused me of having a heart of stone. Didn't we known how much she loved Harry and Brent, the skipper, and the ship? She would surely die of a broken heart if she could not live aboard *Trillium II* any longer. She dropped to her knees, tears streaming down her cheeks, begging to stay.

"Have you no pride left at all?" I asked her.

That was enough for us. We packed her suitcases and set them ashore. "Goodbye, Louise. Goodbye forever." We never saw her again.

**A long
goodbye**

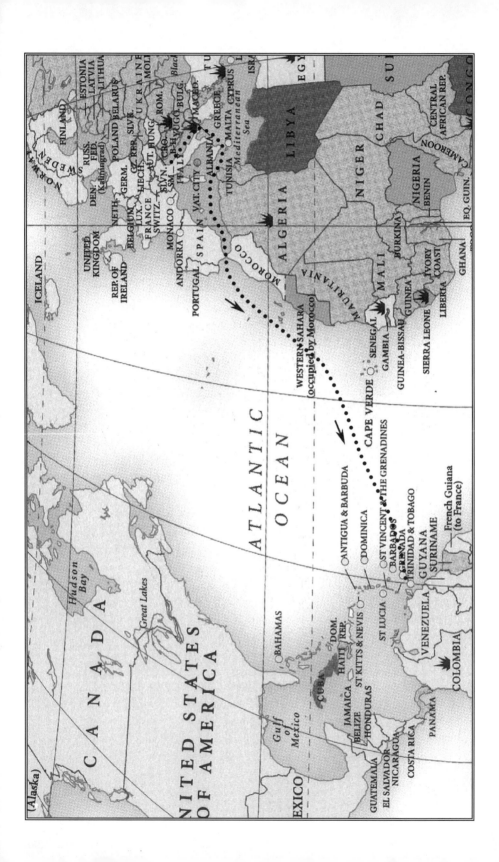

From the Mediterranean to the Caribbean

Last Voyage of Trillium II

I had seen it coming. We had been sailing from Naples to Tunisia with a nice group of young German folk. They had booked for a two-week voyage. On the way to Tunis, we stopped at several Italian islands. Sometimes they were no more than a cluster of rocks with a miniature harbour. It seemed impossible to find a place at the small docks without quarrelling with the local fishermen. For our guests, it was an unprecedented adventure roaming around the Mediterranean.

First mate Harry leaves *Trillium II*

There was Frederike, a dear young woman from Northern Germany, who was on board with her son and daughter. On quiet evenings, while the ship moved under full canvas towards the far lands across the Med, she played her harmonica accompanied by a friend who had brought a guitar. There was always a cheerful atmosphere on our ship.

Hannelore came from Braunschweig. She and my first mate got along very well, so well, in fact, that she stayed on board that summer for a few trips. In September, when her vacation had lapsed, I had a private talk with my son. "Harry," I told him, "you have sailed with me for a great many years,

Concert at sundown on a peaceful Mediterranean. We are on the way from Napoli to Tunisia. At left, Frederike is playing harmonica and her friend is playing guitar.

we have had a good time together. You have seen much and been through a lot. If you want to go ashore, become a landlubber again, I won't stand in your way. If your heart is with Hannelore, go to Braunschweig with her this winter and see how life on land suits you. I'll keep sailing, and I'll manage."

Harry's face lit up. Apparently he had been wrestling with this decision for some time. "Are you serious, Skipper?" he asked. "Are you really serious? I'd hate to just leave you now, you know."

"You bet your life I mean it, my boy. You shouldn't stay on board for my sake. You have a right to a life of your own. I'm so grateful and happy that I've been able to take you along on board of *Trillium II* all these years," I responded.

Dinner on deck of Trillium II *on the way from Napoli to Tunisia. Our guests were from Germany and had booked for two weeks of roaming the Med. We made landfalls on many small Italian islands in the Tyrrhenian Sea.*

"Could I come back next year to sail with you one more summer, Skipper?" he questioned me. "You may, son, you may. There will always be a place for you on our beloved ship, even if it is only to keep your old captain company. We could enjoy a mug of tea between watches again."

Going on without Harry would never be the same. We were so in tune with each other. We were a trinity, Harry, *Trillium II*, and I. How many dangers had we faced? How many beautiful, tropical evenings had we sat together in the cockpit sipping a glass of rum while gazing at a breathtaking, multicoloured sunset? How many watches on the bridge had we shared? How many ports had we visited, how many landfalls made?

We had sailed with an empty kitty, surviving on fish and rice, but also at times when the money poured in, enabling us to purchase new cordage or hoist the ship on shore for a fresh coat of paint.

Yes, I would definitely miss my best first mate and friend very much. We had often had to say goodbye to beloved friends and acquaintances who had shared with us delightful days at sea, and also hard, difficult ones when inclement weather demanded them on deck.

Over the years, hundreds of guests had occupied *Trillium*'s cabins, had stood at the wheel, or cooked and kept the galley clean. We shook their hands when they arrived and again when they left. There are those who have been forgotten, disappearing into the mists of time like ships that pass in the night. Those whom we loved deeply have remained in our memories, never to be forgotten.

Diana, who was part of our first cruises from Harlingen in Holland to Helgoland in the German Bight. She sailed with us to the Caribbean and the Mediterranean.

Frieda from Hamburg, who had been frightened to death on the piers of Helgoland when we entered during a terrifying storm.

Johanna from Amsterdam, the woman with an iron character, a spitfire who didn't want to leave the ship and clung to the skipper when the long cruise terminated in the fishermen's harbour of Oudeschildt in Holland. That farewell was heartbreaking...Isa Lei, Johanna...Farewell.

Catherine from Paris, sweet, gentle Catherine. She was the support and refuge for the captain in that sweltering hell of Port Said and the Red Sea.

Gloria, whom we had to bring to Djeddah in Saudi Arabia. We had to say our goodbyes below deck, because the hostile Arabs detest and revile women, particularly those of the white race. Gloria could not forget her *Trillium II*. Years later she travelled halfway around the world in search of our ship. She found us on Sri Lanka in the roadstead of Trincomalee.

Frederike from Norden in North Germany. Seaman's blood ran through her veins, as well as a great love for nature and horses. She gave the skipper many unforgettable hours and days in Sidi Bou Said, Tunisia, and later on the Luneburgerheide in Germany.

Ingrid, blonde, blue-eyed Ingrid. A deep, tender affinity and love had blossomed during our stay on Kurumba, a small coral island in the Indian Ocean. She wished to come along, but sadly, we left her behind on the white sands of that quiet beach, sobbing uncontrollably.

There were many other memorable characters: Captain Mustafa Hassan of the Egyptian airforce, who resorted to stealing from his own garrison to be of service to us, and had all his men form up at the quay at our departure.

The Immigration officers in Port Said, who bestowed on us smacking kisses upon departure.

The unknown Englishman in Djeddah, who demonstrated unselfish friendship to rescue us from the merciless hand of Arabian port authorities.

We came from a far horizon and sailed on to a distant skyline. Time after time we left much behind, always wondering why it was necessary to say "goodbye" and go on with longing hearts. Why? Why? Love and happiness was here and now. I had asked my oldest son once and he had this answer: "This kind of life was your own choice. You have dreamed all your life to become a seaman, a sailor. Sailors always travel from one horizon to the next—that is their fate!"

But this time, I'd have to say goodbye to my first mate Harry. I'd have to go on without him. He had been on board since our departure from Canada. And now I would sail alone, unable to share watches or mugs of tea with him.

With a smile and an aching heart I let him go, assuring him that I'd manage just fine.

And I did go on. Many paying passengers travelled with me, and we called on numerous ports and islands in the Mediterranean. I maintained my ship at regular intervals, in dry-dock or hoisted on land. I gave her a new coat of paint, and I hired deckhands, but kicked them from board almost as soon as they arrived. I was irritable and impatient when a new crew fumbled with lines and sails. During night sailing I stood grimly on the bridge or in the cockpit. Sure, I managed, but it wasn't the same. I was no longer the man of former times who could never be thrown off balance.

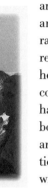

Drinking a cup of coffee on a quaint terrace.

Harry and Hannelore returned the following summer, and for a while I had the illusion that once again everything was the way it used to be. But the season passed too quickly. In the fall, I put *Trillium II* up for sale. I had several potential and prospective buyers. When time came to close the deal, they had no money. Why on earth did those dreamers without cash come whimpering to me? Could I leave a mortgage on the ship? Selling her in the Mediterranean proved to be unsuccessful. For three years we had been sailing there, and Porto Ferraio on Elba had been our home-harbour. Now it was enough. I would set sail for the West Indies, that's what I would do.

My daughter Ellen asked if she could come along on an ocean voyage. Harry had been with me for such a long time, for so many years, and she, too, had a great desire to experience life at sea.

Ellen arranged for a paying crew—an all-woman party of five. They embarked in Gibraltar and we headed directly for Madeira. Sadly, I could no longer recognize Funchal, the time-worn port of old. All the harbour works had been renovated, and a brand new yacht basin was built where once that old, abandoned derelict had moored. Johnny, our "harbour-master," was not there anymore;

however, there was a disco across from the quay. I danced all night with my "harem." They had challenged me, so I danced until 2:00 A.M. Dancing? Well, it was more shaking one's behind, hopping, and jumping. I felt foolish for accepting their dare.

Our next destination were the Canary Islands. Once again I let *Trillium II* rock behind her anchors in the bay of Los Cristianos, and once more I drank sweet black coffee on that terrazzo, where one could overlook the bay, shimmering in a cool morning breeze. This time, not Harry was sitting across the table from me, but my daughter, Ellen. I knew I would never see Los Cristianos, that beautiful place, again. Sadness was in my heart.

The ocean crossing lasted 19 days, a record for *Trillium II*. During this time, the mood on board deteriorated and my daughter was caught in the middle. The old sails needed to be repaired quite often, and for days I sat on deck, crosslegged and sewing like an old-fashioned tailor.

The old sails needed to be repaired and for days I sat on deck, crosslegged, sewing like an old-fashioned tailor.

We arrived in Barbados on Christmas Eve. Ellen and I received an invitation to the New Year's Ball of the local police and customs officials. We were the only white people among the black population. My daughter disappeared quietly, but fortunately a petite police corporal offered to be my escort. Her curly head reached no higher than my shoulder when we danced. Long after midnight the festivities ended, and that curly-headed imp cheated me out of a taxi fare. I stood there, a bit bewildered and disappointed, looking at the disappearing rearlights of the taxi.

At dawn, my all-female crew showed up, including my daughter. Where she had been all night I don't know to this day. She certainly didn't tell me, and I didn't ask prying questions.

From Barbados we explored the other islands in the West Indies, and little by little, I lost my harem. One after the other deserted the ship and stayed behind on islands.

Upon arrival in English Harbour on Antigua, only Ellen was still on board, and she planned to leave for America on the first plane she could catch. As captain, I regretted the loss of my last crew member, but as a father, I gave her my blessing.

"Go ahead, dear, I'll manage just fine." Hadn't I spoken those same words not long before?

Is *Trillium II* still sailing?

I don't know. I sold her in the West Indies for a few miserable dollars. I should have put her out to sea and given her the Viking funeral she deserved. She should have gone down in flames. I considered it, but I could not muster up the courage.

Do not say of this strange Bird:
"Too proud were her exotic travels..."
Perhaps her cradle was close to Paradise....